What's Going On?

Language/Learning Episodes in
British and American Classrooms,
Grades 4-13

What's Going On?

Language/Learning Episodes in
British and American Classrooms,
Grades 4-13

MARY BARR • PAT D'ARCY • MARY K. HEALY

BOYNTON / COOK PUBLISHERS, INC.

Library of Congress Cataloging in Publication Data

Main entry under title:

What's going on?

   Bibliography: p.
   1. Language arts. 2. Language acquisition.
3. English language—Study and teaching.
I. Barr, Mary. II. D'Arcy, Pat. III. Healy, Mary K.
LB1576.W485   428   81–18119
ISBN 0–86709–013–8 (pbk.)   AACR2

For information address Boynton/Cook Publishers, Inc.
206 Claremont Avenue, Montclair, NJ 07042

ISBN: 0–86709–013–8

Printed in the United States of America

    83 84 85 86 10 9 8 7 6 5 4 3 2

For Bill Cook —

who believed that good teachers have much to share, and who helped make this sharing a reality.

Preface

Let's begin by saying what this book is not. It's not a series of assertions and exercises detailing "best" practices, to be tried out come Monday morning. And it's not a collection of journal articles, published separately elsewhere, on one aspect of language teaching.

Instead, here are records of individual journeys by thirteen teachers who asked their own questions about what was going on in their own classrooms. The questions grew from genuine curiosity about their students and themselves as learners when they listened carefully to their students, when they observed them closely, when they talked with them about subject matter.

Each chapter describes an inquiry into how learning happens in a particular setting and what language has to do with it. The settings are varied — from a rural British primary school to an inner city California high school and from a math class to a college composition course. Locales and styles may differ, but the teachers share a common attitude toward the process of education: that it's dynamic, not static; that there is no right way to teach anything; and that teachers need to open their classroom doors in order to exchange ideas grounded in practice.

The teachers in this book write and talk with their students, pursue questions with them, provide audiences for what they write and say. Far from relinquishing classroom authority, they use it to create situations wherein students must formulate carefully, explain clearly, describe accurately, and persuade effectively. Language in these teachers' classrooms serves learning, as students read and listen to find out, talk and write to discover as well as to report. Consequently, textbooks, with their adult and final versions of experience, are considered resources for individual learning rather than prescriptions for what is to be learned. In these classes, teachers frequently ask questions to which they don't know the answers or for which they would be willing to accept alternatives. Students are encouraged to risk mistakes as part of the learning process rather than dodge the possibility of error. Student work is analyzed for evidence of development as well as for effect on audience and for standards of correctness.

Much has, of course, been written about classrooms and language. A growing body of research-based literature indicates the influence school attitudes have on student language development. Other research emphasizes the need learners have to reconstruct new information in their own words so that it becomes personal knowledge. Studies of the composing process itself conducted over the past decade describe developmental patterns which are often at odds with the prescriptions of composition texts and conventional teaching strategies. (The books of people who have had — and continue to have — major influence on us are listed at the end of this preface.)

These research findings provide a background of theory against which teachers can compare their own observations and speculations. Teachers reading the research reports might ask, "Do these ideas make sense, given my knowledge of classroom life, of children, of school pressures?" If some do — at least partially — teachers can use them to refine their own practice. And if others don't, they may be spurred to construct alternative hypotheses, thereby clarifying for themselves the reasons for their own classroom procedures.

The writers in this book are working from ideas about teaching and learning that come from both theory and experience. The reader can follow the emergence of their ideas and see, in operation, the interplay of teachers and students involved with language development. So, too, with the development of this book, which has grown out of continuing conversations among the three of us since 1976 when we met during New York University's summer program at the University of York in England. Since then we have been each other's teachers in many ways: Pat contributing her experiences with London University's Writing Development Project, and Mary K. and Mary involving Pat in the work of the Bay Area and San Diego Area Writing Projects. The connections for the three of us were immediate. We shared similar backgrounds — long careers as secondary English or humanities teachers and as in-service leaders, working with teachers both in their classrooms and in writing project workshops. We had each promoted in-service workshops for the full range of grade level teaching — from early elementary through high school — so we knew how teachers with quite different backgrounds could look jointly at student development. We had all written texts about various aspects of school language — reading, literature, composition — but had come to prefer working directly with teachers in settings where they talk and write to and for each other.

This book, written directly from classroom practice, grew out of those workshop settings. We hope the episodes provoke discussion and encourage the teachers who read them to look at their own classrooms in similar ways. The papers are arranged chronologically so that readers may take an armchair journey through schooling, beginning with the primary grades and ending at the college level. We hope our readers can envisage their own classrooms as places with similar possibilities for using language to learn.

Since we are, after all, both teachers *and* learners, alternately skilled and unskilled depending on the circumstances, there is much we can learn from each other's practices. We offer these thirteen accounts as the beginning of what we hope will be a continuing trans-Atlantic dialogue.

Mary Barr
Pat D'Arcy
Mary K. Healy

1. Armstrong. *Closely Observed Children: The Diary of a Primary Classroom.* A Chameleon Book, 1980. Writers and Readers Publishing Cooperative, (Also available through Boynton/Cook Publishers, 1981)
2. Barnes, Douglas, James Britton and Harold Rosen. *Language, the Learner and the School.* London: Penguin Books, 1971. (Also available through Boynton/Cook Publishers, 1981)
3. Barnes, Douglas. *From Communication to Curriculum.* London: Penguin Books, 1976. (Also available through Boynton/Cook Publishers, 1981)
4. Berthoff, Ann E. *Forming/Thinking/Writing.* Montclair, NJ: Boynton/Cook Publishers, 1978.
5. _____. *The Making of Meaning: Metaphors, Models, and Maxims for Writing Teachers,* Montclair, NJ: Boynton/Cook Publishers, 1981.
6. Britton, James. *The Development of Writing Abilities (11-18).* London: Macmillan Co., 1975. (Also available through the National Council of Teachers of English, Urbana, IL, 1975)
7. _____. *Language and Learning.* London: Penguin Books, 1970. (Also available through Boynton/Cook Publishers, 1981)
8. Burgess, Carol, *et al. Understanding Children Writing.* London: Penguin Books, 1973. (Also available through Boynton/Cook Publishers, 1981)
9. Cazden, Courtney B. *et al,* eds. *Functions of Language in the Classroom.* New York: Teachers College Press, 1972.
10. Dixon, John. *Growth Through English* (revised edition). Urbana IL: National Council of Teachers of English, 1975.

11. Emig, Janet. *The Composing Processes of Twelfth Graders.* Urbana, IL: National Council of Teachers of English, 1971.
12. Graves, Donald H. "An Examination of the Writing Processes of Seven Year Old Children." *Research in the Teaching of English* (Winter, 1975): 227-241.
13. Jacobs, Gabriel. *When Children Think.* New York: Teachers College Press, 1970.
14. Macrorie, Ken. *A Vulnerable Teacher.* Rochelle Park, NJ: Hayden Book Co., 1974.
15. _____. *Searching Writing.* Rochelle Park, NJ: Hayden Book Co., 1980.
16. _____. *Writing to Be Read* (second edition). Rochelle Park, NJ: Hayden Book Co., 1976.
17. Martin, Nancy *et al. Understanding Children Talking.* London: Penguin Books, 1976. (Also available through Boynton/Cook Publishers, 1981)
18. Martin, Nancy, Pat D'Arcy, Bryan Newton and Robert Parker. *Writing and Learning Across the Curriculum 11-16.* London: Ward Lock Educational, 1976. (Also available through Boynton/Cook Publishers, 1981)
19. Medway, Peter. *Finding a Language: Autonomy and Learning in School.* A Chameleon Book, 1980. Writers and Readers Publishing Cooperative, (Also available through Boynton/Cook Publishers, 1981)
20. Moffett, James and Betty Jane Wagner. *Student-Centered Language Arts and Reading, K-13: A Handbook for Teachers* (second edition). Boston: Houghton Mifflin, 1976.
21. Moffett, James. *Active Voice: A Writing Program Across the Curriculum.* Montclair, NJ: Boynton/Cook Publishers, 1981.
22. _____. *Coming on Center: English Education in Evolution.* Montclair, NJ: Boynton/Cook Publishers, 1981.
23. Torbe, Mike and Robert Protherough, eds. *Classroom Encounters: Language and English Teaching.* London: Ward Lock Educational, 1976.
24. Torbe, Mike and Peter Medway. *The Climate for Learning.* London: Ward Lock Educational, 1981. (Also available through Boynton/Cook Publishers, 1981)

Contents

Chapter 1

Learning Through Talking

PAULINE ELKIN

Pauline Elkin is a teacher at Townhill Middle School in Southampton, and when she wrote this paper she was reflecting back over her first year's experiences as a teacher. That year, her class were in *their* first year in the school also (eight to nine year olds).

In September, 1980, Pauline moved to take over one of the two "top" classes of 12 year old students, and she tells me that the differences are enormous — the children are never as physically exhausted at the end of the day nor are they anywhere near as dependent on her as were those in her very first class. Most of them can now read and write fluently and all possess the confidence of being the 'old hands' in the school — experts at finding their way around, metaphorically as well as literally, and full of ideas.

The school was designed for team-teaching with large open areas on two levels linked to six smaller teaching bases that can be partitioned off with moveable screens. There are specially equipped science, art, craft, and cookery rooms, and each of the year-groups has a special quiet room designed for independent reading and other independent work. Teachers work together on a topic basis and the time-tabling is very flexible, much closer to English primary schools than to the more rigidly time-tabled secondaries. Pauline is involved in everything her pupils do with the exception of music and cookery.

To keep track of how every individual child has spent the week, each member of the class has a record folder (weeks at the top, activities down the side) so that what they do can be charted by their teacher as they go along.

Pauline knows only too well that when her 12 year olds move to their Upper School, there is a strong likelihood that they will begin to lose responsibility for their own learning. Their school day will fragment into a scatter of different subjects which they will move into and out of with bewildering speed. Examination syllabuses will impose, almost inevitably, an assembly line approach to learning, and pupils who have worked confidently together will be 'banded' and 'setted' into groups not of their own choosing.

Pauline finds the thought of such changes upsetting.

My interest in how to make children's talking and listening more effective arose from an incident which took place in the second or third week of the first term. I was reading one of the Norman Hunter "Professor Branestawm" stories to the class. I had already read several others to them which, I had felt, they had thoroughly enjoyed. Several children had made up 'in' jokes about the eccentric, bespectacled Professor and in response to one particular story, "An Apple for Teacher," I had been presented with eighteen apples the following day. So, feeling very relaxed and knowing that I was reading the stories well, I started on another. I was now confident enough of myself and the children to read the story at the same time as watching the children's responses. As the story continued, I became aware that although many children were attentively listening and laughing there were also quite a number whose attention had gone. Although not actually fidgeting yet, their eyes had glazed over or they were dreamily looking out of the window. My immediate reaction was an emotional one — I felt extremely irritated with them — why aren't they enjoying it when I'm reading it so well? I felt it was a personal insult and in response to this found myself telling them to listen and springing questions on them and then feeling as uncomfortable and guilty about my behaviour as they did about their inability to reply.

After a couple of days I became worried at the harmful game I was playing and realised that this was something that would only be resolved by bringing it out into the open and discussing the problem. The following day, just as the attention of a few started to wander, I put the book down and started to discuss the matter. I explained what I had noticed, what I felt about it and, above all, that I wanted the children themselves to tell me which of them felt they could listen easily and with enjoyment and which experienced difficulty. After a few minutes' hesitation an honest discussion was under way which proved that the children were as keen to get this problem off their chests and sorted out as I was.

"What happened to you when I started to read?" I asked. A boy who had enjoyed the stories immediately explained the sensation in a surprisingly eloquent way — mind wandering "by itself" to other matters, looking out of the window, sound of the storyteller "floating above the head." I was extremely grateful to him for his immediate and precise response, as indeed were the other children, for heads started to nod in agreement as he explained. Those who had experienced difficulty felt they could build on this and began to fill in the picture even more carefully.

Once this stage had been reached and the nature of the problem agreed upon, the next step was to think of ways in which they could learn to listen more easily. One girl (again a child who hadn't appeared to have any difficulty with this particular story) suggested that talking about the story as we went along might help. This was unanimously agreed upon and for the rest of the year I continued to read a couple of pages of a story, stop, discuss what was happening, and then continue.

This apparently simple incident was the most exhilarating and memorable experience for me during my first few weeks of being a teacher. It was important for a number of reasons. For the children, as well as for myself, I could see the satisfaction of what had been an internal, personal problem (in this case guilt at not being able to listen carefully and being aware that they were missing out on something) become a communal, shared problem because it had been verbalised and could be sorted out and resolved. Furthermore, from that point on, I felt the class was a lot more relaxed and happy because we had jointly established that honest discussions of this kind would be a recurrent feature in the year's work and were positively welcomed and sought by me.

For me, a probationary teacher in a school whose policy and physical structure were very much geared towards individual or small group work, it reminded me early on of the value of the class's functioning as a whole from time to time. The sense of unity and, one hopes, harmony remains and influences the children when they are dispersed and engaged in individual work.

The ways in which the children communicated to me as their new teacher were very varied from the outset; interestingly, group patterns emerged which didn't coincide with ability in other areas: (1) those who had a restricted set of conventional responses, (2) those who grunted and mumbled, (3) those who relied heavily on gesture, (4) those who responded to me with childish familiarity and (5) a minority who had already developed an appropriate way of talking to a friendly but non-family adult.

Of those who tended to slip into conventional formulae Neil, a bright and inquisitive boy, is a good example. Always courteous and formal when communicating with me, he matched exactly the "Yes, Miss Elkin, no Miss Elkin, three bags full Miss Elkin" image of the traditional "English" schoolboy. His questions were phrased in a way which expected a curt, factual reply from me. As a counterbalance to this, he could also be excessively silly and childish — on several occasions in the first term he surprised me and everyone else by throwing his arms around my waist and giving me a lavish hug. Neil was at his best in small groups where he listened carefully to others, was able to explain his ideas clearly, and excelled at helping those who hadn't grasped a point. In a group situation he was respected and trusted. However, in class work he found it difficult to relax and talk to the class and would direct himself exclusively to me. His tenseness made him very serious and he would often become muddled and confused, and the other children were apt to laugh at him.

The most prolific grunter was Lee. He used a wide range of grunts to convey any number of messages or would mumble a response with his head turned away from me. He obviously found any personal contact with me embarrassing and wanted it to finish as quickly as possible. His ideas for language and topic work were good, but his basic mathematical work was poor and his spelling appalling. To begin with, though, he would soldier on in difficulty rather than come to me for help. In a group, although never the one to offer ideas, he would respond to others and obviously enjoyed listening. During class work, however, he would never talk and in a large group had difficulty listening to anything, whether instructions or a story. During the "Professor Branestawm" discussion, though, he seemed pleased to have an opportunity to admit his difficulty in listening.

Peter is another boy I would like to mention. He was the boy who sparked off the original discussion so eloquently by describing the sensation of not being able to listen to the story. He was seen as a natural leader in class work, as he was often the first to talk and introduce new ideas into a discussion. However, he tended to blurt out ideas at the cost of someone else's contribution and was apt to speak rather loudly. At assembly time when responses were invited from the children he had no qualms about speaking in front of three hundred children and adults. In group work and with me, however, he was often aggressively silent, the more so the fewer people he was dealing with. Any questioning of his ideas was replied to in strongly defensive tones as though he felt he was being attacked or belittled.

Darren, a very slow but eager member of the class, enjoyed communicating and would often look to me for praise or help. He was a very physically expressive child and relied heavily on gesture. To begin with I regarded this as an easy substitute for actual talk and, finding myself drawn into this, often had to remind myself to talk to him clearly and fully. On reflection though, and as I got to know him better, I came to recognise this as an early stage in his communication process. He rarely put more than three or four words together, but much was conveyed by 'Oh', 'Well', 'Yeah', 'I see'. He was aware that he was given and was producing a different type of work from the others. This arrangement didn't seem to upset or humiliate him, but it did tend to mean that he set himself somewhat apart from the small group or the class while at work. However, he loved story time and would always listen very carefully.

From the first day Claire talked to me with ease about anything. However, it was often in a tone of such careless familiarity that the possibility of any serious, careful discussion seemed to me to be excluded. I am sure that she treated me much as she did her mother, and would babble on, or sulk when asked to stop. She was a bright, lively girl with many mature ideas as was evident in her written work. In class discussions she would be very eager to contribute but often, when given the chance, would become embarrassed and forget what she was about to say. Perhaps bright children of this type feel that their dignity is too much at stake in such a situation and therefore reserve their thoughts for written work where they know a direct, personal link is made with the teacher, free from the eyes and opinions of the other children.

Emma was one of the few who was able to communicate with me in a way which was friendly and open yet aware of the framework within which one is working in school. An independent, hard-working girl, she was able to take initiatives and work happily by herself. The fact that both her parents were teachers perhaps explained the ease with which she reacted to school life and relationships. She was admired and respected by many, but quite a few were jealous of her and too ready to criticise. When this happened she would quickly defend herself and move away from the person or persons and continue working by herself. She found it extremely hard to work with a small group of children and would usually remain quiet. Her work reflected her lack of confidence amongst others. In class discussions she was expected by the others to take a dominant role, but this she always strongly resisted. Like Claire, she perhaps felt threatened and insecure with her fellow-pupils as an audience, but felt sure of support with me, her teacher.

Grouping the children in such ways and considering their listening and talking behaviour on an individual, small group and class basis, provided me with a framework in which I could see the areas where difficulties and failures were experienced. From that point on and after a term of being with the children, I was able to understand much more clearly first of all the *need* to improve their ability to operate in a variety of contexts and, more specifically, the areas to be concentrated on for this age group.

With my colleague in the first year I had decided to concentrate on developing talk during the Spring Term. With considerable excitement and apprehension I started the second term prepared to put my ideas into practice. I explained to the class the type of language work we would be doing that term — that it would involve a lot of discussing and talking amongst themselves and listening to each other. Their immediate response was one of warm enthusiasm — "great, that means no work!" (What could one say?) Although committed to the idea of individual programmes according to each child's needs, I felt at the time that the class hadn't been working together as a whole unit enough. They had had little chance to talk to a large number of people. So, I started the term's programme with weekly or twice weekly debates.

For years in England the "art" of debating has been practised in the grammar school and private sector of education. Its use in language development has, quite rightly, been attacked by many teachers in that in order to be a successful debater one must learn the techniques of public talk, rather than spend time developing one's own thoughts and ideas.

Despite this, I felt, for several reasons, that debating would be a useful and entertaining way for 8-9 year olds to develop their listening and talking behaviour. For the shyer members of the class I felt that once they were confident enough to talk in front of the other 31 children they would experience the social satisfaction of having internal thoughts sanctioned by a group. Whilst debating, talk is converted into ideas with which one can agree or disagree while learning how to do so without being aggressive or passively acquiescent. The situation requires listening and talking in conjunction, and the way in which voices and the structure of spoken language have to change according to the situation is also stressed. Finally, I hoped that such active class work would unify the class.

I explained the formal structure of a debate and emphasised the fact that one had to be prepared to defend one's point of view and attack the other side's. Many looked perplexed so the actual debate was started as quickly as possible — much easier to learn the rules of a new game by playing it than by trying to explain them beforehand. To begin with, my suggestions for topics were used, the first one being "Children should earn their pocket money rather than be given it." Sides were chosen and speakers put forward, Claire for and Peter against. The class chose who was to be chairman and, rather surprisingly, chose Neil, the traditional "English schoolboy" mentioned earlier, which turned out to be a sensible and interesting choice. The debate started and, rather as I feared, Peter gave a clear but somewhat aggressive speech and Claire's, although not lacking in ideas, was interspersed with giggles and forgetting what she was about to say. The next couple of minutes were rather difficult as no one knew what to do and the majority were rather inhibited by the formality of it all.

Gradually the more talkative members began to get the idea and a reasonable debate was under way. Several difficulties arose, the main one being that most of the contributions were, inevitably, very subjective and did not reflect a shared point of view. Karen, a mature and thoughtful girl, put forward some sensible ideas on why pocket money should be earned, but they were very different from Claire's, and the two girls, both members of the same side, ended up violently disagreeing, with Claire arguing for the other side!

At this point I stepped in and suggested they should discuss their opinions in their groups for five minutes or so. The children went off to do so and returned feeling much more united and sure of themselves; and those who had wanted to talk beforehand, but had been a bit over-awed by the 'talkers', felt confident enough to put forward ideas now that they had group backing. Many children were obviously directly voicing the opinions of their parents. John, an extremely shy and small boy, suddenly contributed a speech about how children should help their mums around the house as it was the children who made the mess, etc., etc., and pocket money should be earned that way. It was a hesitant but quite lengthy speech for him and the fact that he was using ideas heard at home gave him, I am sure, the confidence to speak up. Several children obviously recognised these ideas and felt they could agree with conviction and add to them. This pattern continued over several debates, but as the term went on it was noticeable that having used their parents' views as a confidence booster, the children gradually began to use their own ideas.

The main problem was that about a third of the class — Darren, Lee and Emma included — weren't contributing anything to these full class debates. In order to help the children gain the confidence and de-sire to talk, I decided we would have mini-debates involving groups of five or six people. Each group divided themselves in two and the sides discussed their arguments and decided what point each person was going to make. This meant that everyone had to say something. After a while we reassembled in our classroom and listened to these short four to five minute debates. We then discussed which side had made the stronger argument and voted on it. This proved very successful as even the shyest child felt confident enough to express a few thoughts within such a small group. Furthermore, children such as Darren and Lee were forced to express themselves in full sentences. To begin with they wanted to write down word for word what they were going to say. Af-ter a couple of times, as they realised the other children were listening to their ideas seriously and sensitively, they just wrote notes and head-ings until they talked naturally without written aid.

Once I felt that most of the children were enjoying and gaining confidence during these mini-debates, I took a tape recorder in and said we were going to record them. This caused a lot of excited nervousness, and the children, aware that what they said could now be listened to time and time again, immediately put more effort into trying to express themselves clearly. It also made them more serious about the activity as it made them aware of the importance of what they were saying and how they were saying it; in order to communicate clearly they had to choose the correct words and phrases.

On playing the recordings back, apart from being amazed and de-lighted to hear themselves, they were instantly critical of the lack of

clarity and the poor audibility of their own voices. Pleased with their
response I suggested we re-record the session until everyone was satisfied. This led us on to more technical considerations, making them
aware that their voices had to change in volume, pitch, etc. Learning to
pause at the end of a sentence, raising the voice at the end of a question
and so on, also helped them to understand the need and reason for sentences in written work. "Write it as you would say it" became a common
saying of mine.

Towards the end of term we returned to the more formal class debates but now they had plenty of ideas about what they wanted to discuss. They chose many topical issues such as "Sport is a waste of time
and money," "People shouldn't have the right to strike," "School
should start at eight and finish at one." The quality and enthusiasm of
these later debates hardly compared with the earlier ones. Most people
were eager to contribute in some way, which was a considerable development for the quiet, less eloquent ones, and the quality and structure
of speech used by the talkative ones had also improved considerably.

The more outgoing children continued to be chosen for the role of
speakers and chairman, but in the light of the improvement in the shyer
ones this no longer troubled me as much. Neil was often chosen as
chairman, which gave him a perfect opportunity to use his factual way
of speaking in a situation in which he felt confident and which the children learnt to respect rather than mock. Emma and others like her had
proved to be of great help in the mini-debates and although never
really coming to the fore in even the later class debates were much more
willing to add to an idea and support their side. People like Claire, with
the removal of myself as the central figure in the class, were forced to
contend with the other members of the class as people they had to work
with and consequently became less giggly and less reliant on me.

Another regular activity was the individual talks every child gave
to the class. At the beginning of term I explained that these could be on
any topic they chose, as I wanted the children to feel as relaxed and confident as possible so that they would communicate clearly and happily
to the rest of the class. I said it should last about five minutes as I felt
that would make some of them realise it wasn't just a question of blurt-
ing out a few sentences and sitting down, and that they would have to
think quite carefully about what they would like to talk about. Finally, I
emphasised the fact that they weren't to be read out speeches but that
they could have notes. This was because I very much wanted them to be
aware of, and develop, their ability to shape their ideas and knowledge
while they talked. The rest of the class could ask questions at the end.
Several children gave me agonised looks, "I can't! What shall I talk
about?" So, instead of them choosing when they would speak, I drew up
a timetable, mixing up the different types of children, that is, the children who were confident and enthusiastic and those who might experi-

ence a little difficulty. Everyone, therefore, knew well in advance when they would be expected to talk.

Once again I was surprised and interested by the results. Perhaps the most memorable talk was Tracy's. Until a couple of years back Tracy had been partially deaf and had undergone several quite serious operations. As a result her written work and reading were very poor and she was an extremely withdrawn girl who rarely talked to the other children or myself. Although her hearing was now quite normal, she had obviously got used to not hearing people. During the holidays her family had gone to visit relations in Australia. On her return, amid the noise and bustle of 'first day back,' I asked her about her experience, but all I got back was a whispered conventional response. When the day came for her talk I felt very nervous on her behalf. However, she arrived laden with her maps, brochures, photographs and other mementoes and gave an enthralling and detailed lengthy talk lasting ten to fifteen minutes. The visit had obviously left many lasting impressions on her and she was clearly pleased and proud to be able to share her experience, and to be able to shape her experience into something which the other children would respect her for knowing about and having experienced. Afterwards the other children plied her with questions to which she replied unhesitatingly. The same thing happened with three or four other shy or quiet children. John, an extremely shy and small boy, gave a very serious and detailed account of the history of the cubs and modern scouting. The other children's sensitivity to these more introverted children I'm sure had been developed to a certain extent through the joint experiences of the mini-debates.

An important aspect of such talks for these children was that time had been provided for them to talk. In a class of thirty-plus children it is unfortunately true that the most talkative win and it can be quite a fight to secure a teacher's or group's attention. Nor does the school day often allow the time or the right atmosphere for a lengthy talk about out-of-school activities. Furthermore, the talks gave a dignity and importance to their hobbies and interests and to things that had happened to them which almost certainly wouldn't develop in the playground.

Lee seemed to overcome his embarrassment by choosing a topic which was guaranteed to fascinate the others. Still mumbling, but able to keep the talk flowing, he gave a detailed step by step account of what had happened when he had an ingrown toenail removed. His confidence grew as the squeals of horror grew and by question time he was positively glowing because of the fact that many viewed him as a hero.

Amongst the successes and surprises there were, inevitably, a minority who found this experience quite an ordeal and had difficulty making it last even two minutes. The rest of the class, however, were always extremely sensitive on these occasions and never failed to find questions to ask which eased the situation a little. I certainly felt uncom-

fortable about forcing these children to feel embarrassed, but, on reflection, I feel sure that they would have preferred to have gone through
this rather than be left out, and that it was valuable for them to realise
they could survive such an experience — which must have boosted
their self-image. No one ever said they didn't want to do it, as they
could easily have done.

At the other extreme there were people like Claire and Peter who,
being so involved in what they were talking about, weren't aware that
after twenty minutes most of their audience was getting extremely
bored and fidgety. Both these children were members of the Young
Ornithologists and brought in several highly specialised books to illustrate their talks. Both talks were forcibly ended by my thanking them
for their contributions and saying that it was time for questions. By this
time most of the children were too fidgety to think of anything.

With these two talks, and one or two others, I realised the need for
me, the teacher, to make them aware of the boredom of the other children and to help them to learn from the experience. At lunch-time, after
their talks, I chatted with both of them about ornithology and what
they had said. Peter, in particular, was quick to criticise himself and said
he didn't know how to stop. He was eager to discuss with me ways in
which he could have overcome the lengthiness of the talk.

The most obvious drawback of these sessions was that everyone
only had one chance to talk and therefore there was little or no chance
for individual development. However, as the term progressed (we were
listening to two or three talks a week) the children seemed to learn from
each other and the talks as a whole improved: they became aware of
how long they could interest their audience, how to organise their
thoughts or experiences to a shaped whole, how to finish their talk, and
the advantage of bringing in visual material, if possible. Being a more
informal activity than the debates and because they were by themselves
without group backing, there tended to be a lot of "mm's", "and then
. . . and then" or "then we . . . then we", but, as with all these activities, practice is needed as much as with mathematical computation
skills. Above all, confidence and awareness of one's own ability to create interest need to be proved.

What is given constant practice here is active involvement in listening directed at someone other than a teacher. Interest in a fellow
pupil's hobbies, the fact that they are being given the importance of a
teacher-directed class activity, and the knowledge that they are going to
have to be in a similar position encourage their involvement. Improvement in this respect is marked by the perceptiveness and relevance of
the questions asked.

The arrangement for assemblies in our school is that once a term
each class is responsible for addressing the entire school on any chosen
theme. The attitude of my class towards these assemblies, and how they

spoke and presented themselves to the school, altered considerably after this work on developing talk. By the end of the term several of them, without any prompting from me, decided to speak without notes — something many adults would find difficult to do.

The children's ability to communicate with each other through talking and listening was also being developed in the science work we undertook on the theme of "Time". My main objective for this project was to develop the children's concept of time through experience, estimation and experiment. Jointly conducted experiments were usually followed up by a written report, but the emphasis was placed on the practical aspect of sorting out the problem, setting up a hypothesis and trying to prove it. I wanted the children to learn to co-operate with each other and share their ideas and observations. At that stage, however, I certainly didn't appreciate to what extent their talking and listening ability had to be developed in order for any effective scientific work to take place.

In addition to the difficulty of working with scientific concepts, there were many social difficulties to begin with: the children argued with each other a lot in an unproductive way and were not prepared to work together or accept each other's ideas. There was a gradual but noticeable improvement in this respect, and by the end of the term they were able to work together. This was largely due to the fact that they learnt that the success of the experiment was dependent upon assimilating each other's suggestions and criticisms. Evidence of this development can be seen in the following transcriptions. All of the class had managed to make a candle clock and then I asked four of the brighter children to see if they could make a candle alarm clock. They were able to go into a small room by themselves to discuss and experiment and they could take as long as they needed over it. They spent nearly a whole day on this and I taped much of their conversation. The presence of the tape recorder inhibited them a little to begin with but, after a short time, it had the same effect as with the mini-debates, that is, they seemed to put more effort into trying to express themselves clearly.

The first difficulty in this experiment was for them to think of a way in which a candle with pins in could make a noise at any time, let alone at a specific pre-set time! To begin with they wanted to use an alarm clock in conjunction with the candle and were horrified to realise that the candle by itself had to sound the alarm. Discussing this with them, Ross explains his initial intentions to me and the other three:

ROSS: Yes! I'm going to make it go off!
ME: You're going to make it go off by itself?
ROSS: Yes, well, I'm going to try . . .
ME: How are you going to do that?
ROSS: I'm going to set it, that's if I know how . . .

ME: Ah, but that's using a second alarm clock isn't it? You want to make your actual candle clock make the alarm noise.

JANE: You can't!

ROSS: That's impossible!

ALL: Yes, impossible!

However, after a while, John, a quiet, thoughtful boy suggested the first idea:

JOHN: Make the pin fall onto some more pins, um, make the pin, when it falls out fall onto a pile of pins.

ROSS: But that wouldn't be loud enough, would it?

JANE/JOANNE: No!

John's idea was rejected right from the start as was everyone else's to begin with. After coming to a dead end they decided they had to do something, so they did, in fact, return to John's original idea. This set them off for the day and three or four different clocks were constructed, experimented with and improved upon. The four worked together all day including, by their own choice, through break and lunch-time. At the end of the day they taped themselves explaining how the clocks had been made. These recordings show how they had learnt to work with each other, listen and learn from each other's ideas and co-operate in the actual making of the clocks. Jane, in fact, chooses to talk about the clock Ross started making because she thought it had been the most successful:

JANE: Ross, after we did the one with the bottle tops and the candles, he tried one with two pairs of scissors on a big lump of plasticene, and a tub, with a candle in and, and a piece of string, and it worked! And it made a great big bang when it fell on the, er, tin.

JOANNE: And that was the biggest noise there was out of all the clocks we have made.

Scientific work introduces an extensive new range of concepts and vocabulary which through active use becomes a permanent part of the child's repertoire. For example, words such as "stable", "taut", "attached", "estimate", "testing", "structure" came to be used quite spontaneously by children whose normal vocabulary was comparatively restricted. New language structures arising from cause and effect thinking: conditionals, futures, causal conjunctions, etc. were also demanded and used with confidence by many children. Ross explained his first idea in the following way:

ROSS: We had a trundle wheel at first and we tried to make one with a piece of string, but we found out that if we just let it go the trundle wheel would fall down and the candle would go flying across the room. So, we got another piece of string and attached it to another table and made it stable with two kilogramme weights and a tin and then it stood up. But when the pin fell out it just stood up and didn't work so we banned that one.

Another advantage of sustained discussion in science work is that it encourages children to visualise physical objects and their spatial arrangement on the basis of verbal description and, conversely, to give a precise account of physical objects or processes. For example, how the candle alarm clock actually works. Jane, Joanne and John share the explanation of how one of their alarm clocks worked:

> JANE: Next, we tried to make one with a bottle top and some candles and —
>
> JOHN: Two candles actually —
>
> JANE: Two candles. And we attached the pins on the candles by a piece of string, and a bottle top was on a piece of plasticene in the middle of the two candles, and —
>
> JOANNE: And when the pin dropped out, the bottle top would fall out onto a tin and make, and hopefully make a noise.
>
> JOHN: Then, when we tried that, we lit the candle, one of the candles, and the pin fell out and it worked, but it didn't make much of a noise.

Working in mixed ability groups always has the advantage of increasing the understanding of the brighter members through explanation to the slower ones. Furthermore, in science work where a more factual, logical way of thinking is required, children who are often silent or ill at ease during discussions of a subjective or problematic nature have a chance to come to the fore and demonstrate their abilities. Ross, for example, became a respected and eloquent leader during science discussions. Proof of his commitment and eagerness was the severity with which he reproached Jane and Joanne when they became very giggly during the above-mentioned day:

> "This is not a matter of laughing and fun, this is science."

Looking back on what I have tried to do and learn during this time, I realise that the experience has sharpened my awareness of the listening and talking behaviour of children, and made me conscious of the need for practice to be provided in these areas in a variety of contexts. Variable practice of this kind helps different children in different ways.

For some children, such as Lee, listening to stories can become an enjoyable and stimulating time, rather than a guilt-ridden or, more often, boring end to the day. The mini-debates and individual talks gave confidence to many and boosted their self-image. Providing time for the children to talk about first-hand experiences can increase the often very low level of respect for themselves and for their experiences. As in the case of Tracy, vivid personal experiences can be shaped into something important and exciting for her as well as for the children listening to her.

Talking and listening to others can be of at least as much value as reading and writing when seen as a medium through which learning and experimentation can take place. Ideas and observations can be shared and discussed which can give rise in turn to further learning, whether on an individual, small group, or class basis. In order for this to happen, I now realise, looking back to the Professor Branestawm episode, the teacher has to be willing to be open and to show herself to be open to the class. I had to become aware of my own problems and show interest in their problems. Through discussion, we learnt together strategies for overcoming such problems.

Chapter 2

Only Talking . . .

LEE ENRIGHT

Lee Enright has been a teacher at this Dorset Middle School since it opened in 1977. Like Pauline's school, this one is purpose-built, and its system of management allows for flexible time-tabling of classes and plenty of opportunity for team-teaching. The staff generally see eye to eye with each other and with the headmaster, as a joint article in the Autumn 1980 edition of *Forum** strongly testifies.

During the period that she refers to in this paper, Lee was working closely with the then deputy head, Maggie Gracie, particularly in the use of Bruner's *Man: A Course of Study* (a social studies curriculum). Both teachers were interested to trace the extent to which the course helped pupils to learn from each other as well as from them, and thus to help the pupils understand their own capacities as learners.

Lee has a great sense of humour (which comes in handy!) and her art training enables her to offer children a range of activities through which they can record their responses and illustrate their ideas. As an English specialist I might have missed many of the possibilities that she considers in this paper. In fact, I wish very much that I could have had the opportunity of being a pupil in her class along with all those bright-eyed 10-11 year olds. I know that I would have learnt a great deal from such an experience.

"Listening to other people makes you change your ideas a bit. Like perhaps you have an idea, but as you listen you begin to feel you may be wrong, and so you change what you think." Nicole, aged 12. "Even when you're only listening, language is still used." Martin, aged 12.

"What do you mean you were *only talking* . . . ?"

I believe that time spent on oral work can be considered as money in the bank — its value can be drawn on immediately, or it may be kept

*Forum, Vol. 23, No. 1. Editor: 11 Pendene Road, Leicester LE2 3DQ
*See *Forum*, Summer, 1979, for our discussion of new trends in education.

for the future. Children, though, often remain unconvinced of the value of talk; they feel that unless they have written about something they have done no work. Because of this, it is necessary to prove to children that their teacher values their oral work as much as their written work and regards process as at least as valuable as product.

Another problem for the teacher is the evaluation of a child's progress in spoken language. There are plenty of ways of checking a child's reading development, and apparent 'proof' of development encourages teachers to continue their efforts. There seems to be no clear way to evaluate oral language development, particularly in the short term. Such progress may be irregular, with some children continuing to take a passive role in group discussion, in spite of their teacher's attempts to get them to do otherwise. This does not mean to say that there has been no development — only that nothing has made itself known.

During the first half of the two consecutive summer terms I was with this particular group of children, I kept a diary of each day's events. Initially, the diary was to help me look at learning processes, consider ways in which I could increase the autonomy of the children in my class, and to look at the way ideas moved around a group of children.* The only way to make sure I gathered information that would help me achieve these aims was to write about everything. I wrote the diary every evening, recording as much as I could remember. Another teacher, Maggie Gracie, agreed to help me with the diary. She taught my class and so she was able to contribute her own diary entries. Her special interest in the learning process and her expertise in classroom research, as well as her moral support, were invaluable. My own appreciation of the value of talk and discussion increased when I realised that talking to Maggie about what had happened during the day helped me to sort out my thoughts, consider the part I was playing in the classroom, and also see the connections between past and present events.

Many of the events I describe here happened during my class's work on *Man: A Course of Study*, a social studies curriculum devised by Jerome Bruner, which plays a core role in our school. *Man: A Course of Study* sets out to explore three questions: What is Man? How did he get that way? How can he be made more so? The course materials are drawn from contemporary studies of animal and human behaviour, and provide examples of contrast and comparison to help children develop *their own views* on the three key questions. Bruner's theory that "any subject can be taught effectively in some intellectually honest form to any child at any stage in development" is at the heart of this teaching approach.

In April, 1978, Maggie and I took my class to Brownsea Island to observe herring gulls in connection with their topic work. The following day the children were given a choice between making some sort of record of their day or continuing with their normal assignments for the week.

Brian made a tape recording of what he had done at Brownsea. Brian finds written work very difficult — he is rarely able to write more than three or four sentences, even when he wants to. The tape he made was considerably longer — for him quite remarkable:

At the pier: We all walked down to the peacocks' field. Miss Enright got lost. Miss Gracie took six of us down to Oak Corner. Miss Enright walked through Harley Wood. Then Miss Enright found us. Then we all had dinner. Me and Mark and Stuart went to the cliffs and me and Mark took some recordings. Mark got a good picture of a herring gull's red spot. We all walked up to Pottery Pier. Coming back on the boat some of us got wet. Coming back on the boat we saw a Dutch liner.

Maggie noted in the diary:
"1. He *reads* the tiny print off the map, and clearly *knew* where all the events of the day took place.
2. He gropes for words, corrects himself on the tape, but ends up with a piece of speech, according to Lee, longer than anything he has written."

That same week, Brian tried to make a written account of the day on Brownsea Island:

A long walk to the boat
Me and Roy were lost walking back to the boat and Roy to(ok) a photograph of me by the big white stones. and when me and Roy got back to the tree I was tired and then me and Roy got to the shop and I got on the boat.

I noted in the diary: "Today Brian told us about when he and Roy got left behind on Monday. He related the tale with a wry grin on his face, saying that he had expressed a hope that the others would have left signs for them to follow. He came up to me later when the others were doing their story writing, and asked if he could write about "what happened at Brownsea." I said yes, what would he put? He said he would describe getting lost with Roy. How did he feel when he was lost? Terrified. That he would get left behind? Yes."

The day after that I noted:

'The writing has been started, but today Brian said he couldn't remember how he felt when he got lost.'

Looking at Brian's written account, I am most struck by the obvious effort he has put into it — which appears to be as much physical as intellectual. He wrote in ink, trying desperately to join his letters neatly, and to comply with my normal requests for titles, dates and underlinings. Perhaps getting all this together in one piece of work distracted him from his real purpose — to 'describe getting lost with Roy.' There is no mention of his fear of being left behind or of any search for signs — nothing, in fact, which reflects what *really* happened to Brian on Brownsea in the way his tape recording had done. When he was taping, Brian could think and talk at the same speed and therefore record an accurate picture of his memories.

At about the same time, Mark C was doing most of his 'story-writing'on tape. His written work was always done at top speed — he usually repeated himself, cared little about spelling (he generally 'lost' any spelling notebook I gave him), and almost always included a car crash. He would never allow himself to think a story through, insisting that he 'had to' do it quickly. This is the beginning of a story he recorded, when he used a small plastic model of a man as an audience:

'Hello children. I'm going to tell you another story about this ghost. Once upon a time there lived this boy, and he got *fed* up because they all thought he was scared to death of ghosts. There was this wooden hut right on the top of a hill, so one day he thought he'd go up. Up he went. Knocked on the door. No one came. Knocked again. And the door just swung open. It was getting dark now. He went inside and investigated. He trod on a floorboard — and it *creaked*. A door slammed upstairs! What was going on in this house? Was there a ghost? So he went on up the top. (Sound effect of a crash.) What was that? There was something upstairs. It was coming from the doorway. *Bash* through the door! The window was blowing open. The wind must have blown the door shut. Can you hear the rumbling? "There *is* a ghost in this house," he

This extract is about one third of the whole story — Mark would never *write* this amount — and he recorded the whole thing *without a pause*. Throughout the story, Mark inserts all kinds of sound effects to enhance the ghostly atmosphere. He builds up the story gradually, taking his time, so that the climax is most effective. Towards the end of the story he gets a bit carried away with himself, and the tape is difficult to transcribe exactly, but the story is carried through to its end in a logical way.

said. "What shall we do?!" Didn't know what to do. Stood there. Out the window!!'

Once again, taping offered a way of recording ideas, which was not possible (for this child) in writing. Mark is more articulate than Brian though, and I feel his recording reflects this; it would appear that talk can raise the level of the work being produced by the child whatever his ability.

When Mark and Brian were taping various pieces of work, I tried to make it clear to them and the other children that I did not see taping as an easy way out or as a way of avoiding written work. Tracy and Theresa said they wanted to tape a story too, and this helped me to convince the children that I meant what I said.

Tracy and Theresa both enjoyed writing stories, and this example of Tracy's written work shows that they were not without charm:

'Once there lived a very unhappy duck. Everybody hated him and the things he did. One day he went to play with the goose and they started to argue. Then after that they were not friends. Next day the duck was very lonely so he began to cry. Suddenly a snail came by. What's the matter? said the snail. Nobody likes me said the duck. Well I like you said the snail so they went to play. Him, the snail and the snail's playmates. Next day they started to argue over which sides were which so they broke up. The snails started to run with their little tongues hanging out. Then they slid down a hole in the ground. Some years after the duck was old enough to get married to another duck. Her name was Maggie but he didn't have a name so they called him Martin. His father pronounced Maggie and Martin man and wife. Then they all became friends and lived happily ever after in their little house with the geese and snails.'

By contrast, a tape transcript reveals the girls' ability to consider emotional issues in a much less matter-of-fact manner:

This is the story of Golden Hair.

Once upon a time there lived a girl. She lived in a village and she had golden hair. One day Golden Hair was cleaning out the house and suddenly she saw a secret passage leading through the ground. She opened it and went down. Suddenly she slipped, but she caught hold of a ledge and pulled herself up. Then a voice started calling her.

"Golden Hair, Golden Hair, Golden Hair, come here!"

Golden Hair was very fright-

There are several differences between Tracy's written work and the tape recording she made with Theresa. To begin with, Tracy had an audience and partner, someone to share ideas with and someone to be critical of those ideas.

In her written piece, the action takes place over a number of years but it is encapsulated in a relatively short piece of work. In the tape recording, the events of a few minutes are told at much greater length. The difference here between talking and writing seems like the difference between

ened, and then the wind suddenly shut the passage up, and she began to cry. And a (?) flew over the top. Golden Hair screamed and cried, and the voice just kept on calling:

"Golden Hair, Golden Hair, Golden Hair, come here!"

"No!"

"If you don't come here you'll die of hunger. You won't have anything to eat except the rats."

"No, I want to go home! No, I want to go home!"

"You'll never get out Golden Hair. The passageway is locked!"

"Where d'you want me to go?"

"I want you to come here. Come to me, Golden Hair."

"But I don't want to!"

"Come to me, Golden Hair!"

"Will you let me out after?"

"Oh, I might consider it."

"Alright, I'm coming." (Sound effect — footsteps.)

"Faster, Golden Hair!" (Sound effect — running.)

"What do you want?"

"You are my little child for ever and ever!"

"No, I won't do it! You promised you would let me out!"

"That is what we say, but it is all a lie!"

"No, I want to go home to my mother and father!"

"Your mother and father are dead. Your mother now is *me*!"

plays and operas — in a play a character *says* "yes"; in an opera a character sings a ten minute aria. At some point in our teaching of young children, we give them the impression that they have to tell the *whole* story when they write — can we be surprised when we always seem to end up with a rather flat summary?

The word 'so' occurs four times in Tracy's written piece — this seems to be a very useful word for children when they are trying to maintain a storyline. In the tape recording, the two girls are able to tell their story without such obvious manipulation. They are much more 'inside' their story; because they *are* part of the story, they are able to explore the situations in detail. Golden Hair speaks in a very delicate, girlish voice, her expression varying from terrified to suppliant to angry. Theresa takes the other part, and has a sort of hypnotist expression at first, which changes to a more demanding one, and at the end of this extract she is crowing in triumph.

Taping offers the best of both worlds when it comes to having something to show for the effort. Taped work has an immediacy that is often difficult for children to achieve in their writing — their 'brainwaves' don't get lost between brain and pen. At the same time, the child and the teacher can examine the work in detail when it is finished. It is also easier perhaps to rethink and amend such work than it is to rethink and amend writing.

When a child seeks to express himself through writing, he is often faced with the air of finality of words on a page. When he is talking he has the use of what the Bullock Report* refers to as 'paralinguistic features' — tone, pitch, intensity, timing, facial expression and physical gesture. He is also generally aware of his audience's response, and can modify any or all of these features. Can written work then, especially in the early stages, restrict and possibly stultify a child's ability to explore new ideas and emotions?

MARK: Why have you come to talk to me today, Brian?

BRIAN: I've come to talk to you about dominance.

MARK: Ah! Now, dominance — would you like me to tell you what dominance is?

BRIAN: Yes, please.

MARK: Well, dominance, right?

BRIAN: Yes.

MARK: Is um — now just say, right, there's a load or group of kids.

BRIAN: Yes.

MARK: It happens in baboons — now let's say YOU — know if you were, say — you — you can beat him up, right?

BRIAN: Yes.

MARK: That's how it is. Like you go round, beating people up, and you can say 'Right, I'll beat him up. *I* am in control 'of HIM.' Dominance is that kind of thing.

BRIAN: Yes. *Now* I see.

MARK: There's a group, see — um there's a kind of baboon, right?

BRIAN: Yes.

MARK: Isn't quite an adult male.

BRIAN: Yes.

The flexibility of spoken language, as well as a search for analogies to explain an idea, can be seen in the transcript of a tape made by Mark C and Brian during some work we did about baboons as part of *Man: A Course of Study*. The two boys had spent some time making a troop of baboons out of plasticene. They asked if they could make a recording about how they had made the baboons, and I agreed. They returned about half an hour later and asked if they could make another recording. I asked what about, and they were not sure. I thought for a minute, and then asked Mark if he had understood how dominance was said to operate in a baboon troop. He said he had, so I asked him to explain it to Brian on tape. I was delighted with the results:

I was amazed with Mark's clear explanation of this very complex idea, and am constantly reminded of this amazement when I put other children into the role of 'expert'. They often possess enormous knowledge about things I know little about; these are coun-

*"A language for life." Report of the Committee of Inquiry appointed by the Secretary of State for Education and Science, under the chairmanship of Sir Alan Bullock, F.B.A.

MARK: And it has to go through all these other ones, and these other ones can beat him. In five years he's got to beat *all* of them. Then he can be a proper adult male.

BRIAN: That means it's dominant.

MARK: Yes. Dominant over them. So now you should see how dominance is. O.K.?

BRIAN: Could you show me some of your work?

MARK: (Pause) I'm sorry — could you say that again?

BRIAN: Could you show me some of your work?

MARK: Ah, no! Now that — I couldn't show you.

BRIAN: Why?

MARK: (With laughter in his voice) Because I haven't done any! I don't know nothing about it.

BRIAN: Why are you speaking to me about dominance then? Haven't you got any *books*?

MARK: No! We don't *need* books! If you already know about it, you won't need books, will you?

BRIAN: Course! I didn't *think* of that!

MARK: No, of course you don't. (Grunts cynically)

try children, and many of them have a deep understanding of their environment, and it is often a simple matter to refer other children to them. But this interview showed me that children may well be the best people to pass on new ideas.

I am also interested in Mark's comments at the end. During the week, Mark and the rest of the class had watched a film of a baboon troop, and had discussed it. I had not asked Mark or Brian to write about dominance as I thought they would find it too *confusing*! I felt that building a troop of plasticene baboons would help them understand how the troop was made up, as well as being an activity they would enjoy. At this point, at least, Mark did not consider talking or model making as work — a common idea among children.

A good way to persuade children that talk *is* important is to make discussion sessions a regular part of the curriculum. But, like many other teachers, I had tried and failed to have any success with class discussion — not just with this group of children, but also with the ones I had taught previously.

After various unsatisfactory sessions, I had simply avoided it.

During Maggie's work with my class in *Man: A Course of Study*, she noted that she "found it difficult to get any kind of order into a discussion. Children wanted to contribute at the same time, and did not seem to listen to each other's contributions." We decided to tape record a class discussion — initially to facilitate an orderly discussion, each child having to wait for me to aim the microphone at him before he could speak. When Maggie and I transcribed the tape, we were able to see exactly where things were going wrong. The main problem seemed to be that they were aiming their contributions at us and taking little notice of each other.

One way round this problem is to have small group discussions, where the teacher moves from one to another, to help out where necessary, but not to act as a permanent chairman. Small groups also mean that each child has a greater chance of making his voice heard. These groups generally have a secretary (sometimes chosen by the teacher, sometimes by the children concerned) whose job it is to make a note of any decisions or ideas a group may produce, and to report back to the rest of the class.

The make-up of such groups is often a problem — should one have more or less permanent groupings? Should the *children* be allowed to choose permanent groupings? Should single-sex friendship groups be allowed?

I have tried various methods of grouping, with varying degrees of success. I have come to the conclusion that the biggest factor is not the method of grouping, but the nature of the objective of the discussion. Is it clear to the children? Do they see its relevance? Do they understand what kind of feedback is required? Does it interest them?

I began to understand how important it is for the objective to be clear to the children during some other work they did in *Man: A Course of Study* on the structure and function of various objects. Maggie led this session, and when the small group discussions began I stayed with Mark C, Mark W, and Brian, who often need extra help. That evening I noted in the diary:

"At first they seemed to find the idea of speculating out loud about their structure rather difficult, and simply blurted out possible functions but, as we continued, they began to talk through their ideas together. Brian found it difficult to pay attention to the object *except when he was actually handling it*, so I kept moving it on from one to the other."

I think that children at this age need something that has reality for them when dealing with abstract ideas — whether the ideas are mathematical, scientific or artistic. When Brian talked about Brownsea, he had his memories of the day and a map of the island; Tracy and Theresa acted out the story as they went; telling his story to a little model man, Mark C had his audience, quite literally, in the palm of his hand.

Another problem facing me was (and is) the 'reluctant talker' — reluctant in the sense that he or she is often unwilling to speak in front of a whole class. Three of the four children in the following tape transcript are, to a greater or lesser degree, reluctant talkers. The four make up a mixed-sex, mixed ability group, comprising two sub-groups of friends. The class was asked to get into groups of about four or five — these two pairs ended up being put together by me.

The small groups were asked to design a vehicle which would travel over snow and ice, in connection with the Netsilik unit of *Man: A Course of Study*. They were told they must use fish, thong, caribou antlers, caribou bones, moss and hide. Each group was to appoint someone to draw the design on an overhead projector transparency. They were given about twenty minutes to complete this task, after which they would be asked to present their work to the rest of the class. All the children had seen the 'ingredients' being gathered on film, and were given small picture cards of the various objects to help them focus their discussion. In this group, Mark C did the drawing.

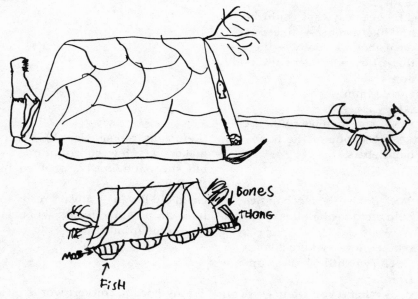

MARK: Well, what can we do with them? Well — well — *string*.

(Reluctant talker No. 1.)

BRYAN: We could use the leather as a —

BRYONY: No, we could use the tent —

(Reluctant talker No. 2.)

BRYAN: Tent —

Speedy involvement of three of the members of the group. No need for long wait to contribute.

BRYONY: And put it on top of the base to make — if it rains.

MARK: Well, first we have to know what body — what —

This sometimes aggressively reluctant talker takes initiative.

BRYAN: Yeah, well, we could make the tent the — body, can't we? Turn the tent upside down —

MARK: So you want the body — let's get the body down then.

BRYAN: Mmm.

MARK: Which way — how do you want the body — like — ?

BRYAN: Just made out that tent leather.

MARK: Let's say that could be — not like a tent — like *that* — what about the body — there — that's how you want the body done.

BRYAN: Mmm.

MARK: *That* —

BRYAN: And then we could use —

KAREN: Use one of the bones for handlebars.

BRYAN: Bones — for handles — hold on to the handles.

MARK: Bones — where d'you — ?

BRYAN: Two little bones, up the front.

MARK: What d'you want — d'you want um — line going across there, going up like that, like a buggy — ?

BRYAN: No, we want a couple of bones, you know, just so they can hold on — sit in the tent and hold on to a couple of bones.

MARK: Aah — so you mean you want — *that*.

(Silence as Mark continues to draw.)

BRYAN: Yeah.

Bryan's first contribution as peace-maker and interpreter between Bryony and Mark. Many more follow.

Mark accepts Bryan's help, and tries hard to get the ideas incorporated into the design.

Bryan makes encouraging, 'chairman-like' noises.

(Reluctant talker No. 3.) Karen makes very few contributions — but she is obviously involved in the task.

Good old Bryan — always ready to look at possible ideas, whoever they come from!

Trying hard to convert words into a picture, Mark suggests a 'picture-word' — buggy.

Bryan is not so easy-going that he will accept an incorrect interpretation. He explains again.

Mark does not normally show willing when it comes to changing his course of action, but here he does so.

MARK: Or do you want it nearer than that?

BRYONY: Nearer, so you can hold on to it.

BRYAN: Yeah, a bit nearer.

MARK: What — about *there*?

BRYAN: Yeah.

MARK: One bone — that one just

BRYONY: What are you going to do for the base?

Now he's *really* trying hard.

Bryan as interpreter.

A reluctant talker getting so involved that she is thinking ahead of the others.

BRYAN: The base. We can —

BRYONY: We could use the —

BRYAN: We could use the antlers.

BRYONY: What as?

KAREN: You could use the fish as the sled.

BRYAN: Yeah, fish.

MARK: What, the fish um skins, go underneath like —

BRYONY: No, you could have the moss — put the moss and put the fish on top so it'd be softer with the —

BRYAN: Yeah.

MARK: You want the moss —

BRYAN: The moss, then some fish skins underneath the moss. The moss goes right round underneath it.

MARK: What — moss bags like *that*?

BRYAN: Yeah.

BRYONY: Yeah, all along.

More evidence of speculation on Karen's part — fascinating idea. Bryan thinks so too.

Bryony is really into the work now, and gets quite excited.

Bryan as interpreter.

Bryony accepts Bryan's interpretation.

MARK: On the sides we put —

BRYAN: And there's the fish skins underneath *that*.

MARK: *Fish* — ? What d'you mean — fish skins under *there*?

BRYONY
& BRYAN: Yeah.

BRYAN: To make it more — comfy.

MARK: Fish skins. Hmmm.

The idea begins to seem weird to Mark, but

He accepts a group decision.

BRYONY: We ought to do some arrows, so when we have it on the OHP you'll be able to sort of see —

Again, Bryony thinks ahead.

MARK: Right, I'll put an arrow to them —

Even without Bryan acting as interpreter, Mark is keen to agree.

BRYAN: And we can use a thong to hold it all together.

MARK: *Moss* — and that . . . .

BRYONY: Fish.

BRYAN: We can use the thong to hold it all *together*.

MARK: Hold on — the string? Mmmm.

BRYAN: Yeah, *thong*.

Bryan tries, gently, to help Mark use the correct word, but is ignored.

BRYONY: Wait a minute — we're doing —

MARK: Right — so say — hold on! The antler! Oh, if we had —

BRYAN: Yeah, we've used the antler.

MARK: If we had *dogs* — dogs could *pull* it.

Mark also begins to think ahead.

BRYONY: Yeah, 'cos we need dogs to pull it — say if we're going up hill.

MARK: How're we going to get going?

BRYONY: Oh we haven't — (Refers to picture cards) — we haven't got dogs on here though.

Bryony works strictly to the rules.

MARK: Mmm — so —

BRYONY: What are you going to use for the seat?

MARK: We'll have to get our men to push it.

Notice the 'We' and 'our' — Mark is right inside his work here.

BRYONY: I know — get the — get the fish to pull it!

BRYAN: *Seat?*

KAREN: Yeah.

(Silence)

MARK: We haven't *got* nothing else.

BRYAN: Mmmm, there's nothing else we can use for the seat unless we use —
(Bryony mutters to Mark about his spelling on one of the labels.)

BRYAN: Unless we use some more *moss*.

MARK: What to?

BRYAN: For the seat.

BRYONY: Yeah.

MARK: So there's a moss seat about *there* — Mmmm.

The muttering never turns into an argument.

Even after the muttering about spelling, Mark is still highly co-operative.
Possible area of conflict here.

BRYONY: It ought to be bigger than that.

BRYAN: Yeah, I think it does.

KAREN: Yeah.

MARK: What d'you mean — 'It ought to be bigger'?

BRYONY: What I *said*.

BRYAN: Rub it out with the —
(Bryony offers to go and get a paper towel.)

MARK: Yes, you do, and *we'll* keep on talking. (Mutters)
Simultaneously

Bryan as interpreter/peacemaker.
Karen voices her agreement.

Bryony won't be budged.
Bryan makes 'helpful suggestions'.
Bryony supports her statement with action.
Mark takes it like a lamb!

BRYAN: If we had more moss —

MARK: See, if we had dogs —

BRYAN: To do the — use the seats and covered with the — bit more fish skin —

MARK: Mmmm.

BRYAN: Comfortable.

MARK: But the problem is we haven't got no *dogs*.

BRYAN: No.

MARK: If we had some dogs — we could use 'em to pull it.

BRYAN: The Netsilik Eskimos could push it up hill.

MARK: (In disagreement) Yeah! They'd —

KAREN: If we had dogs we could tie them with the thong.

The two continue to speculate.

Returns to his previous point

Mark is still using words like 'we'.

Bryan can move 'outside' himself.

Bryony is not around for support but Karen comes up with another idea.

BRYAN: Yeah.

MARK: Mmmm. But we're using this to tie round the *moss*.

BRYAN: They can walk together with the bones — like horses.

Bryan as interpreter.

Mark is able to disagree without getting angry.

Bryan *is* speculating himself, not just relying on the others for ideas.

MARK: Mmmm. *Fish* won't be able to pull it — I'd like to see *them* get up the hill!

BRYAN: No! (Laughs)

The group enjoys a joke which doesn't get out of hand in spite of the absence of a teacher.

MARK: (Laughs) Flub, flub, flub! On we go!

KAREN: They could probably pull it along in the *water*.

Again, Karen comes up with a brilliant idea,

BRYAN: Mmmm.

MARK: Yeah, but how d'you know this'd go across water? (Bryony returns with a wet paper towel.)

Mark remembers the task.

MARK: (To Bryony) Come on then!

BRYAN: It might not — if we had the —

MARK: (To Bryony) Backwards and forwards!

BRYAN: If we had the fish —

MARK: (To Bryony) Come on!

BRYAN: If we had the fish skins underneath — it'd be waterproof then.

Bryan's next idea.

MARK: *You* keep talking. I'll get this thing done again how it was — I know how it was.

Mark is still working as a member of a group — here he is encouraging the others!

BRYAN: It'd be *waterproof*. Covered in fish skins, it'd be waterproof, wouldn't it? (Silence as Mark draws.) (I enter the room to speak with another group of children.)

Returns to his point.

BRYONY: Have you done it?

Does Bryony think I've come to check up on them?

MARK: Hold on!

BRYONY: But what are we going to use the caribou bones for? Aah! I've got a *good* plan!

BRYAN: The antlers?

BRYONY: No! We could use *that* (points to one of the cards) to hold on with, and —

BRYAN: We could use them — you know — fix, say, that in the back so the Netsilik can *push* it.

BRYONY: Oh yeah — no, *pull* it, would be better.

BRYAN: Sort of handlebars — so they can pull — *push*.

BRYONY: Some at — one at the back and one at the front. You know, 'cos if you've got three that are pushing, you can always pull.

BRYAN: Um, we're having the caribou antlers —

MARK: (Muttering) *String.*

BRYONY: (Laughs)

MARK: Gotta put the *string* on.

BRYAN: To hold it together.

BRYONY: It's the *thong.*

BRYAN: *Thong.*

BRYONY: It's not *Tong*, it's *thong.* (Bryan's surname is Tong.)

MARK: Take the 'h' off and then it'd be *Tong.*

BRYAN: We're not talking about Tong at the moment.
(Silence as Mark continues drawing.)

MARK: There's the bone — *that's* the idea.

BRYAN: And then we're using that —
(Silence)

KAREN: We could tie the thong on the front so they could pull it along.

Bryony gets excited again.

The cards seem to have been helpful although they are not often specifically mentioned.

Bryony and Bryan get very involved with the idea of pushing and pulling the sled along.

Still oblivious to Bryan's hint about "thong" being a better word!

Bryony is rather more direct than Bryan.

She turns the episode into a joke.

Mark joins in.

Bryan calls the group to order.

Karen is still thinking hard.

MARK: *Bones*! O.K. Now I'm
gonna —

BRYONY: They could pull it along
with um cari — with um —

BRYAN: Now we're gonna use the
caribou antlers sticking up the
back so they can push.

BRYONY: And at the *front*.

BRYAN: And at the front so they   Bryan and Bryony have reached a
can *pull*.   compromise.

(Silence as Mark draws.)

MARK: Hold on — just putting on
—

BRYAN: Is that — is it finished?

MARK: Nearly. (Mutters)

BRYAN: What haven't we used?   Checks that they have answered
the task.

BRYONY: We've used everything.

MARK: We've used *everything*.

BRYAN: We've used everything.

BRYONY: What about — we
haven't used the caribou bones.

MARK: We have!

BRYAN: We have!

BRYONY: What as?

BRYAN: *There*! Behind — *handlebars*.

BRYONY: Oh yeah.   The group confers and makes sure
everyone is happy before the
work is brought to a halt.

MARK: O.K.?

BRYAN: Yeah.

MARK: Right.

(Tape recorder is switched off.)

I find this transcript interesting for several reasons. The four people involved are not a group I would have expected to be able to work
together easily and productively. Bryony and Karen are close friends,
with Bryony usually leading and Karen following; certainly Bryony is
more prominent than Karen in this group task, and it is this *active involvement* which interests me. In class discussions Bryony is often unwilling to contribute — she says they bore her, although the expressions on her face do not bear this out.

Mark, too, shows an interesting pattern of behaviour. He often
finds it difficult to accept other people's points of view, and nearly al-

ways refuses to change whatever course of action he has decided to take. Yet here, he listens as Bryan explains how he wants some bones arranged in the sled, offers his interpretation which is rejected, tries again, and only then has his work accepted. Later on he accepts, almost without comment, that his drawing is too small. He wipes it off the OHP transparency and re-draws it carefully.

Bryan usually enjoys class discussion, and also plays an active part in this small group. He is ready and willing to provide ideas of his own, as well as being able to support and explain those of other members.

Karen says very little in class discussion, and in this small group made only seven contributions — a tiny amount compared with the others — but they show that she *was* listening to ideas being put forward *and* that she, too, was speculating just as much as the others. There is no doubt in my mind that Karen was thoroughly involved.

Another group, consisting of four girls — Jane, Bridget, Catherine and Sarah — also proved interesting. Jane loves discussion, and working here with three of her friends she became very excited about the work. The other three girls are less willing in class discussion, but in this task they did not let Jane take over. Catherine put forward ideas confidently and was able to cope when they were rejected. Bridget did not make as many contributions as the others, but when necessary she was able to summarise previous decisions, showing that she had followed all that had been said.

The size of the groups was important. In class discussions, reluctant talkers often speak, but so quietly that the chairman does not hear them. They tend to think aloud, but are shy of making these thoughts public. In a small group of four or five, these quiet remarks, often made to a friend, become 'official' and are included in the group's deliberations.

The nature of the task on this occasion was vital. The children had clear limits within which to work, and they knew in advance how they would have to present their results. Yet within this framework there was ample scope for speculation and creativity. There was no one right answer — they were not asked to try to work out how the Netsilik built their sled, only to design one of their own — and this ruled out complete failure. When they later saw the film of the Netsilik sled being built, all the groups were able to make positive comments about their own.

To include talking in the normal week's work of a class is not, I think, enough. Telling them doesn't do the trick either. I found that 'talking about talking' helped me understand something about reluctant talkers, and perhaps made my point of view clearer to them. I was helped in this by the part of *Man: A Course of Study* which looks at talking and learning. During this work, I wrote in the diary:

"I asked if they could think why some people are reluctant to join in discussions. I asked Bridget what she thought. She said nothing, but twitched her shoulders nervously.

Jane said it could be because some people were shy.

I said that I had hoped that after we had been together as a class for two years people might not be so worried.

Jane said that her brother (aged 15) has said that he doesn't join in discussions. It could be shyness or, she said, because he doesn't care.

Bryony muttered, 'Like me.'

I said I didn't believe her.

Mary said that perhaps they were afraid that other people would laugh at their contributions.

I asked Bridget what she thought of this idea.

Bridget said, 'I don't know.'

Mary, one of Bridget's friends, said, 'She said something!'

Mark W said he felt a bit like Jane's brother and Bryony — he just couldn't be bothered sometimes.

Debbie said some people just prefer to listen.

Jane said people won't join in if they don't like the subject being discussed, or if they think it is boring.

I mentioned the discussions I taped last week (sled building) and said how impressed I had been with Sarah C, Bridget and Catherine — the way they stood up for themselves in the discussion.

Martin O, sitting opposite Catherine and Sarah C, said it was because I wasn't there.

Catherine said she didn't know why the discussion had been better. She seemed shy again.

Jane said it was because they were all friends.

Bryony said it was because it had been noisy, and no one could hear what you were saying."

In another discussion, I asked the class how they thought talking helped learning. I wrote in the diary:

"Julie put her hand up immediately, and said, 'If you don't talk you won't learn much, because you can't communicate.'

Jane said talking wasn't always necessary — you could learn without it — you still had your eyes and your ears.

Bryan asked her what she'd be listening to.

Martin O said that even when you're only listening, language is still being used.

I asked the class if they could think of anything they could learn where language was vital.

Roy's hand shot up. 'How to talk!'

Collapse of stout party!"

I have also used the strategy of tape recording class discussions. Tape recorders are as familiar to these children as pencils — they use them almost daily, especially in their Reading/Language small group work. Such tape recording is easily understood by the children — it enables the teacher to monitor each group's work. But tape recording a whole class discussion when I am present needs more explanation. I always told them why I was going to record a session. I said I was interested in the way children learn, and that I thought talking was important. I also told them that I was keeping a diary about things that happened in our class.

When I kept the second diary, I took notes during my visits to small group discussions that were not being taped, as well as during class discussions. This note-taking often led to children contributing in order to see their initials on my notebook, but in nearly every case their contribution was a valid one. After a class discussion during which I took notes, I wrote in the diary:

"Sarah C saw me writing without looking at my note-book, and told those nearby — Sarah T, Catherine, Theresa and Tracy. All laughed.

I explained — *again* — that I thought that what they say is as important as what they write, but they still find it amusing. I get the impression that they realise that I take down the things they say, but they are so impulsive that they forget about it when they speak."

The main problem with talk in school seems to be with its evaluation. I believe that the work I have done with my class has paid off handsomely, but there is no way I could put a grade or percentage mark on the results. I have seen a development in the way these children use their language, but how do I put a yardstick to the way they now approach each other about problem-solving? Or the way they listen to each other in a careful way, helping out where necessary? Or their willingness to explain meaning to each other — and the progress in their ability to do so? Or their ability to have a discussion in which as many as want to can become involved? Certainly over the last couple of months of our time together I noticed that more and more of the class took an active part in discussions, while it became possible for me to "control" discussions by eye contact. I suppose I would also like to think that they have begun to understand that process is as important as product, when you are "finding out" or "learning" about something, but this is probably hoping for too much.

What I do know is that *I* certainly learnt a lot from talking to Maggie *and* the children — especially the 'reluctant' talkers.

Chapter 3

"What If All
the Whales Are Gone
Before We Become Friends?"

LYNDA CHITTENDEN

As a teacher in Old Mill School for fifteen years, Lynda Chittenden's goal has been to encourage in her nine and ten year old students a feeling of competence about themselves as learners and language-users. To this end, she prefers a self-contained classroom where most students will stay with her for two years — a situation which allows long term, integrated subject projects like the whale book whose evolution she describes in this chapter. In the world of her classroom, language rituals abound, perhaps the most popular being the after-lunch gathering on and around the couch in the back of the room where Lynda reads from the current book she has chosen. As a testimony to the power of these daily half-hours "out-of-time," her former students tell her, when they come back for visits, that it's images from the books she had read to them which have stayed longest in their memories of her class.

"What's helped me the most of learning is Lynda talking about whales 'cause books don't get it down in my head. What gets most of the information is the book you're reading to us* and when you make us think how big they are. Every day I go home thinking about that book. It seems like every day I learn more and more about marine mammals."

Justine   10 yrs old

"I'd like to know how a whale is related to a porpoise. When does a whale come to the breeding ground, when does it leave and where does it live after? Also a whale at Marineworld had two kids and they both died. I want to know if she has a problem. How does

*Mowat, Farley. *A Whale for the Killing*, Penguin Books, New York, 1972.

a whale find a mate? What is the whale with the horn? What is the horn for?"

Jason   11 yrs old

"I wish I was rich so I could go out on a boat and go right by one and swim with one. That's what I would like to do. I wish that I could go and hear them talk. I want to learn what they are saying. I want to know what they think. I want to be a whale. I want to swim like one and wave my flukes like one and to spout like one. Whales are beautiful. Yet so much is not known about them. Mom can we go watch the whales? I dreamed once that I was on a island stuck. And the biggest whale came and I climbed on his back and it took me home and everyday I would play with it. I would throw the ball and he would get it on its blow hole and throw it back. Then my mom woke me up."

Jill   11 yrs old

Puzzling, questioning, imagining, dreaming, pondering: these are all accepted mental activities of learning. They are, however, an even more profound part of learning when kids regularly write in learning logs and reflect on the questions, confusions and fantasies that are included in active, involved learning. Also, the learning process is enhanced when kids are surrounded by the language of the unit they're studying: they need to be read good works of fiction and non-fiction that deal with the content; they need to be involved in animated discussions in which they ponder and exclaim over the wonder of the content.

Believing these two principles vital to classroom learning, I consciously made them an important part of a recent study of marine mammals done in my self-contained class of twenty-seven fourth and fifth grade students. I did not anticipate that out of this study would come the enthusiasm and means to publish a textbook on marine mammals!

Our school has a strong science program emphasizing wildlife and natural history, so the kids came to our study well-versed in ecology and basic taxonomy; in addition, they possessed an understanding and sympathy for the plight of many species of endangered animals. Our study would be more than a superficial survey of marine mammals: we would go into the biology as thoroughly as possible. The school community is near the coast of northern California where opportunity exists to view Gray Whales migrating south to the warm lagoons of Baja, Mexico. We would not have to travel far to see elephant seals "hauled out" on land, and be able to witness the mating and birthing spectacle of these bizarre mammals. A marine aquarium is nearby where we could closely view a Killer Whale and actually touch a dolphin.

After discussing several possible science areas, we decided in November to commit ourselves to an in-depth study of marine mammals. We spent December on various fund-raising projects necessary to finance our field trips. We would begin in January because that's when both the Gray Whales and Elephant Seals are locally the most visible.

In January, after returning from the Christmas holidays, and before any reading or discussions, the kids wrote in their learning logs about what they knew and what they wanted to know. Many of these log entries reflected a biological sophistication about marine mammals (m.m. for short):

". . . I also know that the whale is the biggest type of m.m., and that to catch food whales ingulp a big mouthful of water and siphon out the krill and blow out the water. And that dolphins can be as smart as a human. Dolphins are not whales, but they are related."

Peter P.   9 yrs old

". . . m.m. are all warmed blooded. They all nurse their young. They have lungs, but live in the sea. They have different personalities — actually mammalnalities! They live on different foods. Some have teeth, some don't. The ones that don't have teeth have baleen. They are called baleen whales."

Denise   10 yrs old

". . . the Right Whale has a big bump on the top of his neck almost exactly like the Bowhead. The whale or any m.m. reproduces just like us (x rated) and breathes air just like us, but there's one thing that they do that we don't, live in the water. I don't know if whales migrate from north to south or east to west or visaversa, but they do migrate. The whale will beach itself to die. There are other m.m. than whales."

Whitney W.   10 yrs old

While we wanted to study all marine mammals, whales were always the most exciting species and continually became the unplanned focus of our wonder and excitement. Those first log entries in January were on the whole quite sophisticated, but some contained strongly stated inaccuracies: i.e. "I know all m.m. breathe through gills," "all m.m. breathe air through their mouth not gills." There were even some subtle inaccuracies: "the Blue Whale is long with barnacles on his body." (The Blue Whale *is* long, but rarely has the kind of barnacle covering of a coastal species like the Gray Whale.)

The students were comfortable writing about what they thought they knew. They were less sure, however, about knowing what they wanted to find out. "All of these facts can have 'whys' at the end. There is more that I know. *I don't know if I don't know anything.*"

Since my knowledge of marine mammals was only slightly greater than that of the kids, I was only able to respond in writing to these log entries by congratulating them on how much they seemed to know and suggest that as we proceed we should recheck and refine these "facts." I would need to read, study, question and ponder right along with the kids.

In the beginning we all brought into class many resources: public, district and school library books; textbooks written for youngsters and texts intended for a reading audience of older biology students; magazine and journals ranging from the kids magazines *Ranger Rick* and *World* to *National Geographic* and *Ocean,* (the journal of the Oceanic Society); pamphlets from Ano Nuevo State Reserve on elephant seals and monographs from Marineworld, Greenpeace, and Project Jonah.

As we read and talked, we found that there seemed to be conflicting information: Do baleen whales really feed *only* on krill during the warm Arctic or Antarctic months and fast the rest of the year? The older textbooks said so. But a more recently published book* told of finback whales swimming upward in a circular motion "herding" herring together and then gulping them. Moreover, a recent *National Geographic* magazine showed a picture of a humpback whale near Maui, Hawaii, first creating a herding net of bubbles and then actually feeding. We began to read critically, looking first at the copyright date and doubting anything published before 1970.

The more we read and found out, the more questions we had — asking questions about what we didn't know became increasingly easier: Since they have no vocal cords, *how* do humpbacks sing? Elephant seals predictably will begin to arrive at Ano Nuevo in late December, will give birth, mate, and then leave. But, *where* do they go the six to eight months they are away at sea? Gray Whales do migrate from north to south, passing the California coast in late December and January. We saw them. But, the estimated population of eleven to fifteen thousand don't all go to the three small lagoons in Baja, Mexico, that serve as nursery and breeding areas. *What* do those others do? We realized that more is not known than is known about these animals.

After a couple weeks of reading, talking, field trips and note-taking, the kids again wrote in their learning logs. They were asked to reflect on what was helping them to learn and what effect the learning was having on them:

> "I think the two things that helped me most is seeing the m.m. and how they act. I also think that talking in a group helped me a lot because I hear all the opinions of other people. But altogether I think seeing them is the best for me. At home my parents have become very interested in our studys of the m.m. Sometimes we spend all dinner talking about m.m."
>
> Katie   10 yrs old

*Mowat, Farley, ibid.

"What's helped me to learn the most, well, I think the books
helped me. Because I read them and they worked. I also had a
dream. I dreamed that I had a sea lion and I found out what they
eat and what they look like close up, and a whole lot of other
things that I didn't know! I couldn't believe that I dreamed something that I didn't know!"

Cristin   9 yrs old

My primary purpose in using learning logs in the classroom was to
encourage kids to explore and reflect in writing what is happening to
them. Once in awhile, however, I'd fall back to a rather traditional
teachery position and ask them to write "what they learned" rather
than the puzzling, wondering, speculating, imagining, questioning
kind of writing I believe is necessary to real learning.

After a trip to a local sea aquarium (Marineworld) where we were
able to spend the morning with the head cetacean trainer, one student
wrote:

"What I learned about marine mammals is: baby whales, when
they are born, they do not have any teeth. I never knew killer
whales could be so big. I never knew dolphins were so intelligent.
I never knew sea lions could be so huge in a small amount of time
and I never knew that a female sea lion could be so much like a
male guarding his property."

Abby   9 yrs old

This use of the logs has validity when it helps the students recollect and
begin to order their new learning. If used solely for this purpose, however, I could imagine learning logs quickly losing their vitality and
impact.

We chronicled our learning in these logs, but we were also taking
notes. Each of us had a folder, taxonomically organized by scientific order: Cetaceans (whales and dolphins); Pinnipeds (seals, sea lions, wal-
rus); Sirenians (manatees and dugongs); and the one marine mammal
which was the last to return to the sea and whose classification remains
Carnivore (sea otter). We had accumulated and were still gathering an
enormous amount of factual information. What were we going to do
with it all? I began to realize the need to create a focus for our writing.

About this same time, I planned a field trip to a local swimming
pool. We had learned the diving/surfacing pattern of Gray Whales. We
had learned that Cetaceans and Pinnipeds have collapsible rib cages
and exhale rather than inhale before diving. We knew that most marine
mammals achieve great speed using only an up-and-down motion of
their tail flukes and lower body. What would it be like to actually try
out for ourselves those adaptations in a real marine environment?

Finding access to a pool and getting the kids there was easy, but I
had neglected to take weather into account. It was February and the

pool was unheated! Once I got the kids there, I explained what I wanted them to do. Towels, a warm fire, and hot tea waited for them nearby. They didn't *have* to get in that water, but amazingly they all did. Afterwards they wrote in their logs about the experience:

> "Today our whole class went swimming. We were trying to be marine mammals, but the water was only 40+ degrees so no one could stay in very long. I think Lynda should have gone in too. I was trying to swim across the pool but when I was about half-way across I was so frozen that I had to get out. Now I realize how important the whales blubber is. Especially if the sea is around 6 degrees colder. When I was swimming in the pool I was trying to be a whale by making my arms like flippers but I kept sinking that way. I forgot to blow all my air out and instead I took a breath. It's a lot easier for whales to take breaths because they have a blow hole in their head. Whales are very lucky to have all that blubber. *I wonder what it would be like to live your whole life in the sea?* I learned that blubber is more important than I thought. I knew it was real important but I thought that the whales could survive without it. Well, I mean not for a real long time but about a week (or 2). But I could not even survive in that pool let alone the ocean for more than ½ hour. I'd probably freeze!"

> Elida   10 yrs old

The italics are mine, but it was this field trip and log entry that showed me what concept we'd focus on: How *do* these mammals, warm-blooded and air-breathing like us, live so successfully in the sea?

We now had our focus, but what form would the kids' writing take? Many years of teaching had made me dissatisfied with "report" writing. All too often, these reports were written in a dry, encyclopedia-copied language and written solely for the reading audience of Teacher. The kids seemed to feel that a "successful" report was one which was tidy and neat, contained some colorful illustrations, and had a plastic, see-through cover. These reports were rarely ever enjoyable to read, and few students liked doing them. I felt the only learning they demonstrated was of a shallow memorizing/copying nature.

So, how could I broaden the audience for the kids' writing and also give it a genuine purpose? We had access to a great deal of written information on marine mammals, but it had *all* been written by adults. Nowhere could we find anything written by kids about these animals that all kids seemed to care so desperately about. Our fund-raising projects had been quite successful, and we had some money left over after our field trips. So, we'd write a textbook for kids on marine mammals and use our monies* to publish it!

---

*later augmented by a generous loan from the local Rotary Club.

We got busy. A table of contents for our book was drawn up. The orders of Pinnipeds and Sirenians would each be a chapter. The sea otter (order Carnivore) would also be a separate chapter. Cetacean, the ones about which we had the most information and concern, would be split into two chapters: one for just whales and then one for dolphins. All of the writing in these chapters would be focused on primarily answering the question: How does this particular order of animal live so successfully in the sea? We would also have an introductory chapter which would include extended answers to questions like: What is a mammal? What is a marine mammal? Where did marine mammals come from? Our last chapter would be titled "Man and Marine Mammals: Yesterday, Today, and Tomorrow" and would include answers to these questions: What is the history of whaling? What about research today? etc. Consultations with a college-level teacher/consultant with the Bay Area Writing Project had shown me that concept questions are the best way to help students structure and then write about information.

The kids then wrote privately to me telling me what their first, second, and third choices were for a chapter assignment. I then divided them into chapter groups making sure to spread the talent evenly, but also making sure that the first and last chapter groups were particularly strong as I felt these were the more difficult and important areas to write about. After the kids were put into chapter groups, each student chose a specific assignment such as in Chapter Two, Cetaceans/Whales, writing to the question "Why is a whale's body the way it is?" As a group, they talked about what to include and what information in their notes or heads was relevant to each one's assigned question. But before they began actually working on their drafts, I asked them to again write in their learning logs — this time to write what they understood about their chapter assignment, but more importantly what was confusing to them:

> "We have just started writing the first draft of our book. My main subject is adaptation on the dolphin. I don't understand why the size helps it with life in the sea. I understand that its being streamline makes it simpler to live in the sea. The body structure makes it simpler to live in the sea."
>
> Katie   10 yrs old

While writing here, Katie began to explore the answer to her own question. In my written response to this entry, I asked her to think about this relatively small cetacean and compare that size with its speed and agility in the water.

The purpose of the writing the kids were doing was very clear, but many of the kids shared this girl's concern:

> "Right now we are starting to do our first drafts on our book. I understand most of it, but like Justine, I don't know where to start.

Should I start writing on where the manatees live? Or should I start writing about what they eat? I just don't know where to start and I hope you could tell me!! Well, I guess that's the only thing, I pretty much understand every thing else and I like writing in my log, so I guess I'll see ya later."

Cristin   9 yrs old

In my written response, I told Cristin to first write about what a manatee *is*, and then to follow a list we'd developed: body adaptation, feeding, social life, etc.

After the first drafts were written, and the kids had struggled with the organizational and composing tasks of that informational writing, their learning logs began once again to reflect a wondering and questioning:

"This weekend I've been wondering. You see we study whales and sometimes when we find something out, we're just so overwhelmed. So what I was wondering, if whales study us? Like if you're standing watching whales and a whale comes up to your boat. You usually think that the whale is there just for you to look at. But did you ever think that it was there to look at you? Maybe whales already know about us. How we work, how we communicate and maybe they think it mind boggling how we tick. Or maybe whales don't know a thing about us and that's why you see so many of them so many times because they're trying to figure out how we work. I haven't really thought about it but now that I have I don't think I know and I'm getting more frustrated every day. When I was little I used to think that a whale was a whale and they were big and that's it."

Laura W.   11 yrs old

"I wish that I could really be with a dying whale to comfort it, to really try to understand and communicate with it. To sing the song of humans but also of whales, the song of all animals, "life". Unlike all scientists that come to study the whales measures and insides, but most of all to ease a whale's dying. What do other naturalists want to do? Learn about a whales measures or a whale? What do they want to do, see how whales communicate or communicate with them? Can people answer these questions? I have so many questions that can't be answered. I don't know how many millions of questions people have, but I have a lot."

Laura S.   10 yrs old

Listing and ordering new information is necessary at many stages of learning. But I believe that real learning, the kind that changes our lives, comes more as a result of reflection and increased awareness. To me, the kind of reflective writing that the two Lauras did demonstrates an awareness and learning far beyond a mere acquisition of factual information.

As the kids worked on the writing of the first drafts of our book, they often informally checked out their progress with one another. They would read aloud their piece to someone and ask: "Is it clear? Have I included everything? Is my information correct?" But always the one response everyone sought, regardless of the species they were writing about or what question they were answering, was — "Will another kid, one who knows nothing about marine mammals, understand and learn from what I've written."

Because of the kind of response that the kids were initiating and seeking out — this search for clarity and factual correctness — revision became a natural part of their writing process. In the past, when the audience and purpose of the writing was restricted only to Teacher Examining Learning, most kids in my experience felt that whatever they did was written in concrete. They would be reluctant, sometimes to the point of hostility, about any expectation or even suggestion of revision. They were through thinking and a "final draft" meant only recopying what they'd written in their "first draft", with an emphasis on neatness of handwriting and correctness of mechanics.

Now it was different. Their first drafts had been double spaced so there was plenty of room to cross out words, phrases, or whole sentences. There was room between the lines and in the margins to write changes and additions. Sometimes after many changes and additions, I'd hear someone say, "I better recopy this, I can hardly read it." Since they knew that I would type their final draft, they expected that to be the time we'd together make the necessary spelling and punctuation corrections. Our first priority was clarity and factual correctness.

When they felt finished and ready, the kids would sign up for time alone with me at the typewriter. Because of the daily presence of a skillful and perceptive classroom aide, I was able to work individually with kids at this time. First we would read their writing together. By this stage their language was clear and their information accurate, but their piece wasn't finished. Often there would still be organizational and sequencing problems or problems of concept clarity. For example the girl writing to the question, "Why is a whale's body the way it is today?", had correctly grouped together all her facts on body adaptation, but had difficulty being clear about the need for those adaptations and where to describe the need:

"Cetaceans have been in the water longer than any other marine mammal so their body has adapted the best for their environment. Both baleen and toothed whales have developed the same, except their mouths are different. They have developed streamline bodies so they can swim faster. They have flippers to balance themselves. The flippers came from front legs. They have flukes to propel themselves through the water. The flukes came from the rear part of their body. They also adapted for cold water. To adapt to the cold water they developed blubber to keep warm. From having to have so much blubber to insulate, they grew tremendously. That also helped them float. Their nostrils traveled from their face to the top of their head so when they come to breathe they don't have to stick their whole head out of the water. Their ears couldn't be like ours, water and germs would start infections and other bad things. So their ears can close up. The outer opening of their ear is the size of a pinhole. Their mouth changed so they could eat the things they eat now. It became perfect for what they eat. Their eyes changed, they got much smaller because they are not much help in the twilight sea. So they developed sonar. Sonar is sound waves that whales and dolphins send out. They send it out through the melon which is in the forehead section and receive it through the lower jaw. . . ."

> Becky's first draft 10 yrs old

At the typewriter, Becky and I talked about how to improve this piece. Making clear the concept of cetacean adaptation was crucial to the success of our book. Basically her information was correct, but two problems remained: 1) she had not made enough reference to the tremendous time span in which these adaptations took place, and 2) the need for the adaptation was only implied. We discussed this and she quickly supplied the phrases which would solve the first problem, and I suggested that paragraphs and topic sentences would be a handy way to deal with the second. This final draft is a result of our dialogue and was composed as we talked:

"Cetaceans have been in the water longer than any other marine mammal so their body has adapted the best for their environment. Both baleen and toothed whales' bodies have developed nearly the same, except their mouths are different. They have developed streamlined bodies so they can swim faster. They have flippers to balance themselves. The flippers came from the front legs of their land ancestors. Hind limbs weren't necessary in water, so gradually over many millions of years they disappeared in marine mammals. Whales have tail flukes to propel themselves through the water. The flukes developed from the hind or tail part of the whale's land ancestors.

The sun does not warm the sea like it does the land. Therefore, the waters of the oceans are pretty cold. So, whales needed to become adapted for cold water. They developed blubber to keep warm. Also, a huge amount of blubber is what enables whales to be so buoyant in the water and float, and blubber helps conserve body heat.

Whales are mammals and do need to breathe air. It's hard when you're swimming to keep sticking your nose up to breathe. So, *very* gradually over many millions of years, the whale ancestor's nostrils traveled from their face to the top of their head. Then when they surfaced to breathe, they didn't have to stick their whole head out of the water. In a whale, these "nostrils" are called blowholes. Baleen whales have two blowholes, but for some reason toothed whales only have one.

Whale's ears couldn't be like ours — water and germs would start infections and other bad things. So, they developed ears which can close up. The outer opening of their ear is the size of a pinhole.

There is a great variety of foods in the sea. So, whales developed different mouths and teeth which were perfectly adapted for the kind of food they ate. Some scientists think that the first whales were all toothed whales. The teeth were necessary for grasping and holding fish and larger sea animals. Today some toothed whales have teeth only in one jaw. The sperm whale only has visible teeth on its lower jaw, and the narwal's "tusk" is really only a tooth from its upper jaw. The sea is also full of many tiny animals which were available for eating. So, the great whales developed baleen which enabled them to eat all the tiny plankton and krill.

The sun does not light up the sea like it does the land. Therefore, the ocean is sometimes called "the twilight sea" because there isn't much light except at the surface. So, whales eyes didn't get larger the way its body did. Since seeing was so difficult in the dark water, cetaceans developed sonar which is a "sound" way of seeing your world without eyes. Sonar is sound waves that whales and dolphins send out. They send out these sound waves or clicks through their forehead (which is called the "melon"). They receive back or "hear" the echos through their lower jawbone . . . ."

> Becky's final draft   Chapter Two, Cetaceans/ Whales — "How and Why Do Whales Live So Successfully In the Sea?"

Becky's final draft also contains many more specific facts than her first draft. They were needed to better communicate to other kids the concepts she was explaining. These facts were all things she already knew and could supply when she saw where they belonged and the purpose they served.

In struggling to organize their information and compose their pieces, most of the kids came up against the need for topic sentences and paragraphs. One boy, writing to the question "How do toothed whales feed?" wrestled with this difficulty. Writing has always been hard for him, but he cared deeply about his subject. (By this time he was signing all his school and personal papers "Oliver Orca.") When he came to me at the typewriter, I could only applaud his solution. The italics are mine:

> *"All whales feed one way or another.* All toothed whales feed on something bigger than a baleen whale's food. The killer whale, or Orca, eats fish, seals, sea lions, penguins, and even other whales . . ."
>
> Jason 11 yrs old

In addition to writing reflectively in learning logs while they are learning, kids need to be surrounded by the language of the content they are learning. That language needs to be accurate and eloquent, and not always simplified. In the classroom, I've seen the most exciting learning take place when good language was used to explore the wonder of new ideas, and then used to reach for a grand expression of them. Perhaps T.H. White said it best when describing how the teacher, Merlyn,talked to his student, Arthur:

> ". . . The Wart did not know what Merlyn was talking about, but he liked him to talk. He did not like the grown-ups who talked down to him, but the ones who went on talking in their usual way, leaving him to leap along in their wake, jumping at meanings, guessing, clutching at known words, and chuckling at complicated jokes as they suddenly dawned. He had the glee of the porpoise then, pouring and leaping through strange seas."
>
> T.H. White
The Once and Future King

I began reading Farley Mowat's book to the class as soon as we returned from the Christmas holidays. A wonderfully well-written book, it tells a heart-breaking story and is also dense with biological information. It took us a long time to read the book. I would read, we would talk, and sometimes I'd re-read. Here is just a small sample of the quality of language and sophistication of information contained in the book:

> "There are only eleven species of baleen whales, but they rank at the top of the whale's evolutionary tree. About eighteen million years ago, when our own ancestors were abandoning the forests to awkwardly start a new way of life as bipeds on the African savannahs, some of the whales began abandoning teeth in favor of fringed, horn-like plates (baleen) that hang from the roof of the mouth to form a sieve with which the owner strains out of the sea water immense quantities of tiny, shrimp-like creatures, or whole schools of little fishes. It seems a paradox that the largest beast in the world should prey on some of the smallest, but the system works surprisingly well. The proof of the pudding is in the eating,

for the baleen whales are the most stupendous animals that ever lived."

Farley Mowat
A Whale for the Killing

I didn't finish reading this book to the class until March. By then I wasn't sure it was necessary, or even desirable, to read another whale book to them. But then I found the perfect next book: Sally Carrighar's *The Twilight Seas.** Mowat had given us an enormous amount of information and had thrilled us with his writing skill. Carrighar's book, lyrical yet somewhat less biologically sophisticated, tells of the life of a particular Blue Whale. We were at the point where we were writing our first drafts, and now very aware of the language choices that every writer has. This book provided a model of the kind of language to reach for: (In this excerpt the Whale and his mother are trapped by icebergs.)

"For the imprisoned pair this restraint was not being a whale. This was not whaleness. Whaleness was giving a swoop with one's tail and shooting ahead to the boundaries of the earth! Skin glistening smooth sliding through glossy yielding of water.

Whaleness was utter freedom, no gravity and no walls. A body able to curl itself in great arcs or, straightening out, glide forward with effortless ease. Men spoke enviously of being as free as a bird. They should say free as a whale, for birds were limited by the exertion needed to stay in the air whereas a whale's floating was weightless, his swimming simply a wish become motion.

But no longer. Locked in by the ice, the Whale and his mother learned what it was to live in narrow and barren confinement. Sometimes they gave a few thrusts with their flukes just to feel again what it was like to sweep along through slippery water: supremely powerful! But they had to brake with their flippers quickly to keep from striking the hardness of ice. No longer free, no longer knowing true whaleness. Squeezed into a form of nonliving. For a whale a slow, final agony.

Death."

Sally Carrighar
The Twilight Seas

The Whale and his mother do survive this crisis, but some of these phrases appeared on our Graffiti Board. Begun as a way of eliciting language, these large strips of blank paper tacked to the sides of a divider in the class were often seasonal: In October one had simply said "The scariest thing I can think of is . . ." and during the month the kids would jot down responses. (i.e. "my sister in curlers", "waking up and seeing Dracula leaning over me", etc.) But by March the section of the

*Carrighar, Sally. *The Twilight Seas — A Blue Whale's Journey.* Weybright and Talley, New York, 1975.

Graffiti Board labeled simply "Language I like. . . ." was getting the most action. Kids were writing down words, phrases, or whole sentences from books they were reading, from other kids' papers they'd read, and definitely from what I was reading to them.

Above all, Carrighar's book had broadened our awareness of the sea as an environment in which to live. All of the chapter assignments had been given and most of the writing of the first drafts nearly completed. And yet something was obviously missing. Our first chapter began with "What is a mammal?" then "What is a marine mammal?" But we realized now that what should come even before that was — "What would the sea be like as home?"

Many hands were raised when I asked who wanted to write this most important first part. Three girls who'd already finished their chapter assignments were selected and they began by talking together and just writing down words and phrases. Because most kids now needed little help to finish and were busy with other less-demanding tasks, our aide was able to spend a great deal of informal time with these three kids who were full of the responsibility of writing an impressive beginning of our book. She read them selected bits of Herman Melville, Rachel Carson, and John Masefield. Those kids were awash in lyrical language of the sea!

Their first draft was little more than a list of inspired words and phrases that followed a sentence whose genesis perhaps went back to *Charlotte's Web*: "The sea is a radiant water galaxy." (The girl whose creation that was literally glowed and proceeded to use the word "radiant" in every way possible for the next few days.) The rest of their first draft sounded pretty but made no sense. They read and reread what they had, they talked, they wrote some more, tried out different phrases and finally came up with this:

> "The sea is a radiant water galaxy. It's a world of its own in a special way. Under its foam crested surface, there exists a universe of plant and animal life. With the tiniest microscopic beings to the most humungous creature that ever lived, the sea is alive!"
>
> Whitney, Justine, and Laura A.

The combination of constant reflective questioning and wondering while also gathering factual information resulted in some thoughtful and powerful pieces of writing in the last chapter of our book — Man and Marine Mammals: Yesterday, Today and Tomorrow.

An informative piece about the "how" of training some marine mammals in today's public sea aquariums was concluded by this student in a powerful way:

> "One awful thing to think about is — what is it like to be in captivity? You see the Orca jump and perform for thousands of people

only because someone signaled him to do it. But, have you ever seen the Killer Whale when the people are gone and he's not performing? He's there swimming slowly around and around, not able to use his sonar and get the different and interesting sounds of home, but only able to get the same sharp and boring vibrations of his cement tank. But not only his sound world is gone — his beautiful dorsal fin is now flabby and drooped with no beauty anymore. In his tank he doesn't get enough exercise to keep it high and erect like an Orca in the wild.

Next time you see a marine mammal perform for lots of people ask yourself, 'Would you give up the free glistening waters of home for this?' "

Peggy   10 yrs old

The very final thing composed for the book was its title: *Our Friends in the Waters.* That title came from the question that structured the last part of Chapter Seven which dealt with Man and Marine Mammals: Tomorrow. The boy who wrote to this question took factual information he'd learned and combined it with speculations and questions he and others had asked in their learning logs. The result was a powerfully persuasive piece of writing about a concern shared by all of the kids — What if all the whales are gone before we become friends?:

"The future of marine mammals lies in the hands of the children of today. Some species today are so endangered that they might not be around when we're grown.

In Newfoundland and Canada, thousands of harp seal pups are now being killed for their fur. When they are newborn, they have beautiful white fur which is highly asked for by rich buyers. Hunters brutally beat these helpless baby seals to death with large clubs. There is a quota, but it's way too high for them to reproduce enough so they can survive. If this killing keeps up, harp seals are doomed.

Every two years, 8,214 sperm whale males are allowed to be killed by law of the International Whaling Commission. This quota is also too high to keep the species going. Also before they were fully protected, Blue whales were allowed to be killed when they were 70 ft long. But the problem with that was that a Blue of that size is still only a teenager and probably hasn't mated yet. Quotas seem like a good idea, but if the whales being killed are both children and adults, it's just a matter of time until they all die off.

Only 5 species of great whales are fully protected: Blue, Humpback, Gray, Bowhead and Right Whales. However, even Bowheads are allowed to be killed by native Eskimo whalers. Just recently their allowed quota was raised. Some scientists feel that even though they are protected, there aren't enough Blue whales left to recover and find each other in the sea and reproduce. The world should stop all hunting of marine mammals or certain species will be totally exterminated.

If the killing is stopped, the possibilities would be fantastic! We could learn so much about them: We could feed a Sperm whale a fish with a homing device inside that could help us find out how deep this deepest diving whale can really go. We could find out how they are able to stay under water so long. We could even find out what they *do* all that time they're under water.

But the greatest thing that could happen would be for us to be able to totally communicate with our brothers and sisters in the sea! Because Cetaceans have intelligence that has been compared to ours, they'd probably be the most interesting to talk to. A Blue whale could tell us what it's like to be the biggest creature that ever lived! An Orca could tell us what it's like to be the top predator of the sea and not afraid of anything! A Gray whale could tell us what they think of us sitting in little boats always watching them! A dolphin could teach us how to play their games!

We could talk to them. We could tell them our dreams about them and ask them, "Do you ever dream about us?" "Do you ever wonder what we're like?"

But, all this will never be possible if all the whales are gone before we become friends.

Steig   11 yrs old

Initially my intention was to only include in our book the informational writings along with many of the fine line drawings the kids had done. However, after I saw the impact of the learning logs on the final writing product, and then looked again at the quality of many of the learning log entries, we decided to include both. So, in the book two-thirds of each page contains the text information. On the remaining margin in a contrasting type was placed either a learning log entry, which relates to the content of that page, or a drawing. Sometimes there was room for both. The result is pleasing to the eye and to the mind.

Chapter 4

A Seed's Growth

MICHAEL ARMSTRONG

I first got to know Michael well when we were both teaching together at a Senior High School in Leicestershire. His interest in the nature of learning and his enthusiasm for searching out ways of encouraging students to feel the same sense of excitement about the whole process as he did was immediately apparent. He is a great believer in giving students a genuine opportunity to make their own choices and then allowing them a realistic amount of time in which to make progress — and to develop through their own efforts an increasing grasp of the chosen task. He also believes that teachers should allow *themselves* sufficient time (if at all humanly possible) to reflect seriously on the work of their students. As he says in this paper, and in the more extensive book* which his year's research produced, patterns of development only emerge over a period of time and can therefore only be traced by a careful teacher noting the *process* of this development over days, weeks, months. To take a piece of work out of the context of the child's continuous experiences in school, and to assess such a piece in isolation as a finished 'product,' would be regarded by Michael as a highly dubious form of assessment.

Since the beginning of January, 1981, he has taken over the headship of an Oxfordshire Primary School, where the numbers on roll are at present declining steadily. The lowest ebb is predicted in three or four years time — a point Michael is looking forward to, since he feels that the kind of education he believes in flourishes best in small schools.

INTRODUCTION: A programme of teaching and research.

This study of a child's study of a seed's growth derives from a year's teaching and observation in a class of 32 eight to nine year old children in an English Primary School. For the six previous years I had

* *Closely Observed Children* — Chameleon Books, Writers and Readers Publishing Cooperative.

been teaching at Countesthorpe College, an experimental upper school for 14 - 19 year old students, on the edge of the city of Leicester. During these years I had become more and more absorbed by the effort to understand the manner in which adolescent students set about learning. The process seemed to be one not so much of assimilating a body of knowledge as of appropriating knowledge, a matter of reinterpreting, reconstructing, reviewing and recreating knowledge in the course of acquiring it. I began to write about this process, as I observed it in the work of my students, above all in order to understand more clearly what the process involved.* But the daily pressures of the classroom made it hard for me to find the leisure to reflect or the energy to write. I wanted to be released from my obligations as a teacher in order to devote myself more wholeheartedly to study and research. But I found myself in a dilemma; I wanted more time to observe but no less time to teach.

It is characteristic of classroom research, indeed of most research into the processes of intellectual growth, that it excludes the act of teaching from its techniques of investigation. The research worker observes children and teachers, either in a natural setting or in a laboratory, and seeks to interpret, and sometimes to control, their behaviour, but without attempting to participate directly in their activity. It is often assumed that the demands of scientific objectivity force this exclusion upon us as researchers. Yet its effect is to deprive us of vital sources of information and understanding: those sources which depend upon asking children questions and answering their questions, exchanging ideas with them, discussing each other's opinions, chatting and joking, trying to probe their intentions and appreciate their problems, offering help and responding to appeals for help — those sources, that is to say, which depend upon teaching.

It was for this reason that I felt I had to continue teaching children in order to investigate their learning. It seemed to me that the act of teaching was indispensable to the study of intellectual growth; that to refuse the opportunity to teach was greatly to diminish the prospect of understanding the understanding of children. My own interest, in any case, lay in discovering what insights were to be obtained from a research strategy that was almost the reverse of the normal procedure: from continuing, that is, to participate as a teacher in the life of the classroom while seeking to develop a degree of objectivity and a concern for close observation, analysis, and description adequate to the task of examining, in a more or less systematic way, the character and course of children's learning.

* See two essays published in FORUM *for the discussion of new trends in education,* Vol. 17, No. 2, Spring 1975, the second of which is reprinted in *The Countesthorpe Experience,* ed. John Watts, Allen & Unwin, 1977.

Yet to declare such an interest was to face my dilemma. A teacher's manifold responsibilities would seem to curtail severely his opportunities for acquiring or practising the skills he requires as a student of children's learning. In a class of thirty children it scarcely seems possible to become both teacher and researcher. However, what might appear to be impossible for one teacher working on his own might perhaps become manageable for two teachers working together in the same classroom. This was a strategy that had already been attempted in various forms, in the USA, during the educational expansion of the 1960s; I had learnt about it from the work of Bill Hull and John Holt as described in John Holt's study *How Children Fail*,* and more especially from the work of the Mountain View Center for Environmental Education, set up in Boulder, Colorado in 1970, and from the writings of David and Frances Hawkins.** Anxious to explore this strategy for myself, I began to look around for an opportunity to work as an auxiliary teacher in another teacher's classroom, sharing the teaching of the class and yet finding time, in more relaxed circumstances, to make a close study of the intellectual lives of its members.

The opportunity finally arose in 1976 when I was given leave of absence from my teaching post at Countesthorpe College to spend a year as teacher and researcher in a primary school some twenty miles away. The fact that I would be working with children five or six years younger than the students I was used to suited me well. At Countesthorpe I had become exclusively preoccupied with the world of 14 to 16 year old students; I felt that a change of scene would help me to place within a broader context the problems of intellectual growth which fascinated me. For the next year, then, I worked in Stephen Rowland's class of 32 eight and nine year old children in Sherard County Primary School in Melton Mowbray, Leicestershire. Stephen had been teaching at Sherard School for two years and was in his third year as a qualified teacher. He was the one regular teacher of his class although on occasions groups of children might visit other teachers for particular purposes. The class occupied a light, airy room in one corner of the school building. This was where the children lived and worked for most of each school day although often enough their activity would spill out into the shared work area beyond the doorless entrance to their classroom. For some time each day the class would be gathered together by Stephen and taught as one, but for the most part the children worked on their own or, more often, in twos, threes and fours, choosing their own pursuits, sometimes for themselves and sometimes after discussion with Stephen. There were certain common commitments and certain common constraints, but the children had considerable freedom of ac-

*Published by Pitman in 1964

**See *The Informed Vision*, David Hawkins, Agathon, 1974, and *The Logic of Action*, Frances Pockman Hawkins, Pantheon, 1974.

tion. The organisation of the class was informal, its methods progressive, and the school as a whole very much a model of the style and philosophy of education advocated in the Plowden Report of 1967.

The study that follows is drawn largely from the daily field notes that I wrote during the year I spent in Stephen Rowland's class. Each school day I taught alongside Stephen as his auxiliary; each evening, instead of preparing material for the following day, looking over children's work, keeping up to date with records, seeing parents or attending school meetings and functions, I wrote about the day's events, attempting to describe as carefully and reflectively as I could the intellectual activity of individual children in so far as I had observed it during my own day's teaching or heard about it from Stephen in the course of our discussions at the end of the day's work. It was out of these daily notes, the conversations which they provoked between Stephen and me and which in turn led on to further notes, and the samples of work discussed in the notes and assembled for further study, that the central themes of our investigation began to take shape.

Two themes stood out above the rest. The first concerned our growing conviction that it does indeed make good sense to interpret the thought and action of children — eight year olds no less than sixteen year olds — as an attempt, or, rather, a more or less continuous series of attempts to appropriate knowledge to their own use. Time and again during the year's work I was reminded of some remarks of Coleridge, which I had come across several years before in one of his essays and which sought to define the education of the intellect as follows: ". . . not to assist in storing the passive mind with the various sorts of knowledge most in request, as if the human soul were a mere repository or banqueting-room, but to place it in such relations of circumstance as should gradually excite the germinal power that craves no knowledge but what it can take up into itself, what it can appropriate, and re-produce in fruits of its own". Our investigations gave ample evidence of the "germinal power" of the children with whom we were working and of the first fruits of their own appropriations.

The second theme, following on from this first, concerned the belief that intellectual growth can properly be understood as a product or consequence of children's successive attempts at appropriation from task to task over the course of weeks, months and years. It is this second theme which is addressed in the study that follows. The story I have to tell deals with practice: not with practice as drill, as in practicing a piece of music in order technically to perfect it, but with practice as the sustained exercise of skill, judgement and imagination in successive intellectual tasks. It is one of three sketches, written some time after my year's work in Sherard School in order to illustrate, however tentatively, the nature of intellectual growth as it seemed to emerge out of our investigations. The first study was published in the journal OUT-

LOOK, No. 36, Summer 1980;* the third, and longest, forms chapter five of my book *Closely Observed Children*, which develops in detail the themes outlined above.

NARRATIVE: Sarah's diary of the growth of a seed.

At the start of the summer term Sarah began to keep a notebook, or diary, in which she recorded, from time to time, in words and pictures, the growth of a seed which she had sown in a plastic pot in mid-February and put away in a corner of the classroom. She kept up her diary, intermittently and with a certain degree of nagging encouragement from Stephen and me, for some seven weeks, until the plant had withered. Some while later when I began to examine the diary again, I realised that it recorded not only the physical growth of the seed which Sarah had planted but also her own intellectual development as she watched her plant grow and attempted to describe its successive stages.

The diary begins on the first day of term, but it was not until a week later that I described its origins in my own daily notes.

'Monday, April 25th.

My first notes of the term which began last week . . . .

On the first day of term, last Monday, Sarah had been surprised and delighted to find that a bean seed which she had planted some weeks ago and which, up until the Easter holiday, had failed to sprout, had shot up over the holiday fortnight. She decided to begin a booklet recording its growth, together with a graph. [This idea had first been introduced into the class in mid-February when Debra had begun, at my suggestion, a diary of the growth of a seed: a seed which she planted at the same time as Sarah but in a shallow tray of peat rather than a plastic pot of peat and sand. Several children had taken up the idea in the following weeks, but few of them had continued their diaries for long. They made the booklets themselves by folding and stapling together a few small sheets of plain paper.]**

Sarah devoted the morning of that first day to her bean and her diary, and returned to it briefly on the following morning, but thereafter, though she kept a daily watch on the bean, she set aside the diary. Today, at my suggestion, which she took up very willingly, she returned to the diary, having something more dramatic to say now, after a week, since the plant has meantime doubled in height.

(Thus the writing and picture of last Tuesday had been composed under some pressure from myself and with only a glimmer of Monday's

*The Mountain View Publishing Co., 2929 6th Street, Boulder, CO 80302, USA
**Square brackets indicate a later addition to the notes. Round brackets are as in the original notes.

enthusiasm, and all this is obvious in the finished product of Tuesday's record. A daily record was too much for Sarah, the daily transformation in her plant being too small to arouse her interest in recording it. The contrast between last Tuesday's entry and today's is marked; today she has recovered the liveliness of the first entry. I suggested to her later today that, unless the inspiration seizes her, she make her diary and graph a weekly rather than a daily affair.)

The little notebook is entitled "my runner bean". Its cover is decorated with a drawing of the bean, outlined in pencil and black crayon and coloured black with a little red added. Sarah had tried to find a bean lying about somewhere to copy from, but when Stephen had told her he would have to bring one in the next day, she had chosen to draw it from memory, accurately enough, observing the slight depression in the middle of the lozenge shaped bean and explaining to me what a runner bean looked like, with her characteristic and, on this occasion at least, very reasonable, puzzlement about precisely how to put the remembered image into words. This kind of puzzlement, which goes hand in hand with a determination to find the exact word to suit her purpose, has often in the past two terms been a reason, and sometimes an excuse, for Sarah's failure to complete a piece of writing — she has a similar problem as regards her painting and drawing. It is a characteristic which Stephen and I have already had occasion to observe this term; it's what one immediately thinks of when thinking of Sarah and her work.

[At the beginning of the year I was inclined to regard Sarah's somewhat finicky attitude to words and objects as an all too convenient excuse for giving up in the middle of whatever task she set herself. It was only very gradually that I came to see it as an indication of her compositional earnestness. In her struggle with words and images, Sarah was among the most deliberate of all the children in Stephen's class.]

On the first page of her notebook, in handwriting much smaller than usual, huddled up at the top of the page, Sarah wrote as follows:

"On the 14th of February I planted a runner bean. [She knew it was the 14th because she had written a label, stuck to the side of the pot, naming the date.] I got a plastic pot and put some stones in it and then we put some sand and peat in it and I mixed the sand and peat together. After we had done that [the word 'that' was omitted by Sarah and added later by me when I was reading the note over with her] we made a big hole in it and then we put the runner bean in it. Then we covered it over and watered over and left it and then we waited the rest of the term and nothing happened. Mr. Rowland told me to leave it at school so I did and when I came back I went to see if it had grown. It was a much bigger plant than it was when I left it. It had about nine leaves on it. Its roots came right out of the bottom of the pot.

It was 9 cm long.

In the rest of this book I am going to make a record of how my runner bean grows." [The last few sentences were spread down the page, the last two words each on a line of its own.]

Over the page Sarah drew a full page picture of the brown plastic pot, its black peat and yellow sand, the green plant itself with leaves like little stalks, the yellow roots sticking out of three holes at the bottom of the pot, and the label on the pot's side covered in scribble of which only the S and A of Sarah's own name are legible.

The writing and drawing took Sarah most of the morning, the writing being completed with a fair amount of suggestion on my part. I helped Sarah decide what to write — she kept on asking me what she should write next — but it was she alone who decided how she would put it. The tone is personal, going beyond a bare catalogue of events to suggest her own excitement at the outcome. As she tells it, the story is quietly dramatic: "then we covered it over and watered over and left it and then we waited the rest of the term and nothing happened"; "Mr. Rowland told me to leave it at school so I did and when I came back I went to see if it had grown. It was a much bigger plant than it was when I left it"; "its roots came right out of the bottom of the pot". The simple words and phrases are deployed with some skill: see how the word "right" makes all the difference to the excitement of Sarah's discovery of the roots, a discovery duly recorded in her accompanying picture, or how her use of the conjunctions "and" and "then" helps her to build up the drama of events. The last four sentences, briefly noting the chief features of the growing plant and Sarah's intention of recording its growth in the notebook, are separated from each other and from the earlier part of the account, each sentence beginning on a new line, whereas the whole of the earlier part is a sustained grammatical unit, almost a paragraph.

The next day, though somewhat reluctantly, as I've said, Sarah continued her notebook, writing this:

"Overnight it grew ½ cm and yesterday I put it in a pot of water. The leaves have got bigger and now there is ten leaves."

Underneath the writing is another picture, this time cruder and less carefully drawn, showing the pot standing in a larger container, the "pot of water".

Today we began by looking at the plant together, noticing its growing leaves and its new tendrils. "Why are they called 'tendrils'?" Sarah asked me when I'd called them that. We measured the plant again, and then, after I had suggested the sort of thing I thought Sarah could write about it, and had written the date in her notebook for her to start her off, she wrote as follows:

"Monday, April 25th. Last week I put it in some water and now the week is over it has grown twice the size bigger and it had 18 leaves, 8 tendrils.

And it is now 17½ cm high and we stuck a stick in it to grasp around."

On the opposite page of her notebook Sarah has drawn the plant in its pot again and this is her best drawing so far, more precise than either of her previous drawings while preserving, in a more delicate manner, the animation of her first drawing which had been lost in her second. This time the pot is drawn more carefully, with its rim at the top, while the label on its side is no longer filled with scribbles but inscribed "Sarah Salter, 1977, bean". The stalk, leaves and tendrils of the plant are detailed with care, the leaves being of two different kinds and each leaf exactly, though not altogether realistically, veined. Alongside the plant is the supporting stick and two tendrils are already touching it, as if beginning "to grasp around". On this occasion, however, the roots growing "right out" of the bottom of the pot are not shown, the base of the pot resting on the bottom edge of the paper, and neither is the mixture of sand and peat so clearly indicated. We had not attended to either of these features this morning when we studied the plant

whereas we had focussed more attention than before on the leaves and, of course, the new tendrils.

Perhaps it would be a mistake, however, to think of this third sketch as better, in any simple way, than the first. Last week's sketch was more flamboyant and more impressionistic — details merely hinted at, scribbles for the label, short lines indicating leaves — whereas to-day's is more analytical. I'm tempted to suggest that the earliest sketch was a first response to an immediate excitement while the latest represents a more reflective response to a more assimilated excitement.

It was at this time, incidentally, that Stephen noticed that Sarah's runner bean was actually a pea, as he explained, in a comment on the notes quoted above.

'Today, April 29th, Sarah showed me how the tendrils had wound around the stick. There must have been a mix-up at some stage, for this plant is not a runner bean but a pea. Sarah drew me what she thought she had planted — a lozenge shaped seed, certainly a runner bean. I suspect that she in fact planted a pea in one pot and a bean in another, mislabelled the pots, and mislaid the bean.'

Despite Stephen's explanation to Sarah, she persisted in referring to her "bean" for some time, as we shall see. At first, despite his apparently authoritative stance, she seemed to feel that Stephen must either be wrong or that she had indeed planted in this a pot a bean but that it had unaccountably turned into a pea.

The beginnings of Sarah's diary heralded what appeared to Stephen and me to be a new intellectual assurance in Sarah herself. She seemed more frequently absorbed by the tasks she was set, or set herself, and more strenuous in the pursuit of them. Her problems and her puzzlement remained as they were, but her readiness to work through them seemed much greater. It was almost a fortnight before she returned to the diary of her plant, but in the meantime her new assurance had become evident in other aspects of her work, especially in a short but complex narrative about a boy and his pet rabbit which caused her a great deal of trouble because of her anxiety to avoid having the rabbit speak while still finding a way of letting him communicate with his owner and friend. In the past she might have abandoned the story in despair; now, however, she struggled on, with a certain amount of help, until she had found a solution to her problem.

On Friday, May 6th, Sarah next took up her record of the growth of her plant. Here is my own diary entry about the occasion.

'Friday, May 6th.

Sarah wrote about her plant this morning. She had told Stephen, first thing, that she would do some writing and he asked her whether she had written about her plant this week, having spotted the little notebook in her folder. When she said that she hadn't, he suggested that that was what she should write about. She took the plant down from its shelf, not having looked at it, I daresay, all week, and was surprised once more at how much it had grown, observing that the tendrils were wrapping themselves around the stick which we had stuck in the pot alongside the plant. She beckoned me over to look as she took the plant to where she was sitting. A little later she came to show me what she had written:

"On Friday I measured my bean. It was 23 cm and it had 22 leaves on it. I was very surprised when it grew so big because it was quite small the last time I saw it."

At first she had written "On Monday", that being the day of each week on which, originally, we had agreed that the diary should be written. I pointed out to her that in fact it was now Friday and suggested that she might alter the day; she did. I was amused by her continuing reference to "my bean". She knows now that the plant is a pea, and even points this out to others, but she still insists, perhaps half playfully, that it was a bean when she planted it.

She asked me if I thought that she had said enough, and, remembering the problems she had in describing her plant's growth in detail, I answered that I thought perhaps she had, unless she might say *how* the plant had grown. She seemed reluctant but later Stephen told her that he thought she should write more if she could. Both of us feel considerable uncertainty still about how much pressure to put on Sarah when she is writing. The question which I ask myself is how far she had really come to the end of what she wants to say and how far she is merely seeking relief from the pain of writing: for there is no doubt that writing, however simply, is often painful for Sarah. It is difficult to answer the question confidently; usually we just have to guess. On this occasion Stephen seemed to have guessed rightly since Sarah did indeed have something else of importance to say.

After morning play, I sat beside her and asked her how the plant had grown. She pointed to the tendrils wrapped around the supporting twig. "What were they like, what did they look like," I asked. "Like pigs' tails," she replied, but she seemed to think that this wasn't anything you could write down; it wouldn't, somehow, sound right; it would be silly, somehow. I told her that I liked it; they did look curly like that. "What about the leaves?" I asked, suggesting that they were "mottled". She said that they looked "spotty"; that was a better word, she said. Finally she wrote this:

"and the tendrils on the tree (she means the twig alongside I think) are winding round it. It has been 1½ weeks until I have measured it. And the tendrils look like pigs' tails and the leaves are very spotty." (It was after she had written as far as the end of the second sentence here that we spoke about the pigs' tails and the spotty leaves. Then she wrote the final sentence.)'

Although at the time I was pleased to have elicited from Sarah this last sentence, on reflection I am not so sure that the request that Sarah write more was strictly justified, despite the colourful language to which it happily led. The original entry was enough to convey Sarah's chief point, which was the rapid growth of the plant and the surprise which it occasioned her. And there was the accompanying drawing still to come. But the conversation about how the plant had grown certainly drew further attention to Sarah's feeling for words. Stephen took up this point in a comment on another piece of writing which Sarah was engaged on at this time. When I told him what Sarah had written in her notebook and how anxious she had been as to the appropriateness of describing the pea's tendrils as pigs' tails, he was reminded of the description she had written at the beginning of the week in response to an old photograph which he had shown her. It was a photograph of a boy dressed in rags, taken around the turn of the century; he is sitting on a large trunk staring out at the camera with an intense, set expression. He had given the photograph to Sarah and suggested that she write about it. At first, according to Stephen, she seemed to think of writing a story. But this did not work out, as Stephen explained in his note.

'After about ten minutes of thinking she said she could not think of any story to go with the photograph. I said "Why not just write down a few of your thoughts about the boy?" After this she needed very little prompting. I intervened only to say, once or twice, when she was stuck, such things as "What about his body?" "What do you think of his clothes?" At the end of the day, before asking if she could finish off the writing at home (where in the event she added the last two lines), she said that she had really enjoyed doing the writing — indeed that she had enjoyed reading and writing altogether much more recently.'

This is what she wrote:

"The dirty boy.

He was a very dirty boy and very solemn too.

He has not got a happy body.

His hair is like a wig dumped on his head.

His eyes were very sad.

And his clothes were very tattered.

And his box very dirty.

And his shoes were broken down."'

I was strongly impressed by these lines when I read them, especially the second line which seemed to express most beautifully the mood of the photograph. It was the third line, however, which had aroused Sarah's anxiety this time, as Stephen explained:

'"His hair is like a wig dumped on his head." As soon as Sarah had suggested this line to me she retracted, saying that she thought that was a bit silly. I replied that I thought it better to put down whatever she first thought. If she wanted she could always change things at the end. Compare this with her comment to Michael that the tendrils of her pea plant resembled pigs' tails: another beautifully apt description which she almost immediatley withdrew, saying it was silly.'

On Friday, May 6th, Sarah had only written about her plant. The following Monday she drew it again.

'Monday, May 9th.

Sarah, this morning, drew her plant. She didn't have her little notebook since I had taken it home and forgotten to return it, so she drew on a spare piece of paper which I gave her. After she had drawn the outlines of the pot I could see that she wouldn't be able to fit the plant itself into the space she had left so I cut her paper in two and got her to stick the two halves together, making the paper long enough to include the plant as well as the pot. I was anxious that she should not find herself having to start all over again. The finished sketch was large and imposing, twice as tall as her previous sketch and equally fine, although the crayoning over of her pencilled lines has on this occasion somewhat obscured the delicacy of her drawing.

Sarah Saller.
14 th of Feb.
1977
Runner bean.

Jak

It is interesting, now, to compare Sarah's successive drawings. The first was lively and impressionistic; the second, drawn the very next day, rudimentary, a disappointment; the third, one week later, detailed and precise; and today's still more detailed and precise as well as being much larger. Apart from the second drawing, which was no more than a crude repetition of the first, each drawing has been more exact than the one before, more closely observed. The first sketch had a scribble on the side of the pot, representing the label, and simple pencil strokes representing the still half-formed leaves. The third sketch had leaves that were carefully veined and outlined, waving tendrils, and a pot labelled "Sarah Salter, 1977, bean" with added scribbles, apparently representing smudges and discolourings on the label. Today's sketch has still more carefully drawn leaves, some of them drawn so as to suggest a certain roughness of texture, their outlines less conventionally leafy and more painstakingly copied from the plant itself. Sarah explained to me how she had been unable to get the leaves at the top of the plant quite right; she had rubbed this part out several times. The tendrils, looking like pigs' tails, have grown longer and those at the top are shown wrapped around the broken ruler which we have added to the pot as further support for the plant. (Sarah has not, however, drawn the stick which is still alongside the plant, nor has she included the offshooting branch, which would have presented another set of new problems.) As for the label on the side of the pot, this time she has written it word for word as on the pot itself: "Sarah Salter, 14th of Feb. 1977, runner bean". She has even included a graffito - the letters "Jak" — which at some time or other has been added at the bottom of the white label. I pointed out that we knew now that it was a pea, not a bean, but she told me she had to call it a bean because that was what it said on the label. In this sketch she has again included granules of peat and sand at the top of the pot, and the holes at the bottom, though no roots are now showing through.'

It was at this point in time that Stephen and I began to reflect together on the development of Sarah's successive drawings and writings about her plant. The progress towards greater precision and accuracy of representation, which was so noticeable in her four drawings, seemed to be related both to the developing clarity of form — above all, of detail — in the plant itself, and to the act of drawing the same object repeatedly, at different moments of growth. Sarah was intrigued by the changing character of the plant from week to week; the longer she observed it and the more often she attempted to draw it, the more exact she wished her visual record to be and the more exact she was able to make it, concentrating as she did on each new detail as it became clear to her. Her drawings could thus be seen as a record of her own developing absorption as well as of the physical growth of her plant.

Stephen was struck by the way in which the visual record seemed to take precedence over the written record. He noted:

"I have not had as much to do with this work of Sarah's as Michael has, but at each stage Sarah has briefly told me about the progress of the pea. Each point she has mentioned in these brief chats has been represented in her drawing though not necessarily in her writing. It is as if the drawing is the diary (through which she records her observations, showing what developments she has noticed), rather than the writing.'

On reading about another child's diary of the growth of a plant, composed in the Easter term, a friend of ours commented on the sparseness of the writer's record: 'it's almost as though the attitude were "I can remember what I thought and felt if I write down what I was thinking about".' That, however, was not altogether true of Sarah's writing, which included direct references to her own state of mind — "I was very surprised when it grew so big" — and often succeeded in conveying, if fleetingly, a sense of her excitement. Nevertheless, as the diary progressed, it was her drawing, more and more, that embodied and enriched the narrative record, while the writing served to convey a certain amount of raw information and to highlight the occasional detail. Or so it seemed at this particular moment in time. And yet in Sarah's few subsequent entries, which record the brief flowering and rapid decline of her plant, a new balance is achieved between writing and drawing. The writing becomes a little breathless, full of character and of the writer's own particular sense of excitement, while the drawing, too, grows more excitable and intense.

The next entry in the diary is dated May 19th, but I did not record it in my own notes until May 23rd when it had been succeeded by a further drawing of the plant and another brief written note.

'Tuesday, May 23rd.

This morning, at Stephen's suggestion, Sarah worked on her plant again. Last week she had discovered that one of two flowers which had appeared on the plant had developed into a pea pod. She had written about this on Thursday, as follows:

"May 19th.

I measured my plant on Thursday and it was 28 cm long but there was a new thing on it, there were two flowers on it and a pea pod, and now it has 32 leaves on it, but when the pea came through one of the flowers, the flower fell off, but it has not any peas in it yet."

This vigorous account was followed by a very uninspired sketch which in no way extended the range of her drawing as previous sketches had. Perhaps this was because she had cramped the plant into a single page of her notebook whereas the last sketch had been drawn on paper twice as long. [This sketch, still visible behind the paper later pasted over it, is rather similar to her third sketch which was also drawn on a single page of her notebook.] I was so disappointed that I recommended her to try again on larger paper. This she did but at first the result still seemed disappointing. I noticed that the pot was now labelled "Sarah's bean", the exactness of the label as drawn on her last sketch no longer repeated.

Today, however, Sarah completed this drawing by adding the pea pod on its stalk at the top, its seven peas clearly visible — we had

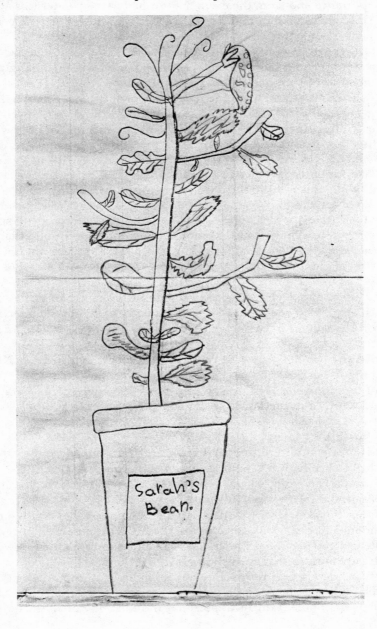

counted them through the pod this morning. In its now finished state
— Sarah decided against colouring it in this time — it does after all
have much of the accuracy of her last drawing. This time she has included the side branches as well as the main shoot. The pod, added this
morning, is especially well-drawn, as one might expect from its novelty
and importance and from the excitement it had caused. Later this afternoon Stephen told Sarah that she should write a little about the pea as
well and she wrote this:

"The other flower has not come off yet but the other pea pod has
got 7 peas in it and it has got 38 leaves on it. Soon I will be having peas
out of it, but at the bottom the leaves are falling off."

Stephen especially liked the nicely personal touch; "soon I will be
having peas out of it", feeling that this made all the difference to the
raw description. Incidentally, it was not quite correct for Sarah to write
that the other flower had not yet fallen off; it did so this morning as
Sarah herself was touching it, taking the pea pod off with it. Perhaps
Sarah had forgotten; the flower had been there first thing this morning
and while she was writing she didn't have the plant beside her.'

When, at the end of the year, I surveyed Sarah's sketches as a
whole I began to appreciate this latest drawing more. In particular, her
treatment of the plant's leaves is more varied and more subtle than in
any other drawing and in addition she has made a brave if only partly
successful attempt to include the offshoots from the main stem. As for
the pea pod it is beautifully drawn and as skilful as any detail throughout her series of sketches. The use of pencil is bolder than in her previous sketch, too, and it now seems to me significant that on this
occasion she should have decided against any attempt to colour in her
drawing.

By now Sarah's plant had come to the end of its growth and was
beginning to decline. The next entry in her notebook, immediately after half term on June 10th, was to prove the last, and recorded graphi-
cally, in words and pictures, the demise of her so-called "bean". Now
for the first and last time she deigned to call it, simply, "my pea."

"June 10th.

My pea was shrivelling up before half term but now the whole
plant has shrivelled up. The only green thing on the plant is the pea
pod. Tonight I am going to take it home. I was hoping that I would have
four peas and then my family would have one pea each for tea."

From the sketch with which Sarah accompanied her writing one
can understand the significance of the tenses in the final sentence. Inside the pea pod Sarah has drawn the peas: and there are only three! We
had already noticed that as the pod grew, the number of peas we could
identify inside it seemed to decline but Sarah had gone on hoping there
would be at least "one pea each for tea."

This final note is the most personal and touching of all the entries in her diary, and in the sketch she drew across the following two pages of the diary she presented a painful portrait of the shrivelled plant, bent sideways, its leaves and tendrils unkempt, weighed down it seems by the pea pod at the end with its three large peas inside. The drawing is again uncoloured and much rougher than previous drawings. It has a directness and immediacy which recalls the lively impressionism of the very first sketch. For the first time the pot is unlabelled. But there is a difference between Sarah's impressionism now and that of her earliest sketch. The apparent scruffiness of her drawing of the shrivelled stalk, tendrils and leaves serves to dramatize the plant's fate while still managing to suggest the close and detailed observation already achieved in her previous two sketches. It is hard to imagine this final drawing as it is without the sequence that led up to it. The image of the plant's decay is an image of Sarah's growth.

On the next page of the notebook is Sarah's last glimpse of the pea, almost by way of an appendix, a coloured drawing of the pod with its three peas and the simple heading: "this is an enlarged picture of my pea after I took it out." She took the pea home on the Friday but I was not in school on the following Monday so it was not until later in the week that I found an opportunity to ask her about it. Yes, they'd eaten it, she said: and that was that.

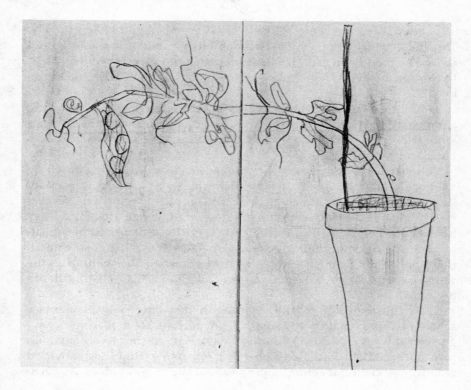

Chapter 5

Pictures Make the Difference

GAIL GUTH

Gail Guth hates the term "remedial reading." The children she saw as a remedial reading teacher in an inner city elementary school in San Diego were learning to read "initially," that is, for the first time ever. Because they spoke English as a second language and had not responded to the basal text approach, Gail promoted their natural curiosity with photography and lots of talk. They began to read and write and learn enthusiastically — and not because of "remediation."

I said, "Tell me about yourself," in November, and Roberto wrote, "My hobby is catching lizards. The food I like is frijoles con chorizo and tacos. The food I don't like is macarone. My best friend is nobody. I will like to see movies. When I grow up I will be nothing. I wish for a mini bike."

In June: "I am a sixth grader. My hobbies are electronics, drawing and fishing. I like hamburgers and tacos. I don't like macarone. I have a lot of friends. When I grow up I am going to work in electronics. I wish I had a mini bike."

Roberto's language power, his self-concept, and my teaching methods all had changed far more than the seven months warranted. Roberto had come to me along with fifteen other "remedial" readers every day at ten o'clock for an extra dose of language arts. Since they had begun their schooling before Lau vs. Nichols mandated bilingual-bicultural programs, their classroom language was in English though they spoke only Spanish. Dropping further and further behind as the years passed, Roberto began to tune out, and his self-confidence dwindled.

As the remedial reading teacher in this inner city elementary school of approximately 400 students, 97 percent Mexican-American, I grasped at ways to make 45 minutes a day create the miracle that would turn on tuned-out kids like Roberto. I remember attending our local reading association meeting hoping to find the magical ideas. As Patricia Hefferman-Cabrera, then in charge of the Teacher Corps project at USC, described the work her students were doing using cameras with migrant workers' children, I felt a sense of relief. Maybe my students could be motivated to read by taking photos, writing about them, then reading and sharing the stories with each other. I'll never forget that first day when I walked into class with a borrowed Polaroid, a roll of film and some high hopes. I'll never forget that first picture either.

I asked only one question: "What would you like to take a picture of?" The response, which could have been predicted, was, "Our teacher!" Impressed with their enthusiasm, I gave directions like, "Ask permission politely," and, "Ask the teacher to come outside where there will be enough light." Then, not being much of a photographer myself, I told them to "point and shoot."

Within a few moments they returned and we pulled the print out of the camera. The three-minute wait before we could pull back the print seemed more like three hours. It struck me during that interminable wait that I certainly had their complete and undivided attention — a feat, theretofore, unaccomplished. We pulled the print from the backing, and there was a moment's silence as the magical mystery of photography captured our senses — only a very short moment — and then we began to roar with laughter. (Illus. 1)

Illus. 1

"Today Mrs. Guth brought a camera to class. She told us we could take a picture of anything we wanted. We went to Mrs. Allen's class and asked her to come outside so we could take her picture. When we came back to class and the picture developed we laughed and laughed. We cut off her head and feet."

As the students commented on the absurdity of their creation, I quickly took notes. After the last laugh, I taped the picture on a piece of tag and began to write on it some of the things they had said, reading aloud as I wrote. Their attention was drawn to their own comments, and they read the "story" several times. Then they copied the sentences onto sentence strips for sequencing.

They made word cards for words they couldn't read and illustrated the reverse side of the word card with some visuals to help recall the word. The word card was then filed in a 3x5 file box to be used later for further study, for phonics analysis or practice with categorizing skills. Students worked in pairs putting the sentence strips in correct sequence to make a story, taking it apart and studying the vocabulary cards. While some of the students practiced putting the story in sequence, I worked with others on specific phonetic or structural analysis skills either individually or in groups according to need. Drills substituting beginning sounds or medial vowels were now meaningful because the words were their own. For those students having trouble with word order because of differences between the English and Spanish languages, we cut the sentence strips apart and compared the word order in English to what it would be in Spanish. The whole experience became the most successful reading lesson to date.

The principal was intrigued with the interest these reluctant learners began to show in school, so when I found a close-out on Mickey Mouse cameras for 99 cents, she somehow managed funds to purchase film. The local film processing plant gave us a discount on developing the film. Roberto's group and I were on our magnificent jour-

Illus. 2

Illus. 3

ney, not really knowing where it would lead or what learning experiences were to unfold.

As we took pictures of each other and life in and around school, we began to develop criteria for successful pictures. Roberto revealed an artistic eye. He was first to point out that you could improve a picture by taking it from another angle. He suggested we stand on a chair or get down on the ground to change perspective. He led the group in previewing several film strips that would help us set up criteria for judging our work. This step seemed important to me, for not only was I aware of the cost involved in a project of this type, but also I was especially anxious that the time with these upper grade students, many of whom would soon go to junior high, not be wasted.

The discussions we had were lively because the topics discussed were real life situations captured in pictures taken by the students themselves.

The first assignments were to take pictures of something or someone important in their lives. (Illus. 2 and 3) As pictures were developed and pinned on a portable bulletin board (Illus. 4), the group discussed each, and the owners of each picture examined their photos to determine how well they met the criteria previously set.

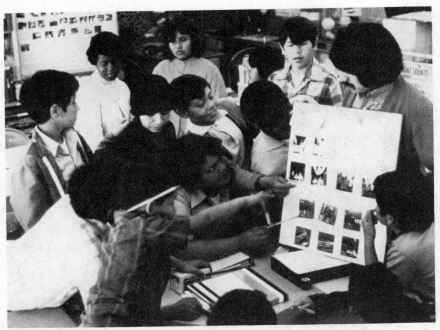

Illus. 4

The first question we asked was: Is the picture sharp and clear?

Each learned that if everything was blurry, chances were the photographer had moved the camera (Illus. 5a). If the subject was blurry and the surroundings clear, the subject had probably moved (Illus. 5b). The group decided whether the photo was complete without distracting extras.

LEADER: What can you tell me about this picture?

STUDENT: It's blurry.

LEADER: Why is it blurry?

STUDENT: Somebody moved.

LEADER: Who do you think moved, the student or the photographer?

STUDENT: Everything is blurry so I (the photographer) moved when I took the picture.

LEADER: What can we say about this picture?

STUDENT: Ricki is smiling and you can see the monkey on the Joy Machine.

LEADER: What about Bernadette?

STUDENT: Her face is blurry.

LEADER: What do you think happened?

STUDENT: Bernadette must have moved since Ricki is sharp and clear.

Illus. 5a

Illus. 5b

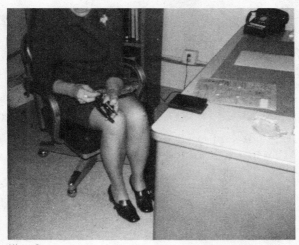

Illus. 6

They eagerly spied the person with the cut off feet and the other missing the top of his head (Illus. 6). The day they found a telephone pole
growing right out of the subject's head and an unneeded chair right in
front of the subject they began to plan for future camera shots so these
errors could be avoided.

The final criterion to be checked was: Is it interesting? All in the
group offered opinions on this question, but only the person who took
the picture could evaluate whether the reason for taking the picture was
a worthy one and whether the special effects sought were achieved
(Illus. 7a and 7b). Sometimes those blurry figures illustrated speed, or
that silhouette displayed a fitting mood.

All of a sudden, these "reluctant" learners were completely en-
grossed in their learning. These English-as-a-second-language students
were active participants in discussions where the emphasis was on the
function of language rather than on the form. Through group discussion, observation, and experimentation, they discovered the ways to

Illus. 7a   Illus. 7b

Comparing these two photos the group decided that 7a was much more in-
teresting than 7b because it was sharp and clear, the picture of the artist was
complete (in 7b they had cut off part of his head), and you could see some of
the students in the audience.

successful form as it supported the meanings they sought to convey. They learned that to get sharp and clear pictures, they would need to:

1. Hold the camera steady.
2. Stay five feet away from subject (two giant steps backward).
3. Be sure sun is behind the photographer.
4. Snap shutter when subject is still.

Illus. 8

To get pictures that would be complete without extras, they would need to:

1 . Fill the frame of the viewfinder.
2 . Separate the subject from the background
3 . Omit the extras like including only an arm or the back of a person, or a chair or other unimportant objects in the picture. Better to move the subject or the photographer to a different position.

Deciding how to take interesting pictures was more difficult because, of course, each student had a different idea of what was interesting. After much discussion, the students agreed that the audience and the purpose determined whether a photo was interesting or not. For example, if the audience was to be a tourist who needed directions, as in a visitors' guide book, Roberto's picture of the city skyline (Illus. 8) probably would not get much agreement as being interesting.
If, however, the audience was to be a class writing about the city or about urban transportation, all might agree that the graceful line of the freeway against the city skyline was interesting. After much debate, they decided that to get interesting pictures they would need to:

1 . Keep the audience in mind.
2 . Shoot while people are busy doing things.
3 . Plan ahead or have the camera ready to catch the right moment.
4 . Try a different viewpoint as Roberto did in Illus. 2.
5 . Include a meaningful foreground that might give a visual clue. (Illus. 9). The picture could have included just the receptionist; however, the students agreed it was more interesting to see the patient waiting.

Critical thinking skills were developing as students defended their opinions and offered suggestions to their classmates. They began to work as a group, to listen to and respect each other. They also developed a respect — almost a reverence — for the equipment they used. When we began, I was reluctant to let cameras go home, fearing loss or abuse. This was a needless worry, for the students were very responsible.
One of the first individual projects was to develop a "Story Without Words," which would be their introduction to story-boarding techniques so helpful in planning slidetapes or Super 8 productions. The assignment was to take a sequence of pictures that would tell a story without the aid of words. For students reluctant to use words, this project seemed too good to be true. As they began to plan and take pictures, however, they realized how difficult it is to convey clear meaning without the aid of words. Roberto's sequence looked like this (Illus. 10).

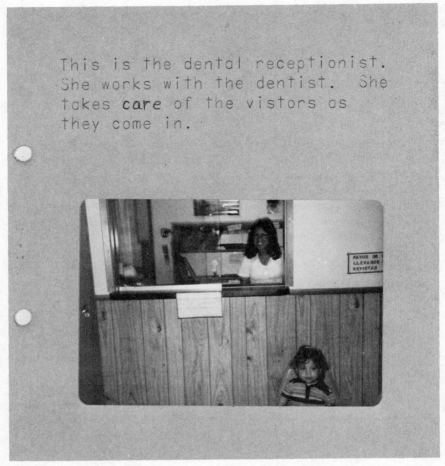

This is the dental receptionist.
She works with the dentist. She
takes **care** of the vistors as
they come in.

Illus. 9

As Roberto tried to tell his story to the group, he found that the sequence he had presented did not really tell the story he wanted to convey. Though all his classmates knew the story was about playing baseball, his beginning and ending were not clear.

To help them see how sequence can affect meaning, I asked them to cut apart and paste on manila paper some cartoon drawings by James Morrow. The students then told their stories to one another, discovering how the same pictures can convey different meanings (Illus. 11).

The talk of the ten o'clock Reading Lab class began to spread around the school as the "school photographers" were called upon to take pictures of an assembly, or the moving of a new bungalow, or an important visitor. They were also asked to create a visual guidebook of the school to help new students get to know the school.

STORY WITHOUT WORDS

Illus. 10

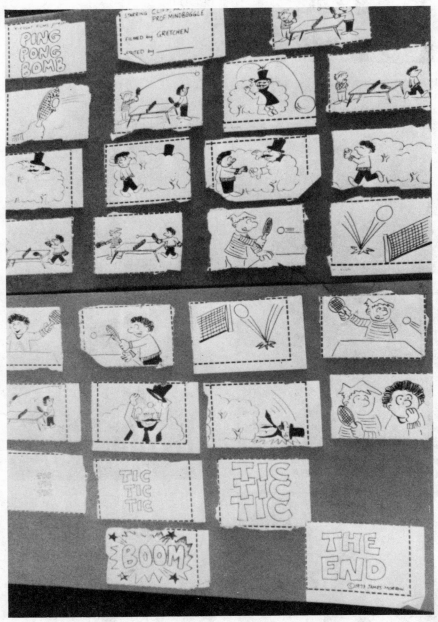

Illus. 11

Several students created a 25 page book about the local Chicano
Clinic "so the little kids wouldn't be afraid to go there to see the doc-
tor." The cover is reproduced here (Illus.12) . The picture on page 78
(Illus. 9) is from this book.

Because the school was beginning a new bilingual program in the kindergarten and first grade, there were many visitors — all of whom seemed to visit the ten o'clock lab class. Time after time visitors would like to know how to set up a similar "program for the gifted." The students became quite articulate in explaining the projects, the equipment,

Illus. 12

Illus. 13

Class book describing participation in Conference of Calif. Art. Association

Illus. 14

Class activity book Wood burned cover by Roberto

and the class. The word *remedial* was discarded along with the inappropriate remedial reading materials. I discovered a very important formula, a formula that I sincerely believe to be true:

Amount of L & R : SC (P+M)

The amount of learning and retention is directly proportionate to the learner's self-concept times the sum of purposeful learning (concrete) plus motivation (abstract). The visual literacy activities provided an intense sense of purpose that inspired self-motivation, which seemed to promote optimum learning and extended retention. (Illus. 13, 14, and 15).

One day the kindergarten teacher rushed in looking for a student to take pictures of a tortoise someone had brought. The result was a display enjoyed by the kindergarten and the whole school.

The principal encouraged expansion of the project, noting the improved self-concepts as well as verbal skills in these upper grade students. The school district added additional funds from money set aside for teacher initiated projects. With more cameras available, Roberto and other students in his class worked with some first grade students. Using the philosophy that you can: say what you think — write what you say — read what you write — hear what you think, the older students wrote down what the younger children said, and students learned to read as

Illus. 15

Lowell students explaining exhibit to visitors during their presentation for Association for Education and Technology

they heard themselves saying the words before them. The upper grade students took pictures of the first graders, then asked them to talk about their pictures as they sat in a cardboard recording studio equipped with a tape recorder. The upper graders transcribed what the first graders said, and the next day the students could listen to their own voices as they saw before them the very words that they had said the day before.

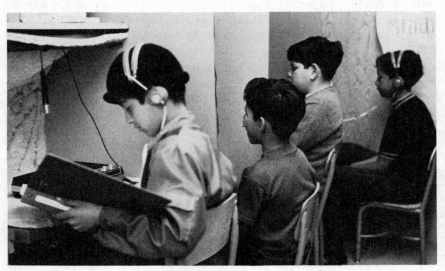

Illus. 16

These first experiments were disastrous, for we discovered our paper box recording studios had walls that were too thin (Illus. 16). Though the pictures were different, the first graders' stories were remarkably alike as each child talked about the subject he was hearing next to him. Then I learned that big, beautiful oak telephone booths were about to be removed from the Del Mar race track, and the community relations division of the local telephone company made arrangements to have six of these booths installed in the language lab bungalow. The phones were replaced with tape recorders and, with light and fan still working, we had marvelous sound recording studios.

From then on, the stories were different and the idea really caught the imagination of the first graders. (Illus. 17). The parents were delighted also, not only to hear their youngsters' stories, but to hear themselves. It became a favorite place to visit, and during Open House it was not unusual to find several members of a family crammed into a telephone booth singing and telling stories, then listening with looks of pure enjoyment.

Roberto was having difficulty with English structure, so we used the cameras for simple vocabulary building, as well as the complicated study of irregular verbs or pronoun agreement.

Mrs. Guth took a picture. I typing my name.

Vitocr

Mrs. Guth did the picture. My name is Victor. I like to eat spaghetti and beans and sopa. Best of all I like carrots. When I grow up I want to be bigger. I like to play ball. After school I go home and brush my teeth.

Victor said, "Mrs. Guth took the picture. I happy, Spagetti, beans, macaroni, rice.

With the teacher or aide, he and his classmates used the photos to play tic-tac-toe (Illus. 18).

TEACHER: Okay, Maria, it is your turn. Where do you want to put your X?

MARIA: In the middle.

TEACHER: What is she doing?

MARIA: *She* is washing *his* face.

TEACHER: Good for you. Put in your X. Jose, where do you want to put your O?

JOSE: Up above that one.

TEACHER: Okay. What is she doing?

Illus. 18a

JOSE: *She* is tying *her* shoe.

TEACHER: You are correct! Good thinking. Lila, where do you want to try?

LILA: This one on the top left.

TEACHER: What is he doing, Lila?

LILA: *He* is tying *his* shoe!

TEACHER: You are right. Ricardo, it is your turn. Which picture shall it be?

RICARDO: Over in the corner — on the bottom.

TEACHER: What is she doing Ricardo?

RICARDO: *She* is brushing *her* teeth.

TEACHER: You are right. Good! Dalila, you are next — the X's next — where Dalila?

DALILA: Over here — the middle left.

TEACHER: What is he doing, Dalila?

DALILA: *He* is tying *her* shoe.

Illus. 18b

TEACHER: Wonderful. That

is a hard one. The boys are next. Alfredo, where are you going to put your O?

ROBERTO: In the middle right.

TEACHER: What is she doing Roberto?

ROBERTO: *She* is tying *his* shoe.

TEACHER: Oh-oh — Girls turn now. Rosa, it is up to you. Where shall it be?

ROSA: Down in the corner, teacher.

Illus. 18c

TEACHER: That is a very hard one. Do you know it, Rosa?

ROSA: I think so — *they* are brushing *their* teeths?

TEACHER: That is close enough, Rosa. They are brushing their teeth. Let's all say that.

CLASS: *They* are brushing *their* teeth.

TEACHER: Tic-tac-toe — three in a row — the girls won!

These tic-tac-toe photo games then became part of Reading Lab games to be used by other students at the school.

With this new found power to read and their new oral fluency promoted by the camera, the students decided to find out about as many careers as they could in the two months remaining until summer vacation. In a brainstorming session, we listed all the questions we would like to ask about a job. With an interview sheet (Sample, Illus. 19) students practiced interviewing each other. Then they interviewed the principal, a teacher, an aide, and the custodians. Interviewers went in trios: one to ask the questions (helped by the others when necessary); one to tape record the interview; and one to take pictures of the person, the workplace, and the tools of the trade.

After this first round of interviews, we discussed once again the interview process. Students noted how hard it was to follow the interview sheet — that sometimes questions would come up that weren't on the sheet. Listening became a very important skill that needed to be

Illus. 19

practiced. They also learned that some persons do not wish to say how much money they earn so they decided to leave that question out and find out the salary range through the public library.

As the students transcribed their tapes and checked over their notes and pictures, I noted the days passing far too quickly. Our grand plans to publish our career pamphlets had to be abandoned for lack of time. It was a big disappointment to the class, but we all agreed that the experiment was very worthwhile and that we had all learned a lot about career choices. More than that, we had learned how much we are capable of learning. For Roberto, especially, it was a memorable experience.

Chapter 6

History Through Drama: It's More than Cowboys and Indians

ROGER DAY

Because Roger Day is now the Drama Adviser for Wiltshire, he no longer works in one school but in many, ranging from one or two class village primary schools to secondary comprehensive schools for a thousand or more students. Roger believes, as I do, that Advisory work needs to be rooted in work with children, inside their own schools, involving their own teachers in their own classrooms. The first time I ever *saw* Roger was a few years before I actually met him, in a film about Dorothy Heathcote's work called *Three Looms Waiting*. I remember vividly that Roger, who was one of her students at that time, was being *climbed up* in the film by an animated group of handicapped children — he was the lighthouse.

Certainly wherever he goes, Roger's presence is felt — most powerfully when he is sitting on the floor, finding out from a class what they want to make a play about. He is a wizard at listening wisely to a rush of suggestions, then taking and weaving a few threads so that the pupils, whether they are five or fifteen, can work together to create the rest.

Wiltshire is a county rich in historic and prehistoric associations, many of which have been brought to life for hundreds of school children by Roger's 'History Through Drama' days — in Tithe Barns or Stately Mansions, at Sheep Fairs, in Long Barrows, along the ancient pilgrims' path, the Ridgeway.

The days themselves are the culmination of weeks of work and careful planning, as he mentions briefly in this account of the District Assizes which brought Ben Black to the gallows. All the schools that agree to take part undertake six to twelve weeks work on that particular period of history. Each school is visited on at least one occasion during

that time by one or two of the 'main' characters (in full costume), whom they will encounter again on 'the day.' These early visits help both teachers and children to take the facts 'off the page' and into a world of the imagination in which they cohere to make a picture which has colour and life and feeling.

Roger knows from experience that a strong sense of 'what it was like to live in . . .' can only begin to coalesce into a living entity for the pupils if on the one hand they are encouraged to take on the task of real research and on the other if a way can be found of *using* what they find out in the reconstruction of 'the day.'

And so the investigations start — into costumes, into pastimes, into the kind of news that might have found its way into Broadsheets and Coffee Houses — and then with fingers crossed for a fine day, all is brought together, like a chapter from a historical novel, on the day itself.

The carriage creaked — ducks waddled hurriedly before us as Judge Ayres lit another pipe of tobacco.

One could think at this speed — observe, discuss, let the horsemen do the worrying.

"It would be ironic," I remarked, "if Black wasn't the only varlet operating in this area and we never arrived to listen to his trial and see him hung."

Ayres peered left and right through the carriage windows sucking noisily at his clay, "Damme, he'll hang, and high!" was his swift reply.

Before us now the road curved and round the next bend flashed the coloured garb of a band of strolling players obviously on their way to delight the crowd with bawdy talk of Ben Black's exploits. One fellow beat a drum while another played a mournful little tune on a reed pipe and I do declare that some brazen dark-eyed wench suggested we walk the rest of the way with them.

Still we were past in a trice and now Lackham Court, my ancestral home, came into view through the trees. Cheering assailed our ears and there with a goodly crowd of at least 300 was Captain Ward of Bristol, waving his tri-cornered hat and capering across the lawns to our arrival point.

I'd seen this crowd in small groups before — each had entertained me with coffee, claret, snuff, tales of Black, songs composed by them, music by the late Mr. Handel and requests that I would do something about the tolls. I, in my turn, had told them of my dealings with Nash and how my cure for gout at the hands of Mr. Oliver of Bath was progressing.

Ward and myself have supped with them and astounded them with tales of London Town and Bristol. We laughed over the fellow

who ate my snuff instead of sniffing it, and now they had all come together — a feat in itself — to see Ben Black, who for the past six months
had been a powerful influence on their imaginations.

The carriage slowed to a halt; Georgian gentlemen and their ladies
greeted me with the deference they knew should be accorded to a
landowner of such stature.

The new Rector of Box offered up a prayer that I should be blessed
not only for arriving safely but for allowing my beautiful estate to be
used for this Country Fayre. "Where is my Katy," I declared, and from
the crowd appeared my intended; taking her arm and inviting the gentry to come and see my new lavender garden, I set off at a brisk walk
towards the main house.

Captain Ward I knew would be busy telling the others where they
could set up their booths — coffee, sports and all the paraphernalia that
went into making a successful fayre. For those of us on the terrace the
roses and lavender had effectively dispelled the odours of the common
folk milling below us on the lower paddocks.

Ayres was in deep conversation with Mistress Katy and I was in
the process of explaining to a portly young man from Bromham my new
statue carved from Italian marble that graced the fountains, when I observed Doctor John Smythe of Rowden Hill approaching. We fell into
quite an animated conversation about the new wine tax, his sadness at
the demise of the late Mr. Handel whose music he so enjoyed, and his
hope that Black, who according to his information had been taken
whilst with a young woman in an Inn at Corsham, would receive his
just deserts.

This ten year old's total involvement not only in my conversation
but in the re-living of the total day was typical of most of the 300 Primary School children who had come to see the hanging. It was an opportunity for "John" to use information that he and his class had
researched in a real context. He offered more, as he realised I knew
about these same facts and could link them with Ben Black and this journey back into the 18th century.

This journey was just one of many that had been made by Primary
and Secondary children in Wiltshire over the past four years. Some had
replayed the battles between Royalists and Parliamentary Forces, some
had buried their Bronze Age Chieftain, others had met Henry the Second in the great forest of Savernake, spent two days at a Medieval Wool
Fayre and paid tithes in one of England's largest Tithe Barns. We had
called these journeys "History Through Drama."

"At least Mr. Handel wasn't killed by some damn ball game," I
said to my companion, picking up a ball and returning it to a fellow
who had removed his waistcoat and carried his curved bat afore him.
We moved down to where the cricket match was underway. The last
time I had seen this "game" was in the town of Calne not a month past,

BROMHAM COURIER,
AND MID WILTS HIRE INTELLIGENCER

STRUCK AGAIN
Ben Black has struck again! With additions by Mr Mofef Breach to ÿ reward, can ÿ mifcreant avoid ÿ courfe of JUFTICE much longer? Our hope is that all BRITISH citizenf, if called to jury fervice, will DO THEIR DUTY!!

COMPOSER DIES in Middlefex
Ÿe death haf lamentably been reported from Edgeware of GEO. FREDERICK HANDEL. Born in 1685 in Germany he foon followed the mufe of Mufic defpite hif father'f wishes that he fhould follow Law. Aged tender 11 he could play upon ÿ clavichord, ÿ organ, clarinet and violin. In 1706 he vifited Italy. Four yearf later he Played before ÿ ELECTOR of Hanover, later our late beloved KING of blessed memory. In 1726 Handel became a British Citizen. Afflicted of late with Blindness he dictated hif Workf to a PUPIL. He is to be interred in ÿ Abbey of WESTMINSTER

THE KING'S ILLNESS
Newf haf come by ÿ latest coach from White Hall Palace of ÿ worfening condition of hif MAJESTY. Grave concern haf been expreffed in Parliament.

STEEPLE FLYER
On Wednefday laft Mr. John Comm attempted ÿ FEAT defying Nature - propelling himfelf upon a board down a rope from ÿ top of BROMHAM STEEPLE to ÿ foot of Church Hill. When ÿ strain upon ÿ steeple caufed ÿ rope to pull away several ftonef ÿ fearless yet foolifh flyer plummeted earthward into a tree which fpared hif life. Henceforth CHURCHWARDENS Edward Crook and Daniel Butler will not allow ÿ church to be ufed for fuch vul fhow as being un-pious, remembering ÿ recent fate of ÿ young perfons of DEVIZES who, taking lightly SABBATH DUTIE did loofe their lives in Drew's Pond.

ASSIZE AT LACKHAM COURT
Our loved PATRON and friend ÿ good SIR ROGER DE COVERLEY will again make LACKHAM his Country Seat, ÿ fair setting for ÿ quarter seffions, to be prefided over by Mr Justice Eyre of Nonfuch, Bromham. Many of ÿ country folk will doubtleff make ÿ day caufe of merrymaking especially in ÿ earnest expectation of SUCCESS to ÿ Thieftaker Captain Fred k Ward in ÿ apprehenfion of BLACK. Sir Roger has been very active in hif encouragement of all MEANS to free ÿ highway of threat. THE LAW muft be UPHELD!

played on the town's green surrounded by ladies who had been val-
iantly carried by stout bearers up the hill in their sedan chairs.

I tried my hand at this new-fangled sport and then moved off to
watch the cock fighting; whilst here I took a pot of beer and, fingering a
garland of sweet smelling herbs, lost a small portion to a gang of motley
rogues.

Wearying of this I passed dozens of booths selling all manner of
goods until finally I reached a coffee shop. Here I partook of this most
refreshing beverage and enjoyed a game of chess; then I had time to sit
back and glance at the Bromham Courier. It was good to see the business
of others drift past me . . . I do declare I must have dropped off!

"Dropping off" was part of the role I had used in many of the pre-
visits to schools that I, Sir Roger, and Captain Ward had made. These
visits had been an opportunity to work with a class in depth to set the
scene and meet with people who could be introduced to the whole
gathering on the day.

Each Primary School we visited had tackled this 18th century project in an exciting and imaginative way: coffee shops, cricket on the
town green, a whole Georgian town built from sheds and greenhouses,
the list was endless.

The sounds of laughter must have woken me, for gathered near
me were a large crowd who watched a puppet show — Ben Black was
portrayed as a hero, I as a doddering fool! Shaking with wrath and waving my silver topped cane, I made towards the booth; luckily for the
puppeteers, my beloved Katy caught me before I damaged their stall
and persuaded me to sit with her as Quincy de Sellwood drew her for
one of his latest portfolios.

Quincy was one of the numerous adults who had become involved
in the project. Besides the children's teachers who had taken roles, there
were Headteachers, parents, other Advisers and the one of prime importance today: "Ben Black," alias Tom Brown, one of our local Teachers' Centre Organisers. All this was a far cry from when Fred Ward,
myself, and a Primary Adviser had sat down in 1976 to plan ways in
which:

1. We could help teachers and children to become more aware of the
   vast local environmental resources — historic houses, barrows,
   earth works, forests.
2. Install some sense of the past.
3. Get schools to cooperate on joint projects.
4. Make project work have a more meaningful purpose.
5. Interest non-drama specialists in a form of dramatic presentation.
6. Develop areas for language work.

The painting of Katy was quite exquisite — Quincy informed me
that he would capture me for posterity at the trial!

The trial — it must be time, for Judge Ayres was approaching, his carriage-wear now changed for robes of scarlet and a full wig. We were escorted by a goodly number of men of the Wiltshire Yeomanry as the crowd was already turning ugly. Taking our places, I noticed anger, fear, hate, elation, on faces as they crowded nearer and nearer the witness seat and the still empty dock.

I felt history was all around us and that it was about people like us. In this "play" there is the opportunity to feel many emotions — anger, tiredness, frustration, in a relatively safe situation — also the opportunity to argue, discuss, disclaim, listen and be listened to.

Being involved by talking, listening and watching, by knowing that even by their murmurings and tangible presence they can change or shape the work in progress is an important feeling for children.

A round-faced buffoon who had caused much merriment in one of the numerous coffee houses was the last to take the oath. As Black was dragged before us a scream of triumph tinged with regret assailed our ears and this once proud ruffian, now bound with chains, awaited the inevitable. Judge Ayres cleared his throat and the trial began.

Each "witness," and there were to be many of them, stepped before the assembled court and told their stories. For some this was to be the first time that others had listened to them; some had to be led as they took their first hesitant steps into story telling. If I or one of the others on the "bench" listened carefully as a description was unfolded, for example, "the horse of his had markings," and then enquired about its fetlock or hind quarters, the telling became clearer, and more experimental language came as the confidence of the child grew.

One witness, on being summoned forth by Captain Ward of Bristol, was asked if he had seen Black perform one of his dastardly hold-ups. "No!" came the reply. Ward's face was a picture.

"No what, sir?" I asked.

"No, I did not see Black perform one of his deeds — but I heard him."

"You heard him?"

"Yes sir, I was truly feared and so I hid in the barn."

"Whose barn was this? At what time of the clock? Why were you there? How did you leave? Did you tell the others of your lucky escape?"

Ask questions! Questions will elicit a response, even a no or yes response can be developed into a saga if you persevere. This witness left believing in the picture he had created.

And others all around the court believed in his picture too. For them this was real; the man could live or swing because of the words they used.

But to swing it was. Ayres once more cleared his by now parched throat, donned the black cap and pronounced in moving tones: "Hung by the neck until dead, may God have mercy on your soul!"

Luncheon — a truly sumptuous affair, with a blessing by the Rector of Box — followed. This lunch was as carefully worked upon as everything else on this memorable day. Children and teachers had fashioned goblets (Coke cans had been leather covered and handles added by one bright drinker), bottles had been covered with papier-mâché and given seals, some had baked their own bread, others had made cheese. This attention to detail helped, not only to create an authentic atmosphere, but to sustain it.

Quincy and Mistress D'Arcy took luncheon with me. Being both hasty folk, they had rushed to the hanging without a morsel to eat, but they were soon brushing the crumbs of an ample meal from their lips. I listened to a fascinating conversation between my Katy (whose every gesture now declared her to be a woman of high breeding instead of one small shy girl from a Village School) and a Headmaster in powdered wig whom she had never met before.

The wine had a somewhat soporific effect, for I was starting to nod when news of a disaster reached my ears. Some bloody kids had pulled down the gallows, the very centre of this afternoon's dramatic happenings! Two teachers and I had spent hours the night before building these and sinking them into the rock hard earth and now some little perishers had pulled them down!! All this to be involved in, I thought. All these wonderful things to see and do and some bloody kids just behave like bloody vandals!! The Aristocratic feelings of Sir Roger had disappeared; I was livid, "Bring the varmints before me," I bellowed, trying hard to re-establish my role.

Soon two quaking 10 year olds were pushed roughly before me, surrounded by a squash of riotous onlookers. "Why?" I asked. Tears welled.

"Because Black came to see us in our village and he is a nice man and he should not swing!" Involvement! It's what I was asking for — and I had got it.

The soldiers led them away to be fined at the next sitting . . .

Captain Ward and others approached; the gallows had been righted, all was well.

The drums began to beat and we started on the long walk to the hanging, only to be interrupted by the players and their version of "Black's life", a fascinating yet irreverent piece of theatre. These actors were a group of 5th year C.S.E.* drama students who, with their teacher, had spent a whole term working on aspects of Georgian theatre costumes and ballads. Their delight in performing was echoed by the delight of the crowd, who 'oohed and aahed' at the characters they knew so well, portrayed for their pleasure and pennies.

*Certificate of Secondary Education

These same 5th year students discussed with amazement at a later date the total involvement and belief of their young audience, not only in their play but in the whole day and questioned why as they themselves had grown up in our school system, their own love of play and make-believe had not been allowed to develop further.

"We could have remembered so much more if there had been a point to it," said one.

The funereal note of the drum once more beat out and we processed onwards towards the gibbet.

Bodies pressed in on all sides as Black was led to the scaffold; with faltering steps he mounted and in a loud voice cried vengeance on Ayres, myself and others of our ilk. The noose was placed around his neck, then suddenly, all hell broke loose — shots were fired — a man sprang from the trees and took me by the throat; a similar thing happened to Ayres — other rogues lifted Black from the scaffold and we were hustled to the river bank.

I was so shocked that the next few minutes were a confused blurr. Coming round, I saw Black rowing for all he was worth into the centre of the stream, the other rogues making off in great haste into the thick woods. Children were everywhere; you could feel that they were glad that yet again, Black had escaped.

"A hundred guineas for his recapture!" I cried, knowing full well that no one would catch him, but it would help the feeling that it was not all over. There would be a chance for follow-up work, not that I felt that more work was really needed. The most important aspect of the whole event was that children had worked on a project that had come to a successful culmination. None of their previous writing, thinking or research had been in vain or just done to fill up a project book. "Dr. John" of Rowden Hill, however, did follow it up. Back in his primary school the following week, he wrote: Lackham Fayre, July 17th, 1759, —

Lackham Fayre   July 17th 1759

As I was riding to hackham my darumed horse threw me off and I twisted my anckle, but I got up and sat back on him. Then we, that is the Peasants and me, saw our first sight of hackham house. We came to an enclosure fence which I easily jumped. I saw all the Peasants and Gentry walking to the hackham fayre. We went into a field where we wated for Sir Roger De Coverly.

After five minutes we saw Sir Roger coming in his stage coach, it was drawn by one white horse. Then he waved to us so we waved back. He came into the court yard and he got out of his coach and started to walk out into the fresh air where he walked through a guard of soldiers. The Parson said a prayer with us and Sir Roger asked for his Katie, she had long blond hair and she looked very beautiful.

Sir Roger then invited us to his garden and Lady Neate was allergic to lavander and she started to sneeze. I met Sir James Montague and Lady Victoria Montague and their daughter who was six years old. I saw a lady that had a big wig on. I saw a lovely pond it had lots of lilies on top and it was surrounded by Goldfish all of the fish were orange except for one that was pure yellow and was the biggest of them all.

I saw my Lawyer John Heath speaking to Sir James Montague and lady Victoria. I went back to my site to sell some papers and to buy some things when I was selling the papers a man came and bought one of my papers for one penny then another fellow with two pence bought a paper. Then I saw a sedan chair that was carried by two men and a man sat inside.

After that we went to see the court and I was on the Jury to tell people if, that Ben Black was innocent or giulty and I said that he was yiulty because he made one slip up. He was sentenced to be hung at two o clock So we went back to have our Banquet I was on a diet so I had two apples, two pieces of bread, two pieces of cheese and a tomato. Samuel Neate let me have some of his wine. The Parson said a prayer to thank God for our lunch.

After lunch I went to watch bowls and lacock lost the first game and the second to my village of Rowden.

A bell rang at two of the clock and we took a lady's arm and led her to the hanging. Where we saw Ben Black. He put his head in the noose but one of Ben Black's accomplices held a gun at Sir Roger De Coverly and led him to the river, where Ben Black escaped in a boat Sir Roger offered a 100 guinnes reward for Ben Black's capture. So then he apolagised for no hanging and we went back to our villages.

Damn me, here I was wandering again, all these thoughts in my head, it must have been the blow from the pistol butt. I had wanted to show that learning could be exciting and that you could come outside your school to learn. That to get children to believe and "play", you as teachers had to believe and play as well, if not better. These things I felt were accomplished at Lackham House. Later a child said it was better than the tele "because it was us." I looked up; one lone sedan chair moved slowly after the crowds who were streaming back towards the 20th century.

Chapter 7

Shaping the World — Through Writing

JOHN RICHARDSON

I always think of John's school as being in the depths of the country; it is certainly not buried, however , although to reach it you have to drive through leafy lanes which wind between steep banks after passing through a narrow tunnel cut deep into a hillside of tall beech trees. To me, this never fails to give the feeling of passing into another world. John's own description at the beginning of his paper pictures vividly the immediate surroundings of his school.

The writing of these 9 or 10-year old children gives an equally clear impression of the vigour and zest with which they savour life. This is no sleepy rural school in which bucolic children suck pens instead of straws; it is a hive of activity of which this writing is only one facet. John Richardson believes that living is a creative act which demands continual celebration in defiance of the difficulties we may encounter along the way. A verse from Browning which I learnt at primary school myself comes to mind:

> The year's at the spring
> And day's at the morn;
> Morning's at seven;
> The hill-side's dew-pearled;
> The lark's on the wing;
> The snail's on the thorn;
> God's in His heaven —
> All's right with the world!

We know, of course, that time can't stand still at seven o'clock on a spring morning, but the children of Wardour School are given a start to their education which carries the conviction that life *can* be celebrated because such mornings do exist.

Wardour School is offically designated as "Wardour R.C. Aided Primary School — number on roll 70" — a description which, though functional from an administrative point of view, sins a little by omission.There has been a school in the Wardour Valley (South-West Wiltshire,near the Dorset/Somerset border and very nearly Hardy country) for two hundred years, and the present crouching grey building, constructed of locally quarried stone, has existed for one hundred and thirty-three years. The valley was the possession of the Lords of Arundel, and much of it, though the title has now passed away, is still owned by their descendants. It was a safe haven for English Catholics during the troubled years of religious discord. It was here, in Hook Manor, that plans were made for the adventure that culminated in the settlement of Maryland, U.S.A.

This area is almost entirely devoted to the raising of dairy cattle, and I can look out of my window now, as I am working, at a glowing herd of pedigree Guernseys. As this was originally parkland, we are fortunate to have around us, studded here and there among the fields, luxurious trees of great variety — oaks, and limes, poplars and horse chestnuts, beech and ash and many many others but, alas, no longer the lovely elms, stricken so tragically by Dutch elm disease in recent times and now burning in our cottage grates as winter fuel. A tiny river takes a lazy route through the fields and a string of artificial lakes extends up towards the conifer plantations which cover the nearest range of low hills. Beyond are the clear lines of the chalk downs, where grain is now once again cultivated just as it was by Stone-Age Man in the birth time of our nation. It is not surprising in such surroundings that we have, living among the old traditional agricultural families, a cluster of sculptors, artists, musicians, writers and potters, whose talents, I'm glad to say, have served to inspire and embellish the writing, singing and art that is celebrated in our village Primary School. My wife and I feel it a rare privilege to teach in such a place (raising our fruit and vegetables, milking our goats and collecting our eggs as a profitable side-line to support our unconventionally large family); I'm sure my other two teachers would echo these sentiments.

The parents here love and respect this school and support it in every possible way. They feel it is theirs and it is in the knowledge of this marvellous support that we try to inject into it an enthusiasm and commitment commensurate with their hopes and expectations.

I must be careful, however, about the use of this word "expectations." At the moment schools are being subjected to a periodic blast from the media demanding a return to the "good old basics," which means, in précis, ten sums on the blackboard and a reprint of all those formidable and uninspiring grammar and comprehension books with which their parents were so effectively innoculated from genuine education not so very long ago. It is my constant aim to raise my parents' sights above the level of that stultifying morass of unrewarding trivia.

As I said, in this village school we keep goats — currently nine of them. We muck them, trim their hooves, brush them, lead them on to pasture, move electric fences, tether, take in at night, give concentrate in right measure to the milking nannies, turn the hay that's cut for us and lift and heave the bales, and throw out the old bedding on to the compost heap to feed the school garden, which is our second venture. We were all able to sit around and watch the birth of our kids from beginning to end — the whole school! This gives us the nearest approach to what I would call our scientific writing. Sometimes the occasion arises for a little research in answer to questions that occur, but we are much more husbandmen than scientists. We end up by knowing how to plant the turnips, broad beans, runner beans, marrows and courgettes, the beet, the spinach beet, the peas, the lettuces, how to transplant, how to stake up the runner beans and tomatoes. Now and again scientific questions do arise but they are not sought out. When a child brings these points up we try to find answers. We watch a little the growing rates and have done some graphing. We write up garden notes, and accounts of things happening to the animals:

> First we picked up the turnips which looked white and I got an aching back after picking them all. We chucked the turnip leaves on the compost heap. We picked some very small carrots which weren't at all big. A few of the carrots we thought were weeds because of their tops. They were orange on the bottom and very small.
>
> Then we picked beetroots which were very successful and we had a job pulling them out. If we had cut them too far down all their juice would come out and they would turn white.
>
> We picked broad beans which weren't very good and we saw that the flowers on them were white with black spots on the middle. In fact it was a poor harvest for broad beans.
>
> The runner beans were our best crop with beans up to one foot long and over. We collected them all and found how difficult it was to reach up because they were so high up, so Tim Rumney came along and picked them.
>
> Our brussel sprouts we haven't picked yet but they are looking extremely healthy.
>
> The bindweed was a very nasty weed which was very hard to get rid of. They were white with long roots.
>
> The marrows were lovely and incredibly big and for the few plants that there were we got a load of them. Their leaves looked like ferns and at the end of the stalk were extremely sharp and prickly.
>
> Tom

The Goat and her milk

The kid inside the goat has no antibodies so he has to drink the milk from her teats to get the beestings. Some people thought all the things were passed through the umbilical cord but it is not so because the kid has nothing to worry about. All the things he needs like warmth, food and drink are all given to him.

The goat has to be milked quite a lot because it will get milk fever. This happens when you feed it too much.

If it gets fat it is harder to produce the baby out of her backside because the womb muscles are made for pushing out the baby but if they are surrounded by fat they can't work as well and thereby it will hurt the goat more and it will take longer to come out and it might die because it might be too big and it will die most likely.

The bag is swollen and you can hardly see the teats. Milk fever consists of hard teats because the udder is rock hard with milk and the temperature goes very high.

Jonathan

Goats give birth

Josephine has given birth to two white hornless kids. We all watched her give birth to the first and she had the other during dinner.

When the goats came out they were covered with yellow slime. The mother soon licks her and the yellow comes off.

It also helps them to get breathing.

When the mother is about to have her baby she is restless and wanders about but eventually she lies down and gives birth.

Tim

My first introduction to "Creative Writing" came through reading a book by Barry Mayberry*, which contained a large number of ideas and, what was equally pleasing, a very good series of examples of the work children had done following his methods of approach. The whole idea, here, is to introduce children to vivid and open situations where they can observe closely and imaginatively and give full vent to their unique powers of expression — and I mean unique, because children have a freshness of eye and mind that appears to be denied to many adults.

I find it useful to look closely at the situation with the children, to do a little talking into it, introducing, I hope, some humour, while sometimes talking mere 'scribble' and at other times hopefully letting flashes of insight come sparking out — and then to surprise the children by saying,

*Creative Writing for Juniors, Batsford.

"If I'd written that down, that would be Creative Writing."
Because I think we ought to get away from the notion that in Creative Writing we are necessarily dealing with "High Poetry." Usually we are not, and can't be, because not all people are poets, nor are all children for that matter, but it's fun to look at things and see what they say to us:

> Broken hinges,
> Worn and weak as if it would fall apart.
> Rusty nails make it rattle.
> Snapped wood comes out of its hold,
> Jammed to the ground, refuses to open and shut.
> Fungi on the cracked wood.
> Unsteady.
> A favourite place for birds. They give it thank you
>   messages.
> Worn away,
> Cracked like an earthquake.
> We have no feelings for it . . . .
> Chippened away, worn through.
>
> Wayne

The youngsters love bringing things in to enhance these lessons. Some of mine have produced huge swords, for example, that some ancestor of theirs left lying about the place with honour's rusty stains about them. Recently a pair of huge snails was brought in and so, reasonably, we looked up about snails first of all, found out where the breathing hole was, saw how they slid along on that foot of theirs, watched their eyes operating on the end of a couple of tubes and how they retracted when an object was put near to them. And then we began to think of a snail existence, what was going on inside that snail mind, how it is to be a wandering appetite over a cabbage leaf, what's coming in through those eyes. My Biro* comes towards them. What's being said to it? The snail has about it that great, blank, incomprehensible cry of all the instinctive little creatures who are exploring a set of meanings away outside our rational, logical comprehension.

Here is what Emily wrote after our discussion:

> Funny when you think of all the different animals
>   on the earth.
> Slimy.
> They look around. So many things to see.
> Hunting for fresh food.
> They long for the fresh outside.
> They slip along leaving a silvery trail.
> They stare at us with strange frightened eyes.

*A kind of ball point pen.

Sick of doing the same thing every day.
They feel lovely and cool.
Slowly they glide along, looking for new things to
    feel and climb on.
The trail has hardened on my arm.
One snail has climbed up the blackboard and is rub-
    bing out the spellings as it goes.
Scared to come out of its secret hideout.
His breathing hole opens and closes.
He sticks to the grass.
.When I lift him up I'm scared his shell might come
    off.
The colour is fading on top of his shell.
What do they see?
How many miles does a snail go in his lifetime?
Proud of being born.
Snails litter the classroom.
It crawls — no, not crawls. It slides along the wall,
    not afraid of the long drop below.
Snails all around. They are small proud animals slid-
    ing like they are on ice.
Nice animals . . . . I think.

Emily

The youngsters, looking at the things and experiencing the situations that I've talked about, in fact are able to communicate, and want to
communicate, great crowds of ideas, and enjoy doing it, and want to
read out afterwards, and let us all hear what they have done, obviously
excited. And I, too, want to read what I've written, let me tell you, because I always write with the children.

It was some weeks after Ken Evans had brought his paintings into
school for us to borrow that I took the painting of the dandelion clock
down from the wall. It had been a familiar part of each day, sitting
there, waiting to be explored and discovered, but in danger of becoming taken for granted.

The children stood round the desk and, together, we looked
deeper and deeper into the picture. I talked with my voice and I talked
with my fingers as they traced the path of the flying seeds. What I said I
do not remember, and the children's work gives no clue to my thoughts.
Their fingers sought the lines of clouds, their minds clothed the leaves
and seeds in different costumes, their pens took the dandelion on magic
journeys.

Old Father Dandelion is losing his grey beard.
Little space capsules floating into space,
    caught in a whisp of air.

A zephyr is blowing.
Black and stormy clouds creep over the face of the
earth.
Gone with the wind . . . .

Daniel

The Wind Carriers

I am the wind, all rough,
Blowing the fluff all day.
The children coming to pick all
the fluff and throwing it into me.
It tickles me a lot.
You wouldn't believe it, but
I am the North Wind . . . .

                                                    Rosalind

The Dandelion

Up, up, up and away.
The S.S. paratroopers with their F.6 42's fall from the
    sky
in a cloud of evil.
The dandelion releases its parachutes.
A desolate landscape . . . .

                                                    Sebastian

The Storm

A storm is brewing.
You can tell by the clouds
The times are changing.
The wind blows and turns the long grass to sea.
I grew as a dandelion.
Yellow dress I wore, but then I changed my dress.
White was the colour then . . . .

                                                    Clare

I'm shaped like a lion in a cage.
Nowhere to go but where the wind goes
I am too far away to say
Goodbye . . . .

                                                    Paul

There was nothing in what I said to produce a stereotyped response, nothing in my tone or manner to provoke imitative reactions.
Whatever I said only stimulated individual thoughts and emotions —
some of them very beautiful indeed:

The Dandelion

Melancholy skies.
The ghostly night trip to darkness.
Ashes to Ashes
    and
Dust to Dust.
What is there to admire in this dark dark world?
"Oh please show me the way to Daylight"
the dandelion seeds call.
The moon rises and all is silent.
The last few gentle rays of the mid-summer sun
disapppear behind a big black cloud.
"Oh Farewell,
Oh come back. I don't know the way out.
Oh well".

Rachel

Although every other lesson I give within the school is carefully prepared, the Creative Writing lesson is merely named as such on the time-table. I do not know from week to week which objects I will use, as the magic of a sparkling frost or the introduction of someone's family treasure may divert me from the intended object. Nor do I know what sort of mood I will be in when we sit down together, the children and I, to talk over the ideas engendered by whatever is before us. It is a verbal dream sequence where thoughts wander and leap at will.

The dandelion picture made the children refine and define, twist and tussle their minds and vocabularies. Their work was, generally, short, but very powerful. Each child saw something different in the picture. Another picture of a man and the sun lubricated their pens. They were itching to get started and their work ranged over pages and pages.

"When time began and when God made man.
He's a ghostly figure.
Pray to Rah, the sun god.
Nuclear clouds.
Sand, sand and sand . . . .

Adrienne

The man just stands there and looks at the rising sun.
His shadow covers the long stretch of sand.
He's alone.
The world has been destroyed. All that is left is him.
Where is he?

A world of his own.
Welcoming the sun.
Red sky at night shepherd's delight,
Red sky at morning, shepherd's warning.
Lonely,
Lost.

                                                                    Rachel

Do you speak English?
Pulling up the sun
Little green man.

                                                                    Dominic

"Here I am and here I stay," says the man.
The red blaze of the sun
is going towards the right.
The edge of the world.
He's at the country of loneliness.

                                                                    Paul

Save me! Save me! is the call he cries.
Nothing to eat or drink.
Up and up and up to the Red Sky.
Dead.
No one can harm him now.
and now he lives on the red cloud.
So beware.
He makes evil spells

                                                                    Christopher

Flames of fire dance about in great waves.
Does the great sun dare come out?
That man bothers me.
What's he there for anyway?
Yes, but it might not be earth.
It might be another world.
Sand, sand, everywhere.
Why is the shadow the colour of the man?

                                                                    Penelope

Fire Sky

Praising his God,
Beginning to end.
Men of first creation,

Skies of fire,
Tresses of the sun.
Lifting the clouds above him.
Ashes lay where the sun
   once stood in the reign of glory.
Atomic explosion from earth into space,
Drifting sands.
The great shadow stands above me.
Is he my self reflection from light?
Great birds of fire fly through the sky.
A golden creature.
Multicoloured glows.
Problem face from earth,
Colostrum yellow.
Reflection burning like saffron everything it hits.
Scientific people of all times
thinking together in a laboratory.
The one and only green man to cover
the face of the earth.

                                         Mercy

The eye, marvellous as it is, cannot tell us everything. We may admire a picture we see on the wall, but we have an affinity with what we touch or hold. Tony Denning knows this, and his sculptures are meant to be touched, moved, rotated, climbed in and out of, generally explored by every visual and tactile means. The inquisitive fingers of the children poke and pry into his pieces, and ideas are stimulated by touch. There are no moving parts in the first sculpture the children wrote about, but the wheel turned in their imaginations, spinning pictures and images for their delight:

A hiding place for ghosts to hide in.
All spooky inside.
"Mr. Witch, can I be small
so that I can sit in there"

                                        Rosalind

Wheels dress me like a garment of silk,
Wobbly ladders stretch up to nowhere.
If only I had a heart.
A heavy weight holds me down
as if I was imprisoned.
I have no soft white skin like some
But instead I wear a coat of metal, cold and hard.

I have no brain with which to think.
I have no eyes with which to see.
I have no nose with which to smell.
I have no life in me to have joy.

Rachel

The Memory Mill

What do you bring back?
Glad tidings for Christmas,
Warm toast with a fire-side melt,
The occasional drink of warm cosy chocolate.
The wife in an upsetting mood.
The cat on the table.
What is the fire-side melt?
What is a degree in courage?
How is spring with buds of lightness?
In your mind, in your heart?
This is what? This is how?
You are what you are.
But how?
Dark Death Dances
In fog-mist snow.
Of a definite snow.
What do we like?
A compassionate lick from the dog.
A cosy bed.
What memories drive us?
The family in the room.
The wood crackling on the open fire.
Crispy bacon crackles and the fat bulges out.
Warm feelings.
Summer sun.

Adrienne

Many of the children, particularly those at the younger end of the class, feel more secure in their writing if there is an element of familiarity about the picture they are admiring or the sculpture they are exploring. Many of the previous extracts were taken from the latter part of a child's work once she had got the image of a mill or an oil rig out of her system and had progressed from fact to fantasy and surmise. An abstract work of art, with no familiar focal points, is a demanding enough rewarding stimulant, which several immature children shy away from, preferring to turn it into a catalogue of its component parts. But all children, regardless of their capacity to abstract, enjoy the initial investigation — spinning coils of metal, handling warm and cold, sharp and smooth surfaces, marvelling at the skill of the sculptor. (And one week, when we had written about a very angular metal man, we complemented our writing and complimented the artist by attempting to make our own out of junk). And some of the children did abstract.

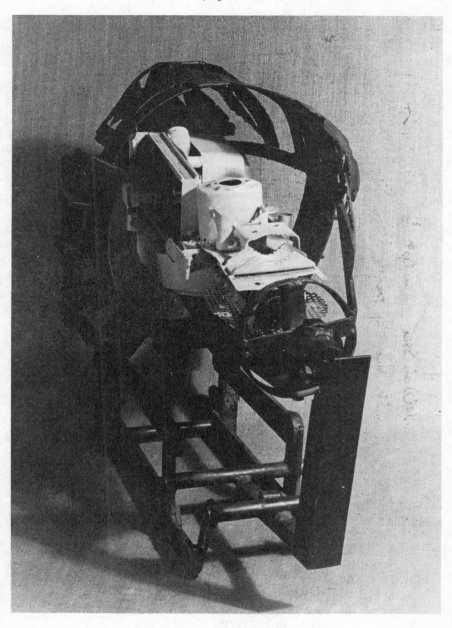

Is it talking to me?
Does it like us?
Nod your metal head if you like us.
It does not move.

Lynn

It doesn't let its love out

Clare

A map of the world.
Funny world.
There's England — that little hole.
Bumps.
Twisting and turning . . . .
I don't know what it is
So I might as well give up guessing.
'Bye, Sculpture.
I might meet you again.

Rachel

Hidden secrets, millions of them.
Something ... err ...
Cold, dusty.
What is he?
Lots of things.
Living or dead?
WANTED
What is he up to?
Turning all about the place ...

Mercy

A ship going round and round
Having open heart surgery.

Adrienne

Mechanical.
I like it.
Twirl, twirl.
Stop, stop! You're making me dizzy.
I like you.
I want to make peace.
Queer looking.
Peculiar.
Odd shaped.
Wouldn't dare fall in love with you.
Blind as a bat.
Doesn't squeak. Very surprising.
Oh, please stop turning me around.
I'm getting a headache ....
He has no brain.
Can't be clever without a brain though.
Spin, spin.
Ooh, I'm not enjoying things ....
.... Everyone's scared of me.
Why? I'm scared and shy of them.

Paul

The additional pleasure the children take in their writing when they know the artists whose work they have available to them in school adds a dimension to the work not immediately apparent to the outside reader. Similarly, when the relationship is the other way round, the children have a confidence in their writing born of the knowledge that their unaltered work will be the framework for a new work of art:

Metal Sculpture

Reaching out with cold fingers trying to find something to imprison in its mind.
Endless passages leading only into time.
Cold . . . .
No feelings in the cold black heart made of stone.
Waiting . . . .
Watching . . . .
Hiding, until the master plan has been finished.
Spinning round on its axis, never stops.
Mouths open, crying out for good, but the heartless object walks by.
Lost . . . .
No one owns it, only the hearts of cruel men.
Push it round and it only springs back into the same position, jeering!
A keyhole, but the key has been lost leaving thoughts whine and scream until they die.
Particles of metal pushed together and screaming out for mercy, but it's never given.
The royal pardon ended, the life sentence begins.
Tormenting the occupants of the cruel black cells.
Surrounded by a heartless atmosphere, but what does it care?
Looking up, out of the cruel heart.
The light of the world unable to penetrate it's resisting layers.
Tunnels not of love, but of hatred.
Still, those fingers reach out, but people have the sense not to go near them.
Telescopes looking at nothing, a waste of time.
Why a waste? Time goes on forever, or will this thing have another idea?
Who owns it? Itself, being its own master, must be fun, but what does it know about fun, the thing who tried to condemn it? . . . .

Kate

The children have been exposed directly to some Eliot, a fair amount of Dylan Thomas, a snatch of E. E. Cummings, a little Lawrence, at least one piece by Sylvia Plath, but no Berryman. I say "directly," because the poets, though they have, as it were, "touched" the children lightly (except Berryman) with their undiluted magic, have also had, I

believe, a great indirect effect on the youngsters insofar as they have influenced the thought processes of me, the teacher. I am attracted by
their immediacy, their tussle with language and form, as though their
minds were in the grip of a frustration brought about by life's inade-
quacy and impermanence and triviality, and that their wrestling with
words personalises these deeper struggles. There is, at times, a rumbus-
tiousness, a pouring out, and, especially with Thomas, a very bombard-
ment, and let the reader beware of flak! And, in Berryman particularly,
a 'chuck-it-away-ah-what's-the-good-well-anyway-it-earns-a-buck!' ex-
terior which disguises — Oh God, it has to disguise! — the whiskey-
burn, the "pals" with all their expectations, and the moon-faces, eager,
in waiting lecture halls:

> Say it for me, John, I pray you . . . .
> 'With arms outflung the clock announced: ten
> twenty.
> Dozens of demons sprang and preyed on Henry.
> All on a heavy morning.
> The baby was ill, the sky was dark, the I
> was Id, somebody put the sky on like a lid,
> somebody who is not returning.'

> Uncollected Dream Songs
> (*Henry's Fate and Other Poems*)
> John Berryman

Without making a "thing" of it all, I suppose I mean that I encourage a carelessness with language, an imprecision, because there is a
carelessness and imprecision all about us, a glorious, frustrating, aggra-
vating profusion, a serious trivia and trivial seriousness. This does not
mean to say, though, that I pay no regard to the mechanical aspects of
my children's writing.

I correct all the written work of the children, but I make sure that
first of all, as far as possible, I read the story with the child and I comment on the story, and its attractiveness and the lovely points it has in it
and the way it's been brought out by the child and encourage the child.
Only very rarely do I say, "No, really, that isn't good enough. You
didn't make much of an effort today. Never mind, after all, we can't all
be good all the time". Mostly it is praise. Then we want to improve the
power that story has to communicate. Now, that power is impaired by
wrong punctuation or by grossly inaccurate spelling — I mean spelling
at the level that is so inaccurate that it's only the surrounding context
that enables one to understand what the word was meant to be in the
first place. And so the child sees why the correction is being done, and
he corrects the errors.

Now, I can't hear every pupil read his work to me, nor can I mark
every story with him. Some of this work has to be taken home, has to be

done afterwards, but a conscious effort must be made to get most of the children to read out their stories, to mark as many of the stories as possible with the children and to ring the changes, so that I make sure I am not always looking at the same children's books every time, but going round the group. In this way, the children grow conscious of two things; first, that for me it is the communication that is important; and secondly, that corrected work is ancillary to the communication — there to make the contact between the writer and the reader or listener more perfect. When it comes to punctuation, we are talking about that part of communication which, to be illustrated, needs to be read out by the child. In this way, the child can hear for himself where he intended the long and short pauses to come and hear for himself where he really announced the fact that he was asking a question by the rise in voice which indicates that a question is being asked.

This reading out by the writer of what is on the page is not only an aid to hearing where the punctuation needs to be. In all kinds of respects it is an intensely learning situation.

You have, on the one extreme, the child who is still at the 'he', 'him', 'her', 'she' stage of writing whose characters are nameless and where we get pure activity with little or no description, where streets, houses, cinemas, cafes are incognito, and on the other hand, with the more advanced children, usually the older children who have experienced this situation longer, we find pupils who are giving detailed accurate descriptions, setting scenes beautifully, starting to draw characters where people are seen through their faces, their clothing, and their dispositions. There's an increasing depth which I never ever analyse, never say, "Look how he did this", "Look how she did that". If the children hear enough of each other's stories and are encouraged to read consistently week after week after week the well-told stories by adult authors writing for children, then this development will come, but it is a natural growth. The seed-bed for it is not the seed-bed of analysis. You don't get, for example, the right use of adverbs, adjectives, adverbial clauses, adjectival clauses, noun clauses, be it what it may, by lessons on these, by sentence analysis. You get this development by constant practice in the art of writing, by constantly hearing each other's efforts, by constant immersion in good children's literature. No way can you draw out a linear "Curriculum of Langauage Development" for this kind of work. As a teacher I am aware that I am surrounded by a group of individuals each at his own level of development, each possessed of his own vocabulary, each developing his own style of expression in the light of his own imagination. Yet each of us is gaining from the others in the group subtle and invisible influences which tend to improve and embellish our efforts the longer we share a celebration of the creative pieces produced by all of us. And the matter does not rest there, for the child receives particular instruction from his teacher, as and when the teacher thinks it appropriate so to assist him. Let me give you an instance. It is quite legitimate, when the child first starts to construct cohesive stories of his own, that he should string together the separate sentences with the phrase 'and then', but there comes a time when the teacher feels it appropriate to indicate that 'and then' or 'then' is too indefinite a time-lapse indicator and he will suggest to the child that such expressions as 'a moment or two later', 'in a short while', 'after many hours', 'after the passage of many years' and so forth, would more accurately describe the message that he was attempting to transmit to his readers. What we are really waiting for is that moment, different in the case of each child, when sufficient fluency and confidence has been achieved to allow for what is, after all, a level of subtle criticism. This really means that the child is now eager and willing, as well as able, to accept such refinements of his writing without feeling that his heartfelt efforts are being in any sense denigrated.

The reading system used in this school starts with the Initial Teaching Alphabet, i.t.a., as produced by Pitman's. The most excellent thing about this method of introducing reading is that children are quickly able to read up to the level of their known spoken vocabulary. This, in turn, means that the youngsters are also able to express their thoughts readily in writing:

"This is Witch and the Witch past in one snaek, too snaels, three wirms, for spieders, fiev rats and sterd it up and maed a spell and sed

> snaek in a draek
> a snaeyl in a taeyl
> a wirm in a ternip
> spieder in a greder
> a rat in a hat".

Catherine

I am sure that the fluency our children possess in written language by the time they leave our school at the age of eleven is in large part due to this early rapid reading and writing experience. Of course, were it not for the admirable work done by the Infant teacher and the teacher of the younger Juniors in encouraging the children to read widely and to express themselves in vivid and exciting ways, the progress I have eulogised would not, in fact, take place. Although I have written chiefly from the point of view of the teacher of children between the ages of nine and eleven, it is important that readers should realise that the systems and methods I have described are used throughout the school, though in a measure appropriate to the age and development of the children.

I cannot over-emphasise the importance of regular writing to the development of reading. Whenever the child writes he is revising and consolidating his grasp on our language. Just as it is true that we first learn to drive a motor car by grasping a series of sequential techniques and actions which, later, amalgamate to produce a unit, the parts of which we cease to analyse — and, indeed, it is dangerous to do so if our aim is to keep death off the road — so it is equally true that the 'written language', which initially stutters along with word following painfully-recalled word, after a while develops a flow which is not only a facet of the writing itself but also of the reading which is a concommitant of the writing. The child who is a writer himself is more likely to appreciate the written word. You know how easy it is to pass over a magnificent portrait produced by a great artist until you have drawn your own pin-man and crowned him with a mane of lunatic yellow hair. Once you have become involved directly, your ability to appreciate is considerably increased and, if you have any gifts, you start to see not by analysis but by intuition and by the absorption of technique as a result of constant contact with it, how your own efforts can be improved and refined. In short, you must read in order to write and, if you write, you'll want to read and then write again.

Chapter 8

Using Writing in Teaching Mathematics

JUDITH SALEM

Judy Salem's interest in the use of verbal language for explaining processes in mathematics began when she was the only math teacher on a school-wide committee examining curriculum issues. Her attempts to explain mathematical concepts to teachers of other subjects taught her the value of using non-mathematical language in order to clarify operations for others. Simultaneously, in her own classes, she broke her long habit of grabbing her students' pencils and *demonstrating* answers to their questions; rather, she made a verbal explanation, thus forcing her students to translate her words into mathematical formulations themselves. As this practice seemed to aid their retention of processes, she moved next to the uses of writing described in this chapter.

What does writing have to do with mathematics? Twenty years ago I would have answered, "Nothing." That's one reason I chose mathematics as my major in college. I found very little use for discussion, written or oral, of problems or theory, but learned by intuitive leaps and discovery of patterns. Many students who find mathematics challenging but not difficult probably learn the way I did. I imagine many other teachers learned that way too. Is it any wonder then that many of our students find mathematics so mystifying?

I can't count the number of times I've found myself introducing a new concept, reaching the critical point of the new idea, and standing speechless, chalk in hand, because I could not verbally breach the gap between what I just said and wrote and what I was about to. The way out? Do a lot of examples, until the students who could see patterns picked up the idea. When they had given the idea some credence, I'd go back to point out the pattern to the others. But for those students who relied more on verbal explanations, I had never made the connection.

Another example brought home the realization that there may be a large number of students who don't learn math, maybe can't learn it as I did, but could learn it through a more thorough and consistent use of language. Returning to San Francisco after an unsuccessful trip to the roulette tables of Reno, I was attempting to convince my friend that a bet on the reds had no better chance after five blacks in a row than did a bet on the blacks. For two hours I attempted to convince him with diagrams, arithmetic computations, and analogous examples. No luck. Finally I managed to put the right sequence of words together in a simple sentence, and he said, "Of course, why didn't you say that in the first place?"

I am convinced that many students could better understand and use mathematics if we gave them more opportunities to write about and talk about the subject. Writing is a tool for learning that mathematics teachers have long overlooked.

Learning Logs

One of the major objections of students, who are looking for reasons to dislike mathematics, is a lack of warmth, of personality, of human content. Those of us who love the subject cannot deny the charge. The things that excite us most involve structure, the creative reorganization of dry bones. Bertrand Russell described the ethereal thinness of mathematics when he said, "Mathematicians never know what they are talking about nor whether what they are saying is true." Unfortunately, when mathematicians deliver the results of their creative efforts, they do not tell us of their frustrations and false starts. They deliver clear, concise, clean, cold proofs of results. Textbooks tend to do the same.

Introduction of some of the history of mathematics and biographies of mathematicians helps, but to verify the students' own flesh and blood involvement in the exercises they are doing and the skills they are learning, I have begun requiring that they keep a journal.

In my first year algebra classes the journal (we call them our math logs or learning logs) serves two purposes. First, the log is a notebook. I ask students to write down explanations and examples that I write on the board. They will have these for reference as they do their assignments at home. I often disagree with the method or explanation a text presents, but, more important, I think it is valuable for students to write their way through examples rather than just read them or watch me do them.

Second, the log is a personal record. The last five minutes of each class period, or at the end of the week if I forget to allow time each day, students write comments on how they are doing and whether they are understanding, criticism of the material, the teacher or their fellow students, or anything else that may be on their minds.

Their first entry in the log is a statement of three goals for the semester. Then in the last entries of the quarter and of the semester they will assess whether they accomplished what they set out to. Goals for the first semester all tend to look the same:

1. I will get an A in algebra.
2. I will do my homework every night.
3. I will pay attention in class.

—Mike

The second semester their goals become more realistic but sound even more like promises:

1. I have to get at least a C in this class.
2. I will not miss any more classes.
3. I will stay after school for extra help.

—Sandy

or from a student who did better:

1. This time I'll get an A, not a lousy A-.
2. I won't bother Antony so much.
3. I will not make any more dumb mistakes on tests.

—Craig

I try to read the log entries once every week or two weeks. They give me another way of assessing how well students are understanding what we are doing in class. Also, since some find it easier to write criticism of assignments which they found confusing or irrelevant, the log gives me a continuous evaluation of my teaching. If there are errors in the notes they have taken, I correct those, but the only grade is for keeping the log up to date. I often respond in writing to comments or on points of confusion.

For most students the log is a running comment or chatter about how they are doing. One of my goals is to get them to write more about the content of what they are learning and a little less about their grades.

Friday, Oct. 20

We had a quiz on the distributive property today. I think I did OK.

Monday, Oct. 23

I got a B. DAMN. I understood it but I didn't factor all the way, and I made a dumb mistake on the first part. $2x(4y - 6x)$ isn't good enough. You have to go $4x(2y - 3x)$.

Others are more cryptic:

Tuesday, April 3
Got a lot done today.

Thursday, April 5
Fooled around today.

Friday, April 6
Blew it again today. Clay was really weird.

—Tom

A few write more personal entries, and some use the space to inveigh against algebra. The girl who wrote the following entry did well in the class but . . .:

Math is DUMB and algebra is the DUMBEST. Why do we have to do all these things with exponents. I want to be a doctor. When will I ever use this stuff? I HATE ALGEBRA. Besides it's boring.

Barbara

Sometimes I answer these in writing:

Looking at it from your point of view I'd have to agree, but you are only seeing little pieces now, pieces that don't seem to mean anything by themselves. You're right. They don't. But algebra is the language behind most of the rest of math and a lot of science. Unfortunately it's hard to appreciate the pieces until you take the next math course or a science course where you need to use them.

J.S.

But this time we spent some time in class discussing "why algebra".

While students groan when it's time to take notes, most say they look forward to writing down their own comments. They often remind me to allow time to write in their logs, and few have raised questions about the value of doing this type of writing in a math class.

To introduce students to writing accurate descriptions and directions I started with an example which I consider related to mathematics, but which does not fit in with the material contained in most high school math courses. I wanted our first attempt to be something different and to provide a chance for everyone to succeed. The exercise includes using Cuisenaire Rods to build something, then giving instructions on how to build the building to another student who cannot see it. The fact that building is a linear, step-by-step process makes it a fairly easy process to describe, and the "how to" approach to this problem is very similar to what I will ask them to do with mathematics problems later. I have used this exercise in basic and remedial classes as well as with first year algebra students.

I divide students into groups of three and give each group two containers of Cuisenaire Rods. One person will build, then he will give directions to the second. They will need to set up some kind of barrier with books so the second person cannot see what the first is building. The third student is an observer and should have a view of what both the others are doing. After the first student has built something she may use any descriptive words she wants to tell the second student how to construct her building. The second student may ask questions if the instructions are not clear enough. The observer makes sure the builders don't talk with their hands and warns them if they are getting too far off the track. Then students rotate roles so each has a turn at each position.

After each has had a chance to be architect, builder, and observer, students isolate themselves to build something to describe in writing. I collect the results and have them typed, leaving off the writer's name. A few days later we bring out the blocks again, and I randomly distribute the typed directions. After they have built according to the directions they have received, they try to find their own buildings. If they are successful they congratulate the builder, who also criticizes the directions and signs the typed copy.

They gain an appreciation of the need for detail, precision, and order; nevertheless, most students succeed because they can adjust the complexity of the building to their writing skills.

The smallest block is a white cube. Next is a red one equivalent to two white cubes, then a light green one, then magenta (some call it purple or violet), then yellow, then dark green, then black, then brown, then blue, up to an orange one which is equivalent to ten white cubes. Some student examples:

> Take four blues. Stack them horizontally with the side facing you. Then take two purples. Put one in the middle, horizontally, so that the end faces you. Take the other piece and put it on top of it, horizontally, so that the side faces you. Then take four white ones. Put two of them on the lower one. Put them on the end, and then do the same with the other two on the upper one. Then take two green (light colored) and put them standing up on the ends of the top blue. Take two more purple and put one from each green to a white.
>
> Vince—Algebra

1. Take four oranges and form a flat rectangle.
2. Put four reds on end inside each corner.
3. Put two blues across the reds sideways.
4. Now put two blues the opposite direction to form a blue rectangle. Put a black one across the middle in the same direction.
5. Put two blacks across in the opposite direction (close enough together so you can put three yellows across them).
6. Now put in the three yellows.
7. Put two dark greens in the opposite direction.
8. Put a red on each end in each corner. Now put four whites in a row next to the reds (on the two dark greens).

Cary—Math Lab

1. Place one yellow upright on the table.
2. Place one black one directly on top of the yellow.
3. Balance two rouge blocks on the two ends of the black.
4. On the left side place a blue block upright so that it is parallel to the end of the black and the rouge. Place a small white block on top of the blue.
5. Do the same as #4 to the right side.
6. Place a large orange block over the tops of the rouge and white. Place it evenly to both sides.
7. On the left side put a brown block next to the blue and a black next to that and a dark green block next to that and a yellow block next to that.
8. On the right side do the same as #7 but reverse the direction.

Susan—Algebra

Ifill Tower

Starting at the bottom with the orange blocks lay two orange blocks lengthwise and two more the opposite on top to make a square. Do the same with the blue, then the brown, black, dark green, and yellow. When you get to the purple you should use all six, light green all eight, red use six, white use two.

Dan—Math Lab

Many students discovered the simplicity of describing buildings with symmetry and repeated patterns. Others discovered the importance of the choice of those little words, the prepositions. (The secret to understanding several of the definitions of calculus and analysis lies in the appreciation of prepositions. No harm in starting early.) I thought this exercise was an excellent introduction to using writing in a mathematics class. My algebra students, however, were not quite so sure, as many of their log entries indicated.

Algebra was fun today. We got to build things. I don't know what it has to do with algebra, but it was better than factoring. Whoever tries to build mine will be mad. It won't stand up.

John

We didn't do any algebra today. We played with blocks. It was fun.

Beth

Such entries made it abundantly clear that I had some explaining to do. I'm not sure I could have made my reasons for this lesson clear at the time they did it, but later when we did some other assignments that involved writing directions, I made an extra effort to tie it in.

I've tried using writing directly as a means for learning algebra in what, by hindsight, looks like three different ways. There are, I think, a lot more ways to use writing in a geometry course, but I've not had the chance to teach that class since the writing bug bit me.

One use is what I call chatter: students talk to themselves on paper as they do a problem. They had to pause a moment to decide what to do, write down what they have decided, then do it. For example, to emphasize that solving a simple equation means undoing what is done to the variable, I ask students to first think what is being done to the variable then state what they will do to reverse that.

$\frac{x}{3} + 7 = -13$	The student should think, "x is divided by 3 then 7 is added."
Subtract 7	Is the first step to undo that.
$\frac{x}{3} = -20$	Now think "x is divided by 3."
Multiply by 3	To undo that.
$x = -60$	

Some one-step multiplication or division problems are the most difficult for students to deal with. They often feel like they are guessing about what to do. I have found that requiring students to put their thoughts into words and to write down what they are going to do before doing it resolves the confusion for many.

$\frac{5x}{8} = 80$	The student may say to himself, "This is the same as 5/8 times x."
Divide by $\frac{5}{8}$	Then the student should think "But that's the hard way."
Multiply by $\frac{8}{5}$	
$x = 128$	

In another approach to the problem the chatter still helps.

$\frac{5x}{8} = 80$	Another student may say, "This means multiply the variable by 5 then divide by 8."
Multiply by 8	To undo the division.
$5x = 640$	Now all we have is 5 times x.
Divide by 5	
$x = 128$	

Students usually strenuously oppose having to write these directions to themselves, but I remain adamant in requiring that they do to the point of including them on tests. In a standard problem set I usually choose three problems on which I require them to write out both the "think" and the "do" steps. Then I require only the "do" written out on about one-third of the rest. The improved understanding of the solution of equations is well worth the battle, but I've more than once referred back to these learning log entries when I needed to convince myself.

> Hooray! Mrs. Salem said I didn't have to write the steps on problem set 22 and 23. Maybe I can catch up with the class by tomorrow.

> I missed more than half of the answers on 22. Now I have to stay after school for help. But I have to take a French test.
>
> Beth

She knew how to do the problems when she left class, but she got confused at home. When she came after school all we had to do was start writing down the steps.

For some students the ability to write a set of directions on how to do a problem may better demonstrate their understanding than their success or failure in getting a right answer. So my second direct use of writing is for explaining how to do problems in addition to or instead of actually doing them.

Before starting to work with rational expressions in algebra, I asked students to pretend they had to explain how to add fractions to a younger student who had not yet learned the operations with fractions. The younger student knew all the other basics and knew what a fraction was but was not very familiar with the vocabulary relating to fractions. New words would have to be explained. I suggested that for this exercise students limit themselves to explaining "how." I see this task as very similar to the building directions but harder because it is not quite so linear. I was surprised at how well the first group of students did.

When you want to add two fractions together like:

$$\frac{1}{2} + \frac{2}{3}$$

you have to get the two bottom numbers the same, so you say to yourself, "What number do both of these numbers go into?" If you want, start from one and count on up until you find a number that both of these numbers go into. This number is the Common Denominator. The Common Denominator in this problem would be six. So then you might write the problem like this:

$$\frac{1 \text{ x}}{2 \text{ x } 3} \qquad + \qquad \frac{2 \text{ x}}{3 \text{ x } 2}$$

'cause then you have to multiply the top number by the number that you multiplied on the bottom to get the six. So now you would have:

$$\frac{1 \times 3}{2 \times 3} \quad + \quad \frac{2 \times 2}{3 \times 2} \quad = \quad \frac{3}{6} \quad + \quad \frac{4}{6} \quad = \quad \frac{7}{6}$$

now multiply and then add, but you never add the bottom numbers. Seems complicated, huh!

Katie

O.K. now. Do you know what a fraction is?
That's good.
O.K. Write a fraction for me. 2/6. Very good.
All right 2/6. The bottom number is called the denominator. You can remember this because it starts with a D. D for denominator and D for down. The top is called the numerator. I'm going to teach you how to add two fractions. Start with 2/6 + 1/3. When you add fractions you need a common denominator. First take the largest one and see if you can divide it by the lower one. And you can. 3 goes into 6 two times. So both denominators become 6. 2/6 + /6. 3 goes into 6 two times so 2 x 1 = 2 so it's 2/6. The other fraction that already had the denominator of 6 stays the same. The problem is ready to work 2/6 + 2/6. O.K. One more thing, you only add the numerators 2/6 + 2/6 = 4/6.

Greg

Greg, who is in the English department's study skills class for students who need to improve their writing skills, made an unfortunate choice of fractions so what would already be a difficult paragraph to follow becomes harder. In the future I'll give an example like 2/5 + 1/3 = 11/15, so the problem itself won't confuse the issue by repetition of numbers and so students do not have to reduce the result.

Mike asked if he could try to do the assignment without using any numbers instead of trying to teach a younger student.

First you take the two bottom numbers and you find a number that they go into evenly. Then you take that number and find out how many times each bottom number goes into it. Then multiply the top number by the number of times its bottom number goes into the first number. Then put that number on top of the first number. Do that to both fractions. Now add the two top numbers together and keep the bottom the same.

Mike

Of the seventy students who tried the assignment the first time all but five succeeded. Two students clearly demonstrated that they did not know how to add fractions, and I had an opportunity to offer them some extra help right away. The other three students wrote such things as, "Find the common denominator and add." One of these could not elaborate. The other two I had failed to convince of the value of writing math. For the most part, though, both the students and I were impressed with their efforts. As they finished writing and reread what they had written, they realized that they'd succeeded at doing something pretty complicated, and they started to gather around me as I worked with individuals so I could read theirs right then.

As I read their papers I was struck by how difficult they were to read in spite of the fact that they were correct. Reading mathematics is probably one of the most difficult tasks a math student faces. I used to shock my advanced math students by telling them that in one graduate math course I had a textbook that was essentially prose, no numbers, and my reading rate was three pages an hour, maybe five on my best days. In any case, I am hoping that by writing and reading what they themselves have written, students may better appreciate the intricacies of written math and learn to read it slowly.

I have used this assignment of explaining to a younger student for several other mathematical operations in first year algebra. I am convinced of its value as a learning tool which allows students to better organize their information and as a diagnostic tool that lets me know immediately who needs help. William Geeson, in an article in *The Mathematics Teacher,** recommends asking students to explain how to do problems as an alternative to just having them solve problems on tests. I plan to do more with that idea this year.

For students to succeed in writing about mathematics, the task must be very clearly stated and very specific. This next use of writing in mathematics I call "failing." About a week after the students were so successful in explaining *how* to add fractions with different denominators, I decided to really push my luck and ask *why*? Why do you add fractions the way you add fractions? Now, I knew it was a hard question, so I said they could work together in groups of four and produce just one written result for each group. But I made that inexcusable mistake teachers sometimes make. I did not do the assignment ahead of time myself. To this day I've not been satisfied with any of my own attempts. The students discovered very quickly that before they could write anything, they had to draw pictures, pies or rectangles to be cut into pieces and the pieces compared. Then, basing their writing on the pictures, a few managed to get something down on paper.

I had hoped that the results would include more words and fewer pictures. By the end of the period the level of chaos was just what you'd expect from thirty-three ninth graders who can't do the assignment. But, in spite of the fact that no one had really succeeded, the effort of trying to put an explanation into writing had forced most students to get a much clearer notion of the reasons behind the mathematical oper-

---

*Geeson, William, "Using Writing about Mathematics as a Teaching Technique." *The Mathematics Teacher*. February, 1977. Pgs. 112-115.

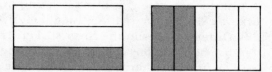

1/3 means one out of three pieces and 2/5 means two out of five. The pieces are different sizes. So you have to cut them up smaller to get all the same size pieces.

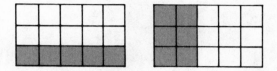

1/3 is the same as 5 out of 15, 5/15. 2/5 is the same as 6 out of 15, 6/15.

Group 4

All together there are eleven small pieces. 11/15 is the answer.

ation of adding fractions. Because of that I went ahead and asked my second algebra class to do the same thing. It was later in the day, and the result was even more chaos, but I became even more convinced that this assignment was worth doing badly.

I've used writing in these three ways: as chatter, to explain how-to, and to attempt but not necessarily succeed in explaining why, throughout algebra and more sparingly in the less and more advanced courses I teach. In more basic classes I've used the "how to" more than the others. Explain how to add the decimal numbers 2.86, 5, 1.3, and .007. In second year algebra and pre-calculus classes the chatter approach helped at least one student do a lot better with trigonometric identities and made reading them a lot more fun for me because I could see the false starts and their method of thinking about the problem right down to the last "aha!" The "how to" explanation is good with polynomials. How would you go about finding the zeros of this polynomial? The student who is error prone and misses a zero because he made a mess of the synthetic division can still demonstrate that he knows what to do. The "failure to explain why" approach suggests many possibilities I've yet to try. One I have asked is why should a polynomial of odd degree have at least one real zero? Students don't really fail to answer this. They do a fairly good job.

Some students are going to rebel at having to write in a math class. For some students the writing probably adds nothing to their understanding. But it certainly doesn't hurt, and for those it helps it is well worth the effort. Just this afternoon, as I was standing in line to buy a Thanksgiving turkey, a *Reader's Digest* article caught my eye. "Why Men and Women Think Differently," said the cover sticker. The article was "The Other Difference between Boys and Girls," a condensation from *The Brain: The Last Frontier* by Richard Restak. The article suggests that girls tend to think more verbally than boys. Now I don't know whether that is true or not. Remember, I started by saying I did not rely on words for learning. However, I do believe that many people do rely on verbalization for understanding and we math teachers must make an effort to include that option for learning.

Chapter 9

Dracula Rides Again

PATRICK JONES

From the outside, Hreod Burna school looks a bit like a modern factory — rectangular lines and flat green roof. It is situated on the outskirts of Swindon, half in, half out of the industrial zone; the 'reedy brook' which gave it its Anglo-Saxon name still flows through the school grounds — and through rather scrubby fields on either side.

Inside, the sense of being a factory rapidly disappears, especially in the cluster of rooms which belong to the English Department. Here, the English 'team' work closely together, sharing ideas, helping each other sort out the problems which any full-time teaching job entails. Pat has taught in the school since 1971, two years after it opened, and he would be the first to say that he was fortunate to take over the leadership of the department from the original H.O.D. with whom he shared the same aspirations for the students and the same beliefs about teaching and learning.

Sharing has always been the keynote of this department. They are unusual as a department for two reasons: they teach all their 14-16 year old students in mixed ability groups throughout the 4th and 5th years, working towards Mode 3 examinations, which are based in some cases entirely on course work, and they retain a team-teaching flexibility which offers students a choice of different teachers and different courses at regular intervals, although each teacher has particular responsibility for one group.

Pat Jones believes firmly that every student has 'immeasurable' potential and that the teacher's job is to plan as far as possible to find the sort of opportunities in the classroom that enable students to surprise themselves as they make fresh discoveries about what they can do. Such a philosophy requires careful and constant planning. Monitoring and directing individual progress is in many ways more demanding than making provisions for the class as a whole.

Cooperation is essential. The success of this closely-knit group of friends (it would be impossible to teach in this department in lonely isolation), not just in terms of outstanding examination successes across the whole ability range, but more importantly in terms of the students' social and intellectual confidence, provides a convincing demonstration that this approach to teaching and learning really works.

It may be worth mentioning that these materials and the ideas for using them are a good example of the many jointly prepared sequences of work which the department have collected together between them. The story tape, and the cloze comprehension, and the sheet of possibilities were all drawn from their own resource bank to which additional materials are continually being added.

Making Use of Horror Stories in the Classroom

Silence (well *nearly*); a darkened room. 25 heads perched in the gloom over glimmering scraps of computer print-out paper. What's he up to? After a burst of dramatic violins a voice crawls out of the tape recorder, sinister in its mid-European, husky tones:

". . . In the far dark corners of every human soul there lurks a black, crouching spectre; the ghost-like shadow that waits; a shrouded thing that pulsates with malignant evil. The name of that ghost is fear . . . (violins). Fear is born of the devil. It has no beginning, no end; it is eternal, omnipotent. Fear is at your side as you listen to a half-heard sound (sound of rats). It is here - a finger-touch away. It is always behind you, especially when you are *alone*. (Bats wings flutter off into the dark. Piercing female scream). And giving substance to fear are the legends that surround it. The most dreaded one of all was conceived in a nightmare. It rose from the very bowels of hell: the Prince of Chaos, Master of the Undead, Ruler of the Damned, Lord of the Vampiric Hoards — COUNT DRACULA. (Drums, orchestral climax, lowering to an eerie winding of oboes.)

In a remote area of Transylvania, beyond the plains of Marosh and the slopes of Gorginia there is a narrow road which winds through the foothills of the Valachian Alps. There are no milestones along here; there are no signposts to point the way. Some believe that it is a road without end, others that it disappears amidst the swirling fogs that mantle the woods, but there are a few that tell you in hushed tones that it leads to castle Dracula (wolves howling, lightning strikes); and they will swear that at dead of night four horses may be seen pulling behind them a hearse, thundering along, nostrils flaring, hooves pounding, but with no coachman at the reins. And inside there is only . . . a coffin (lightning strikes, funereal bell booms out)."

(Then a description ensues of how a coach got lost on the road "towards the end of the last century" and broke down. It contained a young man and his "radiant" bride-to-be).

> "As the coachman and the young man inspected the damage, the girl stepped to the side of the road, for she had seen the dull glimmer of a watery light through the curtain of trees (sounds of radiant bride-to-be heard moving through dense undergrowth — silly girl). She moved slowly towards it, thinking it might come from a woodman's cottage (howl of wolf). Before her was the grey bulk of a silent, towering castle. Windows stared down like eyeless sockets. Dead, hollow, sightless. The dim light emanated from a doorway, beckoning to her, drawing her in. (Lightning. Histrionic creak . . . echoing footsteps) . . .

At the end of the tape I asked them to continue writing the notes I had asked for at the beginning of the session, which were:
1. To note down any experiences when they had felt really afraid.
2. To note down any films/books/stories they had read or watched that they had found scary.
3. To make a list of all the ingredients necessary for a corny horror story.

I'd used this "noting down" technique after finding that discussion can fall a bit flat immediately after a particularly arresting tape, which can create its own entrancing cocoon-like world. Once the tape is switched off and the lights on, the students find it hard to come back into the "real world" to discuss in a mundane way. I've found the same problem with good TV programmes. Noting down important things during and after the tape provides five or ten minutes lone concentration whereby a student can make an easy transition from the "world" of the tape to the world of his own thoughts and experiences. The step to the public world of shared classroom experience is then a much more manageable one.

> "Right then . . . would anyone like to tell us about times they have been scared? . . . times they have been afraid? . . . you know . . . perhaps on your own at home." . . . Silence . . . embarrassed twitchings show on the faces of the most communicative students . . . Have they *never* been afraid? . . . of *course* they have! Teacher's got it wrong again. These are 4th Year students, fourteen or fifteen. No one really wants to admit being afraid until the discussion has "warmed up." I should have started with the "easy" one . . . "OK, let's come back to that and go on to the one about things you have read or seen that are really scary. What's the most scary film you have seen?" 2, 4, 10 hands shoot up. Phew. We're off. "Jaws . . that was really good" . . . (Yeah, Yeah). "Can you tell about one bit from the film that stands out?" Chorus of voices . . . one holds on . . .

"When he finds that body at the beginning Sir . . . He's like walking along the beach . . . They know a body's there somewhere. Then he sees this funny looking pile of stuff and when he gets there, it's half a body of this woman . . . Yes, Sir then he's sick all over it. (Urrr!) No. that's the book . . . Hey when that bloke under the boat in the cage gets attacked" . . . (Teacher losing control.) "OK, OK, one at a time please."

A good discussion ensued. Good, because the kids were involved, committed, keen, if inarticulate. The tape had been the springboard. The group were together as only a mixed ability group can be. These moments are hard to achieve and need a lot of work and a lot of failure before this can happen regularly. Eventually they talked about a wide variety of films and we began to focus on exactly what the best films did to be frightening. "Psycho" had been on the television the previous month and we talked about how Hitchock had "built up" the suspense with a series of hints. *Great* help here from a book of stills from the film. Eventually we *did* get on to the personal experiences. A terrifying story (later re-told in a fuller version at the request of the class in connection with the supernatural topic of "The Supernatural" we covered) about a girl hearing knocking from the attic and no one believing her until her mother finally slept in the same room as her and heard it too. What's more, Dad refused to investigate until daylight!

Bell goes. Good lesson. I know in my guts it was. The kids were still talking about things as they went out. But this is an article and reactions like that aren't very helpful. What were we really doing and why? How should I respond to a mother who says she doesn't approve of horror stories for her son . . . and why don't I try to teach him to spell better so he can pass 'O' Level . . . and they read these stories anyway.

To explain this, I need to probe in some detail into the aims and methods of the department I work in.

We had decided early on to teach in mixed ability groups all the way to the public exams. By implication this meant a rejection of standardized work from textbooks or coursebooks, yet we did not wish to cut out whole classwork from our approach, as we felt that one of the benefits of the mixed ability situation is that students can live, work and breathe together, sharing important moments, though inevitably following up private interests and activities. Individual programmes of work are readily available and relatively easily produced, but we felt that we did not want our students to sit in blinkered isolation, following endless work cards.

Instead the teachers worked together to develop a core of ideas to use in class that we felt would be successful, and which would lead to students being able to work in ways that would "stretch" everyone and that would involve them encountering and developing a wide range of linguistic resources. The ideas are now well-documented and kept in a set of ring-files, a flexible enough format to be added to and changed in order that they don't go stale. The Horror Stories sequence is one of the most regularly used and it would be safe to say that all the teachers now use it with their 4th or 5th year students.

It was chosen and developed for a variety of reasons.

A major reason was that the Horror sequence taps an important vein in their consciousness; it is an area they know and understand. They all watch horror films and talk excitedly amongst each other at morning registration after a particularly good one has been shown on television the night before. Many of them read horror stories avidly and, for some, collections of pulp fiction horror stories have replaced the more sedate household libraries of yesterday. How well I remember reading and re-reading "1001 Ghost Stories" in my parents' collection when I was about 13. I wanted to bring this part of their world to the classroom and to get them to examine it closely in the context of the English lesson.

What would they take from the sequence? What in particular would be the benefits for the development of the students' skills and abilities with language?

Little would probably be learned about human behaviour from the sequence — or rather from the angle we were going to approach it from. The growth points of the Horror Stories sequence are to do with words, style, involvement and structure. We want our students to encounter a wide range of words and kinds of writing. We want them in their own word usage to experiment with, become familiar with, and perhaps to master as broad a spectrum of kinds of written and spoken language as they can manage. We want them to develop language strategies as flexible as they can, so that they can stray from the well worn paths into the less safe, but more challenging and exciting experimental areas. This implies that hesitant, perhaps unsuccessful, experiments will be received kindly, for these are the growth points.

The best horror stories contain a sophisticated, stylised use of language and a wide range of vocabulary (see the opening tape) but one which it is quite possible for the students to experiment with. The style of such stories is often dramatic in its punctuation and in its ritual sense of audience — techniques we are keen for our students to develop as both can make for more effective communication.

We felt too that writing a horror story would encourage the intense imaginative involvement of the students which would enable such growth moments to happen. For language does not develop in casual or dispassionate moments, nor in the context of isolated exercises which may involve the pen and the book, but not the full engagement of the student's faculties.

The best horror stories are technically very competent and sophisticated pieces of writing with careful structure, a patient build-up of style and detail, and an economy and relevance to the main effect. All these qualities were ones which our students could usefully build into their own language strategies.

The stories which resulted would, I hoped, be of high enough quality to go forward to the final folder of work to be presented for examination at the end of the 5th Year. I suppose this is the most superficial justification of the sequence, but one which tends to appeal readily to the students and their parents.

So . . . .

Next Lesson

We did a "cloze" comprehension together. This involved students supplying the missing word in a piece of writing with regular omissions. Classically, the technique is used as a test of readability, but I have found it very useful in other ways. Here, I had made not the strictly regular omissions of the readability test but I had concentrated on the descriptive vocabulary, sometimes leaving two gaps at a time to encourage the students to think in terms of pairs of adjectives and adverbs. There were two passages, both taken from past students' writing, one a classic horror story with obvious connections with the tape we had listened to, and the other with a more homely situation:

1. "The road _____ up the mountains, through the _____ and jagged outline of the pine forest, _____ in mist,_____, _____ and silent. Near the top was an outdrop of rocks, from which _____ the _____ castle with its _____ walls, turrets, and its battery of _____ windows, all _____, all _____ all inpenetrable. Deep in the _____ of the castle, a shadow_____ detached itself from the darkness and glided _____ towards one of the tiny windows. The dark hood was thrown back to _____ a face pale as _____, and eyes glinting and black like _____ A malicious smile _____ on his lips as he heard the jingling and _____ sound of the approaching coach and his smile revealed his _____ line of white teeth — sharp teeth, _____ teeth.
   The next victim was approaching."

2. "I sat, _____ and warm, _____ my hot cup of cocoa, watching the late night movie, Hitchcock's film "The Birds". As the screen _____ in front of me I remember thinking this is an easy way to earn two quid. At that moment an _____

draught _____ over my face. The steam from my cocoa _____ sideways. I heard a _____ rustling sound and turning round in some terror, I saw the curtains _____ outwards. _____ with fear, I sat staring at the curtains. As they _____ sideways I heard the _____ of metal _____ against the wall and found myself looking into the black _____ of the garden. Thank goodness! It was just the French windows had blown open. With some _____, I crossed the _____ pile carpet and closed them tight. My feelings of _____ came back as I returned to my _____ chair and cocoa, but the feeling was short lived as the lounge _____ into darkness, and the tele died. A fuse? Again I sat _____ watching the huge _____ shadows thrown on the wall. Silence. The clock _____ on into _____ And then a new sound — the _____ grating of a door handle. Inside my stomach a _____ seemed to _____ and I bit my lip to stop screaming, and then I could see clearly in the _____ light of the fire, that the handle was turning, and the door was opening.

Students could attempt either or both and could work in groups of 1-3. Groups were asked to discuss choices and compare, but not necessarily to agree on the same one. There are of course no "right" answers to a cloze comprehension such as this. The exercise is a purposeful one with plenty of scope for the intelligent involvement of the individual, without having to endure the mechanistic ritual of the standard comprehension. As such, the technique is ideally suited to mixed ability classes.

They spent 20 minutes in groups, discussing animatedly, fumbling in dictionaries, asking teacher and each other about half-known, half-remembered words. They began to get enthusiastic about elaborate and archaic words, hesitating over misspelled and mispronounced guesses, straining at the limits of their linguistic ranges. These are the important moments when vocabulary growth happens, sometimes imperceptibly, sometimes in great bounds.

We spent a further half hour discussing choices with the whole class whilst I banged unusual words up on the board for them to note down for later use. Finally two or three people read their "finished" versions to the whole class. This was important as the whole exercise was tied together and we could savour the (usually quite impressive) final product.

Next Lesson

End of week. First I told them a horror story, a terrible one that I had heard about a girl babysitting who had a series of anonymous calls and when the operator finally traced them she realised they came from the extension phone upstairs. ("As she slammed the phone down she heard heavy footsteps thundering down the stairs. She ran straight through the French windows into the blackness of the garden.") Promise of another worse story about murder. Meanwhile I let them loose amongst a pile of horror stories, horror film books, novels such as "I'm the King of the Castle", "1984", "Jaws" even. I had asked them to bring in any horror books from home and about a dozen had appeared — a very useful supplement. I had a collection, too, of about 20 stories from past fourth and fifth year students, some of which had been presented with illustrated covers. A long quiet involved reading session followed in which I found I could read too without constantly flickering my beady eyes round the classroom to spot what was going on.

Next Lesson (2nd Week)

Having told my horror story in the last lesson, I gave the students a sheet of titles for horror stories, but I explained that I would much prefer them to create their own. (I wanted this to be an important personal achievement, not just a routine please-the-teacher-with-2½-sides-on-his-topic-session-of-writing). In fact, about half used their own subjects. Examples of titles used are:

"It seemed like an ordinary butcher's shop; it was just that the meat was a bit cheaper here" (Title intended to have blood and *humour* in it).

"It was past midnight when I realised that I had left my notebook in the church crypt. I remember having qualms about returning so late. I wish now I had heeded them." (A lot of guidance here — a lot to go on. This title is often used by those who find story ideas difficult. It has touches of the kind of vocabulary I was hoping they would try — "qualms" "heeded" — and it enforces the first person narrative, something which usually makes for a more involved story.)

"The first time I realised that something was wrong with me was when I saw the look of amazed horror on my younger brother's face as he woke me up" (Touches of *Metamorphosis* here!)

"Room 101" (*1984* extract available).

"Count Blood bites again" (For the humourists again)

I suggested strongly that they begin the stories in rough and show them to me once they have written about ten lines. This is a useful approach to any kind of story writing. It encourages students to make drafts and re-write. It also makes them think harder about the opening and enables the teacher to make suggestions to get the style and approach on the right lines before they are half-way through the story and committed to any particular approach.

For the next two lessons they could read, or write their horror stories, but they were told clearly, twice a lesson, that I would collect the stories in at the beginning of the next week. (So those who chose to read most of the week did most of the writing at home and, usually, were happy to do so.) I played tapes and atmospheric records (Pink Floyd highly recommended) during these lessons to help with atmosphere. I also provided coloured paper and felt tips for illustration and to make covers. Some students can do this superbly.

The following Monday I collected in most of the horror stories. Some students were absent — Monday is always a bad day. Some asked for extensions. At least two grandmothers had died, dogs and hamsters had eaten up a couple of efforts, and one student claimed I had given him until the following week.

As I started on a long session of marking that evening I could begin to judge the success or otherwise of this two week sequence. How could I judge it? To be frank, at the time my judgements were instinctive, but writing this article gives me time to reflect more methodically. The specific kinds of language development I was seeking to foster were as follows — and not all these goals were appropriate to all students, but at least some of them were to each individual.

1. Committed writing, in which the writer was deeply involved in the story, sharing its excitements. This would show in the imaginative depth of the story, as well as in the use of realistic detail.
2. A sense of audience, appropriately sustained in the development and structure of the story and the characters, and in the tone of the writing.
3. The use of an appropriate style (and not all the titles suggested an ornate, stylised use of words — some suggested a casual, conversational tone — e.g. the first one). This would show in vocabulary, punctuation, sentence structure and tone.
4. Attempts to use ambitious vocabulary.
5. A story where all the parts added up to a whole, where the purpose (to thrill) was sustained by the style, the structure, and the characterisation.

We had listened to and discussed three horror stories, two of them oral. We had spent a lesson discussing vocabulary and a lesson reading professional and amateur horror stories. Had that been enough to "tease out" at least some of the above qualities in some of the students? (And I'm not naive enough to be disappointed with a less than perfect success rate. I'd be pleased if half the students showed signs of development. I'd only start to worry if it was the same students who failed to respond every time). In the event I was very pleased, as it seemed to me that at least half the students produced work that showed real signs of development.

The majority of the students selected the horror stories they had written as going towards their folders of best work at the end of the year. I looked through those folders to choose "typical" (the inverted commas come from my flinching from generalisations about students — something ingrained on me by mixed ability work) examples of stories written before the sequence as a means of comparison. These "typical" stories are what both the students and I were reasonably satisfied with at the time. To facilitate a close comparison, I have chosen stories that had a horror element in them, or at least one was implied in the title. '

Hazel

(Aged 15, a very pleasant, quiet girl who had been doggedly average and uninspired in her written work so far).

Extract from "The Old Manor House" done in March as an examination piece for the 4th Year Exam the term before. This was a longish story (650 words) and I had been fairly pleased with it.

"All three of us stood outside the massive front door, poised. Wendy was staring at the strange gargoils, they seemed to be glaring at us. I stood up on the first step and glanced at the other two. "Come on then" we slowly stepped up to the fifth step Eric pushed the door open and stood back; looking inwards there wasn't much to see so rather bravely Eric stepped in, Wendy and I followed only to see dusty covered furniture, boarded up windows. Eric turned on his torch "Well" he said, looking very pleased with himself, "what do yer think?" Wendy gave me a funny look, I shrugged my shoulders. Eric looked at us from one to the other. "What's up?" he said, rather taken aback. Wendy stoutly replyed "you stand there makeing a silly statement with a stupid smile on yer face" "Well I found this dump, didn't I?" Eric rather nastily added the last bit. "No, it's been here for years" Wendy spoke quite sharply. "Don't be so bitchy, Wendy" Eric then began imertating her. "Now on you to" I said rather impatient with listing to them. "Yes, lets get exploring".

Wendy stayed to look around down stairs, Eric decided on up stairs. I followed him upstairs and saw some more stairs to you up into the attic. I began the climb up the stairs, I stopped at the top and pushed open a door, its squeaked back, I stepped slowly into the room. It was completely black. Not the sort of black you can see in, jet black. I switched on my tourch, there were paintings and chests, and chairs, skattered all about the room.

I walked over to the nearest chest, and opened it. It cracked open. Inside were two mirrors, very small but deffinitly mirrors. I picked one up and looked into it but no reflection appeared. I threw it into the chest and shut it tightly. I stood back, panting, I was affraid, but I didn't know what of. I felt somethink by my foot, I moved back, nothing was there. I shone my torch all around but there was nothing. I decided to go down and join Eric.

I shut the door behind me and began down the stairs, I got to the set of stairs that led to the ground floor, I went into the bedroom, the room was completely bare, I looked in all the other rooms they also were bare. They hadn't been bare when I'd gone past before."

There are definite "tries" here for an interesting, stylised vocabulary, and some good imaginative touches. I was pleased by "poised", by the "glaring gargoyles," and by the mirror without the reflection. The opening up shows distinct signs of a sense of audience with a careful if conventional use of detail. In particular the dialogue was quite pleasing, showing the odd attempt at "phonic" spelling (yer) and qualifications to the speech ("rather taken aback", "looking very pleased with himself") which could have been induced by an earlier session on tapescript writing.

Yet in the end it wasn't very involved writing. Note the way that at the beginning there "wasn't much to see" (by whom??), and then after looking at the "dusty covered furniture" the torch is put on. The second paragraph is marred by a dreary sequence of commas, not through excitement, but, I fear, as Hazel was losing interest and sharpness. The repetition of upstairs and stairs in the first few lines of this paragraph shows little awareness of style. Descriptions generally are undeveloped and lacking in convincing imaginative touches. The moment of fear when "somethink" touches her foot is described limply and blankly.

The final paragraph is very dull and repetitive, and I, as the reader, was fast losing interest at this point. Character had not been firmly or clearly drawn, though the dialogue had been useful here, and the overall style was neither very gripping nor very controlled.

After

Hazel's horror story, written six weeks after the previous piece, was twice the length of the earlier one. Though quantity is no yardstick of success, I felt that the story was long not just for the sake of it, but because the writing was fully involved and committed; the pressure of the careful, stylised build-up made it essential for her not to rush the story, but to develop it in a leisurely, though tightly controlled way — very much in the vein of the stories we had examined.

Here is the opening to the story.

"Strange Circumstances"

Angus Macdonald slowly and carefully lowered himself in his

arm-chair; he grunted as he finally managed to get himself comfortable. Just then his butler, Jenkins, a rather dignified, upper-class person, came swiftly, but silently into the room. Angus looked up, slightly startled by the cough from behind him. Jenkins smiled and handed Angus a small blue envelope. Angus looked puzzled. Jenkins caught the puzzled look, "its just arrived, special delivery, sir". Angus nodded to himself and with a flutter of his fingers sent Jenkins away.

Angus stared at the blue envelope; the hand writing didn't correspond with anybody's he could think of, off hand. He opened it and a folded blue letter fell out. Angus unfolded the letter, it read:

I was really pleased by this. In general it had a thoroughly professional, confident air about it, as though the writer is fully aware of an expectant audience whose appetite must be whetted. The patient build-up of relaxed, natural detail reads effortlessly and the writer seems practised and sophisticated. This is, I feel, due to Hazel's complete imaginative involvement in the story, combined with her appreciation of some of the necessary skills and effects she needs to work on.

Most interesting of all, to me, was the fact that her style and punctuation are *much* more controlled here, though the piece was written only six weeks after her earlier effort: the comma is no longer overused; the first sentence of each paragraph uses the semicolon neatly; and the second sentence with its swift note about Jenkins (in parenthesis), struck me as very poised and sophisticated — "Caught the puzzled look" and "a flutter of his fingers sent Jenkins away" are both beautiful touches. She is there, seeing events clearly. Character is drawn clearly and convincingly throughout. Later the protagonist arrives at a strange door. Comparison with the first piece is interesting. Here much less is made of the door squeaking open and the dusty interior. Instead she concentrates fully on the characterization, maintaining a sense of mystery and including some very deft touches.

"Angus knocked at the big front door of the house, still shocked from the sad news. The door opened and a tall, elegant gentleman answered.

"Angus Macdonald? I hope!" inquired the man. Angus rather taken aback, nodded dumbfoundedly. "This way Mr. Macdonald, we've been expecting you." Angus was taken into the front room, a small, shiverled up man, rose to his feet. He was dressed completely in black. Shirt as well.

"arh, Mr. Macdonald, please do sit down." Angus sat himself down by the window the tall gentleman who'd let him in sat down on the sofa, and nodded carefully at the small man."

The comparison with the second piece continues as Hazel describes another box being opened. This time she describes the event in full, confident detail, and with a developed sense of audience.

"Angus stopped and placed the key inside the lock, and turned it to the right. The lock moved with great ease, much to Angus's surprise. Angus pushed the lid up to reveal a box full of papers and odds and ends, the little man looked to interested for Angus's liking, so Angus inquired, "haven't you looked in the box then?" The man quickly withdrew and added "No, we've only got the key this morning, for the will was read out last week. Angus still felt rather dubious but said nothing."

Note too the concentration on character here and the definite attempt to use appropriately sophisticated vocabulary:
"reveal" "withdrew" "dubious"
The final paragraph in this 1,500 word story rounds it off nicely and is evidence of the sustained control over style and character.

" "Congratulations Angus" said David, as he raised his glass high in the air. Angus smiled and said "just like old times ah David?" They both laughed and gulped down their whiskeys."

P.S. Her spelling was better too, wasn't it, Hazel's mum?

Caroline

(15, very attractive. Boyfriends' (apostrophe is right) names all over her folder. Monday morning usually spent adjusting them and adding new ones. Never misbehaved, yet her work was a real disappointment. Sketchy, uninvolved, undeveloped and no regard for audience. She generally wrote neatly and accurately yet rarely produced stories of more than 300 words. Here is a story typical of her best effort up to the horror story sequence.)

Before

I Can See Again

"As I lay in my hospital bed I feel really proud as I can see again. I was really proud because when I was 2 I became blind and my only dream was to be able to see again and now I am 16 and I can see again. My parents help me to save money for a very important operation for me to see again and it has worked out fine. I come out of hospital today at 2:00 o'clock and its now 1:30. First thing I will do is to go round to Chris's house, my boyfriend, he thinks I don't stand a chance and mum hasn't told him the result. Oh look here is mum and dad now.

"Hi mum, Hi dad," I greeted them with a kiss.
"Hello darling" they both reply. "Ready to go"
"Yes" I answer.

As I walk along the white corridor I can see people walking past me, some sitting down in chairs. I can see the end of the corridor where we have to go through two big doors. As I walk through the doors we are outside and the sun is shinning down on me and I feel really excited, down the stairs across the car park. I say to myself everything is going to be different now I can see and I jump up in the air with confidence."

That's all. A girl has had her sight restored. Exciting experiences and relationships beckon, but Caroline dipped out after 150 words. She doesn't even bring the boyfriend into it. Touches of Mid-Atlantic vocabulary from the radio and her teenage mags stick out: *"real* proud" "worked out *fine"*. The repetition of "see again" in the first few lines shows scant attention to style and audience, and her lack of involvement shows through too in the change of tense of "greeted." A bland, flat story.

After

Caroline was particularly keen on this sequence of work and confessed to being a horror film addict. Here is her story, which can be printed in full as it is not as long as Hazel's though it is double the length of her longest effort:

Clare

"The church stood in the deep mist of the night as the church clock struck twelve. The gravestones stood out like figures in the dark. A full moon perched in the dark sky shone down onto the earth. Silence was everywhere except down Old Mill Lane. The lights stood very still and dim but one light stood out against the rest; at number 8 a party was being held. Music blared out from every angle and the voices sounded as though everybody was having fun.

In the house people were dancing, drinking, talking, but one person sat alone. A girl. This girl seemed strange sitting alone her long brown hair covering her shoulders, a pretty sort of girl. She sat shyly with a glass in the left hand and a handbag laying down by her side. Everybody seemed to be enjoying themselves that they didn't notice Clare (the girl's name).

Clare sat alone for another hour but still nobody noticed her so she decided to go. As she walked out of the front door she felt the cold, eerie air outside. She walked out of the gate and started walking along the dimmed lighted street. As Clare approached the church it struck two o'clock. Lights in the main street became lighter. To get home Clare had to go through Chicken Alley. Chicken Alley was called this as somebody was meant to be attacked. But Clare did not believe this. Clare decided to go down there.

As she entered the alley she looked down into it. It was dark and the bushes rustled a little. Clare walked on into the alley. Half way was a bar which was almost invisible but Clare could just see it as she approached the bar. As Clare ducked under the bar she heard two footsteps crawling upon her. Clare looked back and saw a tall dark figure walking behind her. The figure was tall with a long black coat on with short trousers on which did not touch his ankles. Clare began to walk a little faster as she looked round when she arrived at the end of the alley, there was nobody to be seen. Clare took it as her imagination.

The street was deserted and nobody was to be seen All you could hear was the footsteps of Clare walking loudly down the street. Clare walked out into lonely street and stood there looking at the end of the street. The very last house is were Clare lived, number 14.

There was a few bushes before her house, the bushes shaked furiously as the wind beat against them. As Clare walked down past the bushes behind her a hand came out from the bushes and grabbed Clare by the back of her neck. A hand drew forward towards her face and she tried to scream but her terror couldn't help her to scream. In the hand of the person lay a knife. A voice said "I will kill you".

The knife struck into Clare's heart and the blood trippled down her slim body very slowly. Dark red blood was over the person's hand as he slipped his hands back into the bushes.

The morning came and the birds were singing sweetly high in the street. Nobody was awake yet. By the bushes lay a small, swollen, blooded dark body. Clare was DEAD!"

Alright, it's not brilliant, but it carries our interest along, has poise, shape and it *is* finished. For Caroline, it is a very patient, controlled opening with a sense of the need to build up atmosphere and situation before the story or the characters begin to be explored in earnest. She shows some very neat imaginative touches in the first paragraph. The gravestones are threateningly personified and the transition from the street lights to the party lights is deft and sinister. In general the contrast between the dark, silent, menacing atmosphere of the graveyard and the bright, noisy, secure feel of the party is very well handled and very important both to the build-up of tension and atmosphere in the story. Clare is very neatly and clearly characterized (much more definitely than the girl in the first piece), and the description of her shows both involvement in the story and a sense of relevant detail. "She sat shyly with a glass in the left hand and a handbag laying down by her side."

There is clear evidence, too, of Caroline becoming more ambitious and imaginative in her use of words: "ducked," "footsteps *crawling* upon her." Some of the mistakes may well arise from a greater involvement in the story; she is getting carried away.: "The bushes shaked" furiously as the wind beated against them." Is "trippled" a coined phrase or a mistake? Either way, it works. Though the middle of the story is a bit soggy, the description of the hand coming out of the bushes is done well, with a sense of tension, helped by the short, clipped sentences, and the anonymous voice.

The last paragraph was the most pleasing of all to me. The contrast between nice and nasty begun in the opening paragraph is sustained. The sense of audience is real, the style is varied and dramatic; and very importantly for Caroline, the ideas in the story have a sense of completeness.

The story was a turning point for her. I raved about it, and since then she has continued to develop a more committed attitude to writing.

Dean

(15. Appeared to be a lout, rarely read anything, yet had a good imagination)

I have chosen, in Dean's case, to show how the sequence triggered off in him the desire to experiment with ambitious words and structures and helped him develop a sense of audience, which he sustained in later months.

His work had up to now been lively in a colloquial sort of way, but he had rarely strayed from the paths of his own linguistic patterns and those of his peers.

Here is an extract from an earlier, autobiographical story that will give you the flavour of the best of his work up until this point. He is describing breaking into a school:

> "We entered a classroom and gazed at the pictures on the walls they were everywhere, loads of faces, all looking at us, it was pretty creepy. We soon left that room and entered the Gymn we quickly started swinging on the ropes and climbing up the wall bares, then suddenly we heard voices coming nearer it was the caretaker and his son quick I said out the window, we all dashed quickly out of the school and started home, "Mission accumplished over and out."

There is a kind of breathless excitement here and one very effective touch (the pictures on the walls looking at them). The seeds of ambition are in the vocabulary ("gazed", "dashed") yet his resources are not tapped deeply enough in "*loads* of faces" and "pretty creepy". There is a "routine" feel about the whole story, enlivened by the final flourish, which does at least show a sense that someone is listening. The lack of control of punctuation (particularly the grammatically undramatic arrival of the caretaker) lets the piece down somewhat in its total impact.

Here is the opening page of Dean's horror story.

"I lay in bed staring at the bleak damp ceiling. So tempted to explore the forbiden room!

Eventually the urge overcame me, and I slowly sat upright in bed. 'Shall I, or shall I not'. 'Yes'. I quietly slid on my somewhat tatty slippers, and crept to the door. The handle slithered round like a decaying water wheel, and before me gloomed a vast, dark shadow-stricken passage way. I slowly but hesitantly, tiptoed down the vast corridle, that lay ahead, and there before me stood a mistifying, towering door, succur and immovable.

I glanced up, and to my astonishment, I saw a corroding key, hanging like a condemed victim. Then some unknown force, mysteriously began drawing me towards the key. Then to my surprise I was standing amazed and nervous, with the somewhat rusty key clasped in my hand."

The first thing I noticed was the control of punctuation to very dramatic effect, something he had just not managed before. He is in command of his effects and hence his audience. There are very sophisticated touches, surely inspired by his listening to and reading some chillingly controlled stories ("my somewhat tatty slippers", "to my astonishment").

The final sentence of the second paragraph shows a real control and sense of mystery. Comparisons are ambitious and dramatic to the extent of perhaps seeming a little strained ("like a decaying water wheel") but witness the very sophisticated use of a highly appropriate simile in "a corroding key, hanging like a condemned victim". Vocabulary too strains at Dean's mental limits, to the extent that he is tempted to coin words and phrases ("gloomed", "shadow-stricken"). Overall his intense imaginative involvement has, I feel, prompted a leap forward in his command of ambitious language.

But could he sustain this? Would this leap forward be followed by a "retreat" to his earlier world? Once a student has produced a piece of work like this, can the teacher expect all subsequent work to begin at this standard? The answer is, of course, no. Dean still wrote pieces very similar to the first one, but a detailed examination of his subsequent work shows that he has indeed assimilated the techniques he has learned into his linguistic resources and he can use them when appropriate and when he wants to. Here are some extracts from his subsequent writing.

"The scorching hot sun beams upon by back, as I stumble and drag myself across this unholly wilderness hopeing to find some sort of sivilization. As I turn my head and look behind me I can see my somewhat hesitant footsteps fading away miles into the distance over this flat, barron wilderness."

The control of sentence structure is very much evident as is an ambitious vocabulary. "My somewhat hesitant footsteps" is surely an echo from his earlier piece.

Here is a piece called "Our Backies" written as a short descriptive piece four months later.

"The Sun out of sight, as I look along the stained, *shadow striken* alley way of buildings. They stand like warriers waiting for battle.

Now out daited but once modern, just a complement of past technology.

The chimneys stand so tall and dominant, smoking like an anni-hilating cigarete. A far off bark echoes along the mist sprinkled alleyway of relics.

The brick work, the shed roofs, the windows, all looking like a mathematical book of equations. So ugly yet so beautiful, one day to be destroyed."

I find this fascinating. The subject might perhaps tempt him to adopt the casual colloquial tone of his earlier piece. His more ambitious approach to style and vocabulary, which first really showed in the Hor-ror Stories sequence has led him to a more profound and philosophical analysis of his environment. It is the tool enabling him to review his picture of his surroundings in a more complex way. This is a powerful piece.

In January, six months after the Horror Stories sequence, Dean produced his first poem, on which he worked very hard. I believe that there is less experimentation here (except perhaps in "cadaver") be-cause his use of ambitious vocabulary, comparisons, and dramatic stylis-tic devices has been internalized as a now conscious part of his linguis-tic resources.

Hero's Ha!

The Corpses lies dead and solidified
The once active body now a
Cadaver
A hero of before
The Trench, Protection! Ha!
Now his grave.
The mud encloses the withered
bones like sinking sand.
The fork every man dreads

Poised waiting to pitch him
Onto the truck of Death
HERO'S!

I feel that the sequence produced clear evidence that the majority of students were able to make significant advances in their ability to use words. It is difficult for me to be precise about what process is at work when such developments take place, but the nearest explanation that I can offer is that the sequence "unlocked a word-hoard" that already existed in their heads. For years the pattern of language used in horror stories and horror films had been washing over them, attended to with varying degrees of involvement. The shape of sentences, the texture of the vocabulary were slowly beginning to form in their heads and the Horror Stories sequence provided both a burst of sustained attention and a source of inspiration for them. Finally, primed with the language patterns, they were given the opportunity to experiment with them, to give birth to them, to clarify them in their own stories. Once a linguistic pattern has been made "your own" in this way, I believe that it becomes part of the resources you can bring to bear in coping with the language demands you are likely to meet.

It is not easy to account for the pretty well universal appeal of Horror Stories to teenagers. I don't believe that they are all innately sadistic or psychopathic. The three students I chose represented a very wide range in the spectrum of social attitudes and abilities. Hazel was conventional, diligent, rather conservative in her approach both to life and to lessons. She stayed on to the Sixth Form. Caroline was very much a trendy teenager, moulded by the "pop" world, tolerating school until she left to become a secretary at 16. Dean had a police record and a history of confrontation with teachers. He was expelled from school two months after writing the poem I quoted.

Yet they were all only a short step away from both childhood and adulthood. The fears and fantasies of childhood where monsters could be very real things was still very clear in their heads. The Horror Stories sequence provided the opportunity to look back at this world, to contemplate it, and in a sense to master it and grow out of it. At the same time, in their own way, they were struggling to come to terms with strong tides of feelings within themselves. I mean not so much sexual promptings, but waves of frustration from and even hatred of, authority figures — parents, teachers, police. To a certain extent the chance to read and to write horror stories channelled at least some of these feelings in a useful and constructive way. Many of the stories can easily be interpreted symbolically as a purging of strong, often violent feelings towards figures in their lives.

Chapter 10

At the Beginning

KERMEEN FRISTROM

Punky Fristrom teaches the academically talented high school student. His students come to him over a three year period for English and history in a tutorial and seminar setting which operates within a comprehensive school. Punky knows, as few do, how to respond to these bright kids — separated from their fellow students by institutional design and natural prowess — so that they take the risks necessary to move beyond the appearance of knowledge.

"Have another drink of orange juice?" I asked the only quiet person in the room. She was sitting alone while everyone else seemed to be talking at the same time as they drank their juice and ate their doughnuts, the welcome back gift I give to my classes on the first day of school each year. The atmosphere was definitely relaxed and friendly, except for this one girl who sat somewhat apprehensively looking at her chattering classmates.

"Did you go to Dana or Collier?" I continued, hoping to draw her out a little. "No," she replied, "I just moved to San Diego from Ohio."

A small insight, but still significant. No wonder she was so quiet. All of the other students had gone to junior high together and so had many friends and acquaintances to support them on their first day of high school. I glanced at the seating chart the students had completed at the beginning of class.

"Lori?" She nodded, indicating that I had read the correct number of seats in the right row. "Welcome to San Diego. I'm an immigrant from the Midwest, too — from Chicago. If you hated the winters in the same way I did, you'll love it here." She murmured something about how she hoped that she would, and I moved on to try to get to know a few more of the students.

Later in the hour, I finally got the group to settle down and we continued the process of learning about each other in a different way. The game that day was an auction of different futures. All students started with five hundred "dollars" and could use them to bid on items that appealed to them. Some of the items for "sale" were serious, some humorous. High scores on SAT tests, 5's on Advanced Placement tests, admission to Stanford, a date with a rock star, a starting position on the football team, a 4.0 grade point average, a lifetime pass to the movies, a starring role in a motion picture, one hundred gallons of ice cream. The list went on. Bidding for most items was short but furious. I noted as carefully as I could who bid on what items, which bids were serious, which were jokes. As usual, a girl won the starting position on the football team, but her bid told me something about her. Lori was quiet and didn't make a bid until a "polished writing style" came up for sale. She entered a low bid and then kept after the item until she won it at what I thought was a ridiculously low bid of only two hundred dollars.

Soon the auction was over and I announced the twist. All students who bought items had to write a brief statement about why they had bought their particular items, and all of those who didn't buy items had to write about why they didn't. The class groaned, as usual, but the good feelings generated from that hour seemed to overcome their negative reactions, and the year was off to a good start.

The Heart of the Matter

If getting to know each other and to understand each other is the first and primary concern of any class, then introducing the journal is second and not far behind in importance. If my students are to improve their writing, the journal is the most important method they can use.

A student, honest but unambitious, once came to me and asked, "I don't have time to do all of the writing you ask for your course. I'll be glad to do what I can, though, so what is the most important?" After a few minutes of discussion concerning his goals and the proper way to achieve them, I admitted to him that if he couldn't do everything required, then the best thing he could do was to keep a journal and neglect the more formal writing. The bad news is that that is pretty much what he did for the entire year. The good news is that he passed the Advanced Placement Examination with flying colors, although he had been only an average writer at the beginning of the year.

The journal is, indeed, at the heart of the matter. Unfortunately, it's also the most often ignored part of the writing process, the part where the ideas are generated, where the experiments are conducted, where the writing can be the most fun and the most personal. It's the realm of "expressive" writing, to use James Britton's term. At its best, the journal will contain hundreds of pages in a year's time. It will show the daily writing of students when they are the most free and creative, writing for themselves and not for a critic, either teacher or student. Freed from most of the external pressures of writing, the student can use the journal effectively as a language laboratory in which to conduct experiments with words, and as an intellectual record of the developing ideas and concerns which fill the mind during these years.

In order to meet these goals, the journal must be used in ways which will help the student gain the greatest benefit. Most important of all is that the journal belongs to the student and is safe from any unauthorized eyes. The journal is above evaluation, and so no risk is taken by any writing that is done in it. This rule does not mean that the teacher will not look at the journal, but that the student's permission is necessary before the teacher can read any part of it. Even when the teacher reads the journal, no grades, no correcting, no marking of mistakes will be offered. If given permission, the teacher is free to comment on the experiments and ideas expressed, but with as little judging as possible. There's a place for grades and comments and corrections, but the journal is not it. Nothing will kill the free flow of ideas in a journal faster than the heavy hand of disapproval.

One of my students wrote in his journal: "Biology is a disaster. The doddering old fool uses notes that are twenty years out-of-date. He stammers and drools all over his shirt. It's absurd that such men should be in teaching. The class pays no attention to him. Stupid, senile son-of-a-bitch." After reading that comment, I couldn't resist replying in the margin: "Your comments are totally inappropriate for a statement about a teacher, or any adult for that matter. I am really disappointed that you don't show more good sense in what you write." He was stuttering with anger when he came up to me after class the day I handed back the journal. "You said that we could write what we wanted in the journal and that you wouldn't grade us down for it and that you wouldn't criticize us for it and now you do this," he said, waving the offending comments I had written in my face. "Well, if this is what you are going to do," and the notebook once again waved through the air, "then I'll never write in a journal again." And he didn't. For three more years he was a student in my classes and we lived an uneasy truce concerning journals. He did the other writing required for the course, and did it well. He was excellent in discussions, usually well-prepared and able to participate actively, but the journal remained a point of contention that he mentioned only in moments of frustration when he would remind me of my folly and broken faith. He was right. I had done what I should not have done. But once done, the damage could not be repaired and the value he might have gained from writing a journal was lost.

Fortunately, I learned from that experience and have been careful since not to repeat it. The journal does belong to the student and I intrude on it only tentatively and with great restraint. First, the student controls whether or not I read it at all and which parts I read. A note, "Do Not Read," at the top of a page is respected and the page is not read. The entire journal may be kept from my reading if the student so desires. At such times the teacher in me still requires that I have the opportunity to skim through the pages rapidly (one student even claimed that I was a speed reader and could read a journal while flipping through fifty pages in ten seconds, but most believe in my word) simply to see how much has been written and if the student seems to be writing regularly.

Comments that I do write are carefully non-judgmental, unless they can be positive reactions to what is written. The problems caused in stifling writing are almost always caused by negative statements, not by commendation. To the student who wrote, "I'm becoming an automaton again. I do all my work, go to all my classes, do everything that I'm supposed to and it's as if I have no feelings at all. I really can't stop to think about how I feel, because if I do, I will get all self-pitying and I won't want to work at all." I responded in the margin, "I know that feeling. The best thing about it is that it usually only lasts for a short time. I have found two tricks that sometimes help me get out of it. One is to focus on very short-range goals — something that I am going to get done tomorrow that I will be glad that I have finished. And then I find another goal for the next day. When I am really bad, the goals are even closer — what I will do in the next hour. And second is the reward. I tell myself, 'Get this done, and then as a reward you can do something you enjoy, read a murder mystery, watch a baseball game, listen to a favorite record.' That entices me out of the sense of futility."

I'm also careful to write in pencil in the journal so that the student can erase what I've said if so desired. The pencil is not as obtrusive as ink, especially as red ink, and the very appearance reduces anxiety. The informality of the pencil matches the informality of the journal. When grades and comments do go on a student's writing, then that is done in ink, always blue or black to avoid the connotations of red.

Once I've explained that the journal belongs to the students and the rules for my looking at it, then we're ready to talk about the writing and the kinds of things that can go into it. It's important that each student write something every day, even if it's simply, "I don't have time to write today." The regular writing produces more writing, in most cases, and a wider variety of writing as students explore different ideas. Regular practice builds self-discipline and encourages students to use writing as a means of exploring all parts of living, rather than using conversation or thought alone to do it. It's helpful for students to date each entry, not only to see how regular the writing habit becomes, but also, in the months or even years ahead, to place the contents in time.

With some classes, I use ten minutes of class time every day for students to write in their journals. It's a time when they must have their journals on the desks and their pens ready to write. I'm never as happy with this method as I am when they find time on their own to write, for the writing in the classroom makes it belong as much to me as to them. They're performing according to my rules and needs, not to theirs. But if I find that a class, when left to find its own time to write, writes little, then I'll make class time available because the writing is necessary however it's done.

The nature of the content of the journal is important. Any writing that the student does is of some value, but the writing that is most valuable is that which focuses on the twin goals of the journal, to become a language laboratory and to provide an intellectual record. A diary of events, a calendar of dates, a listing of items of current gossip is helpful, but not as helpful to the students as attempts to record and analyze the contents of their mind and to perform the stylistic experiments that lead to increased mastery of the written word. Students find it helpful to have suggestions that they can fall back on when their own sources of ideas dry up, so I give them a list of ideas which they can put in the front of their journals and use if necessary.

Suggestions for Writing in Your Journal

1. Stepping Stones and Stumbling Blocks — key points in your life.
2. Roads Taken and Not Taken — key decisions in your life.
3. Goals — real and imaginary.
4. Fears — obsessive and casual.
5. Ideas — yours and others.
6. Colors — how they affect you.
7. Dreams — asleep and awake.
8. Twilight Writing (Ira Progoff, author and psychologist, uses this term in his book *At a Journal Workshop**) — allow your mind to wander freely.
9. Events — what has happened and what was behind it.
10. People — good friends and casual acquaintances.
11. Fragments — overheard conversations and remembered bits.
12. Conversations — real and imaginary — with self, with famous people, with parts of your body.
13. Books — what they say and what you think about them.
14. Plays, Films, TV — what you have seen and what you have thought.
15. Experiments in style.
16. Puns.
17. Concrete words and concrete poetry.
18. Poetry of all kinds.
19. Stories or parts of stories.
20. Outlines for essays.

This list contains suggestions used more often at the beginning of the year than later on when the journals seem to acquire lives of their own. The list does suggest the variety of topics which can be written

*Dialogue House, 1975

about in journals, but it's much less than what the students actually do write. The real journals show an amazing variety of the interests and abilities of bright young minds.

As the year went along, Lori came to typify that particular class, not because she was average, but because she was the best and represented what I hoped every one of the students would be. Although she was marvelous in discussions and showed her creativity in dozens of ways, it's her writing that I remember best. I provided a structure, gave her nudges here and there and a lot of encouragement, and then she took the opportunity to produce wonderful writing of many kinds.

We kept up a year-long dialogue in and about her journal. Many of her entries came from the suggestions which I had made at the beginning of the year, but others developed as we did different kinds of writing throughout the year. A sampling from the journal shows the variety.

Being a methodical person, Lori began her journal with an entry based on the first suggestion, to write about the stepping stones and stumbling blocks in her life. In talking to the class about writing in the journals about this topic, I had suggested that they think back to early events in their lives in order to try to have some perspectives that time might bring.

My formative years were spent in an environment of extreme pressure, a veritable pressure cooker. I learned just to expect success, thrive on it, and if — heaven forbid — I fell short, to suffer for it. The unspoken rules also had a painful corollary: never reveal vulnerability. Talk about a recipe for an ulcer — this technique was haute cuisine. I had to be perfect, and combined with my impatient streak, I had to expect perfection from those around me. And getting things accomplished from four year olds is an often frustrating experience.

Building on the pressure mill was my parents' preoccupation with success. Although my brother and sister experienced it to some degree, I was the most heavily confronted with the effects of my parents' intensive drives. Any expert who maintains that very young children are blissfully unaware of the events swirling around them is almost tragically off base.

The most devastating aspect of driven parents is a sort of insidious neglect. After my sister and brother went to college, I spent countless evenings dining alone on microwaved food. And I am probably oversensitive to the little things, but it was depressing to have my parents overlook my birthday or to get a call the night before junior high graduation to the effect that my father just couldn't get back from Washington to see me give the valedictory address. The big psychological question is just how does a 4 year old (or 8 year or 12 year, for that matter) cope with an exceptional situation like that. The answer for me was quite simple. I dug down within myself and found enough personal strength to more than counter any disappointment.

I told Lori how impressed I was by her brief remembrance. We talked for a while about the pressures we both felt from childhood, how I felt that I always had to volunteer to do the most difficult jobs, and then how I hated myself for having volunteered. I said that I still had a hard time saying no, but that I had decided that I would be more miserable if I didn't take on all of the extra work and headaches than if I did. She said that she was the same way, that she was always trying to be involved in doing old things better and in exploring new things to do.

The opening which she gave me was a natural one. "Why not use your journal to try to organize what you want to do, and to keep track of what you have done?" And so I soon found the following entry:

Planned course of study for exploring questions
Asia — read *Stilwell and the Am. Experience in China*
    I hope to read the *Best and the Brightest* and attend World History's Southeast Asia seminar
Economics — continue reading Sorenson's *Economics* textbook
    expand my reading of Galbraith to *Affluent Society* etc.
English History — read Churchill's history of Britain, post-Richard III
    read *The Once and Future King*
Latin — continue translating Virgil's *Aeneid*
    master all passive verb tenses, keep watching *I, Claudius*
    learn irregular noun declensions, read some R. History, move on to deponent, infinitive, and subjunctive verbs, keep working in *Latin: 2nd year*; finishing by Feb.
Color — integrate color into my papers
    read *Scientific American* Nov. & Dec. articles on perception of color and 4-color may be problem
Science — continue reading *Scientific American*
    read selective parts of the Biology textbook
    continue Sociology study; read *The Hidden Dimension, Design for the 3rd World*
Misc. — read *Roots*, monitor South African events
    continue reading English classics (like *Lorna Doone*)
    keep reading periodicals
    read *Blind Ambition*, move on to White's *Breach of Faith*
King Tut — see the King Tut exhibit again
    read Drury's novel.

I wrote back to her: "I'm glad that you are young and have lots of energy. Your menu is marvelous, but it certainly is extensive. It proves that you really do have a drive for perfection — and then some. but it also shows the tremendous strength you have. Just to conceive of such a program is evidence of your drive. I notice that one small part of your program is to use color more in your writing. How about starting by making a list of unusual colors? Combine colors that are not normally combined. Be sure to be as specific as possible. Remember that when we talked about your review of your childhood, I commented that it would be even stronger if you used more specific incidents and details."

The next week the journal had this section:

A scarlet mahogany bleeding stallion
olive green khaki fatigues
a metallic ice-blue gaze
rusty crimson autumn leaves
a French blue ivory drawing room
a granite grey pigeon flavored white Millard Fillmore statue
an electric blue chartreuse teen's room
an Irish green orange battlefield
an apple red complexioned, baby blue-eyed ingenue
a butterscotch, marshmallow-eyed pre-dinner boy
auburn streaked chestnut locks
an institutional green corridor
a steel hospital white surgeon
a bamboo lacquer red temple
a black velvet, merging into midnight blue, sky
a primary red, yellow, blue elementary school room
a leather brown oak study
a moss vibrant green forest
a grape, cherry mustachioed kool-aid drinker

"Great," I wrote. "I see that you have checked the ones that you managed to work into the story you wrote last week. Look at the effect when you leave out the 'ands.' They really are not needed, and unnecessary words often interfere with meaning and with effective style."

Not only was the journal helping Lori become a better writer, but it also was teaching me a lot about her as a person. Her challenging mind and her sense of whimsy both came through in her discussion of a math class:

When Mr. Smith was speaking about number lines, he said that between two points on the line there is always another. For example, between 2/8 and 3/8 there is 5/16. He said this applies ad infinitum. I think this is impossible on a number line. A number line obviously consists of a series of close, yet *not* contiguous, atoms of various elements. So, if this act of determining a 'between' point is narrowed to finding a point between two atoms, the theory runs into a problem. At given points in time there will be a total void between the two atoms. With their electrons spinning, occasionally there will be no mass between the two closest nuclei (10th $-$, 10th $+$).

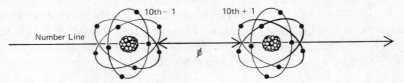

Therefore, there is no graph (point), which is a requirement of a number line — to coordinate with the 'between' number. Although the former Ohio University professor and math book author, Dr. Morton, would rip apart my faulty logic, it is always fun to challenge the mathematics hierarchy (no matter how ephemerally).

The journal can also be used to respond to what goes on in class. I am a shameless Freudian, and few discussions go by without at least an oblique reference to one or another of Freud's major tenets. After we had finished a unit on *Crime and Punishment*, during which we had focused on the dreams in the novel, and also during which I had talked about the psychosexual nature of the dreams, Lori answered back, not directly, but by a journal entry that gently questioned my views.

Iceland

Last night I had a rather unsettling dream. I dreamed that I received a draft notice in the mail. I was not terribly upset by it; I called several of my friends and we began systematically checking colleges for admittance. It was only after the army prohibited college deferment that I became alarmed.

For some reason CO's and the like were not available; we then resorted to a conference. There seemed to be about 20 people, all of whom I knew, seated around a large oval table. They were as worried as I, concerning our alternatives. The meeting just plodded along until I suddenly started talking.

I began to urge these people to renounce their American citizenship and to accept Icelandic citizenship, which for some reason was being offered. When some expressed doubt about becoming expatriots, I practically coerced them into doing so.

The last event in my dream consisted of this group madly dashing about with a few belongings in tow, at an airport waiting to board an airliner.

It surprises me that I was being so militant. It's also rather amazing that all of these people were so easily persuaded to leave. I have no idea if there is any significance to this dream, although I seriously doubt if there is any Freudian explanation for it.

"Dig into your own minds," I had practically shouted at the class. "Look at what Joyce has done in *A Portrait of the Artist*, but you keep writing about times and places that don't belong to you. Your writing is good, but somehow it doesn't belong to *you*. Remember how Joyce dug into his own childhood and tried to catch his own relatives. Why not try to do the same with your memories?"

The challenge was too great for most of the students, although several of them tried with varying degrees of success. Here is what I found in Lori's journal:

> My mother. An endlessly fascinating person with almost exactly the opposite background from my father. She was raised in a one-parent family for fourteen years, and suffered under the discrimination of a more privileged older brother. Uncle Dick was quite a tap dancer, even as a teen, and the already strapped family budget was strained even further to pay for his tap, music, and voice lessons. My maternal grandfather was not there to contribute, because he left the family when my mother was a baby. She is still very bitter about his action, but the alternatives were highly limited for all unemployed washer salesmen with three dependents. After the crash, he couldn't cope with his failure as a provider, so he left. The family didn't hear from him for years, and almost had him declared dead. Then when my mother was about 16, he wrote them from a trailer park in Texas and sent several pictures. The story that followed was a poignant one. He continued to wander around the country and once missed seeing Mother by a few minutes when she was vacationing in San Antonio. She never did get to see him, and to this day he remains a fascinating enigma in my mind. One of the few restless spirits in my family, he pursued a transient lifestyle until his death from cancer in the 1960's.

"That's the right idea. Now keep thinking about these people, talk to your mother about them, get to know them as though they were still alive and lived next door. Then you will have some exciting material to write about."

At times, Lori would use her journal to develop materials for papers that were due in my class and in other classes. I found the following section that eventually became a paper for a history class:

> 'Monolithicism and the Author of the *Ugly American*.' Lederer wrote the Ugly American in 1958. He reflects the philosophy of that time in his book: Dulles and his policies of containment are tacitly yet profoundly present. Lederer clearly injects his feelings into his characters, especially Father Finian.

Finian says, 'The evil of Communism is that it has masked from native peoples the simple fact that it intends to ruin them. Americans do what is right and necessary; they are doing also what is effective.'

Lederer holds the belief characteristic of the 50's. He holds that all Communist aggression is directed by Moscow. He ignores nationalism as impetus for a Viet Cong's action. Rather, Moscow's tenuous fingers prod the villagers into rebellion.

I think, in some respects anyway, that Vietnamese were justified in their resentment of the colonialistic France.

Incidentally, the Ugly American is actually a hero in the book, contrary to popular references to him.

"The 'incidentally' is not incidental at all. That's the heart of the idea and of your thinking about the book. See if you can make that the central part of your paper, with all of the other points following from it. Don't be afraid to consider carefully such afterthoughts or random impressions that may not seem to be important at first. Sometimes they are the main thing."

And journals certainly don't need to be limited only to writing.

October 1962: To really survive in this family you have to be wide awake — and even at the age of thirteen months — I'm no exception.

"If I could only get you as wide awake in class!"

But the journal has to be fun, too. It has to be a place of playing joyfully with words. Lori never let her interest in ideas and in books keep her from trying different kinds of experiments in her journal:

> Mnemonics help mnen
>   who have minds to amend
> Mnesiac mnen
>   mostly depend
> on mnemory aids
>   for their good grades.

My response:

"Mnever have I had to mnegotiate through such a mnarrow opening as that between the mn and nm in your poemn. I can't remnemnber such a thimng sinmce I was kmnee-high to a grasshoppernm."

Shortly after that, she came back with another poem:

```
                    I
                   A M
                  O N E
                 G I R L
                B E I N G
               A F R A I D.
              P U Z Z L E D,
             T R O U B L E D,
            W O N D E R I N G,
           F R I G H T E N E D.
            S E A R C H I N G,
             Q U E S T I N G
              S E E K I N G.
               B E C A M E
                A W A R E.
                 W E R E
                  Y O U
                   A S
                   I?
```

My comment had to be:

```
                    I
                   D O
                  S E E
                 T H A T
                H A P P Y
               J O Y F U L
              E N G L I S H
             T E A C H E R S
            R E C O G N I Z E
             S T U D E N T S
              H O L D I N G
               M Y T H I C
                I D E A S
                 J U S T
                  N O W
                   A S
                    I
```

"Excuse the redundancy and the lack of creativity, but I needed to try to match your poem, even if I can't do it."

Once when we were writing septomes in class, I found the following exchange in the journal. (A septome is a seven line poem in which the number of syllables in each line is determined by the writer's telephone number. A number of 222-4528 would produce a poem with two syllables in each of the first three lines and then four, five, two and eight syllables in lines four through seven.) In Lori's journal I found not only a septome she had written, but also one written by a friend:

> The birds
> Who sing
> In the trees don't seem to
> Pay
> Much attention to
> Us, but
> Why should they with the songs we produce?

To Lori   From Amy

(2	If you're
2	looking
5	for very unique
0	experiences, there are only two
8	worthwhile activities to do:
1	read;
5)	play the piano.

The journal is opened up and is no longer just a personal and private record, or even just a dialogue between Lori and me, but now can be a record of relationships between Lori and many people.

The journal cannot be a group teaching device, carefully planned in advance with known checkpoints and pre-determined goals. It must be a growing relationship between the teacher and the student in which the teacher sees opportunities inherent in the student's writing and guides rather than leads the student.

Making Relationships

My goal for Lori in her writing was to help her to make relationships. Like many gifted students, Lori was already well along in making relationships in the narrowest sense. She could spell well. She knew the conventions of the relationships between subject and verb and pronoun and antecedent. She needed to work on the relationships which made words into rich sentences, sentences into rich paragraphs, and paragraphs into well-structured essays. Once Lori was able to move to the point of seeing such relationships, then it was my job to disappear as a teacher and to become an equal, working with her.

My job was not to work with Lori on one piece of writing, but to show her that each piece of writing was part of a continual process. The process in Lori started long before I knew her, and would continue after she left my class, but I could be an important part of it. I was fortunate in having relatively few students so that I could work with each one as an individual and not be reduced to an editor or proofreader as so many teachers are because of the numbers of students they deal with every day.

I wanted Lori to write a series of short essays in close contact with me and with other students rather than to write a single long essay that was done almost entirely on an individual basis and without constant feedback from others as the writing process went along. The process is so complex that to see it in its entirety requires that one live it.

However, we can abstract a part of the process and look at it closely as representative of the whole, using the development of one idea through a series of essays as indicative of what happens on a much more complex level as many ideas are interwoven. The beginning may be as simple as a passing reference in a journal that would have been forgotten if the teacher had not called attention to it. Having just finished *Antigone*, Lori wrote in her journal a series of reactions to the play, one of which was, "I really felt sorry for the guard, even though he wasn't a very important character." I noticed the sentence when skimming through her journal and suggested to her that she think further about the guard's role in the play. I wasn't surprised at what happened in her seminar later that week.

The seminar is the key to the entire process of reading, discussion, and writing. It consists of small groups of students, no more than ten, but usually fewer, who have decided to join the group because it offers the opportunity to read, discuss, and write about specific selections of literature chosen by the seminar leader. The leader may be a teacher or a student, and has a great deal of freedom in structuring the seminar's work. Each seminar meets three or four times a week for a period of four to six weeks. The students read the assigned works, then talk about the reading, and then write about what they have read, what has been said, and their own ideas concerning it. During the process of writing, the seminar functions as a read-around group and offers comments to the writer about the work in progress. Ideally the writer gives a copy of what has been written to each member of the seminar for careful study and commentary, but sometimes it's necessary to pass a single copy around the group, to project it on a screen, or to read it out loud. Each of these methods can work depending on the length of the work being considered.

At times the read-around will talk about a single student's writing, and at other times each of the members of the group will bring something for the group to discuss. A required stage is that each member bring the introductory paragraph to the group for comments and guidance. After that step, members are encouraged to bring more fully developed essays to the group, but are not required to do so. Because they soon discover that their essays are better after the group has critiqued them, most students do ask for more detailed comments on their entire essays.

Lori brought the following introductory paragraph to the group:

> The friction between laws of a state and the natural dictates of conscience has created conflict through the ages, as *Antigone* by Sophocles demonstrates. A guard, Creon, and Antigone embody the polarized concepts. The tragic nature of the play stems from the collision of the two perspectives. Responsible man-made laws are derived from consideration of the potential benefit for all members of society. The values which a man develops emanate from his uniqueness as an individual. Poorly synthesized laws, however, can produce repression and injustice. The guard is insignificant in the city of Thebes and realizes this. Lacking a justification for a dynamic life, he becomes oriented toward survival, and his rigid compliance with the state results. This moral obligation to others and the responsibilities of their trust become secondary to his drive for self-preservation. When Creon, the Theban head of state, threatens him with death should he fail to find the defier of Creon's decrees, the fearful guard is confronted by a major threat to his security. He therefore betrays the guilty Antigone to the King, saying, 'To have escaped from ills oneself is a great joy, but 'tis painful to bring friends to ill. Howbeit, all such things are of less account than mine own safety.'

The group jumped into the discussion with numerous suggestions to her. Bob said, "You've got more than one paragraph there. You not only have your introduction, but also the first paragraph on the guard."

Amy continued, "*Antigone* only demonstrates that there was a conflict over the laws of the state and the dictates of conscience two thousand years ago. It shows nothing about conflict through the ages."

Then John joined in, "Your second and third sentences need to be combined into one sentence. As they are now, they're both thinly textured sentences that will bring the stamp on them (I own a stamp that says "Thinly Textured" on it which I use with red ink when appropriate).

Bob added, "You can create a better sentence by adding a word before "laws of a state" to balance the "*natural* dictates of conscience."

Susan showed her close reading, "What's that 'this' which the guard realizes? I don't know what you mean by it."

Finally Maria said, "How can the guard 'betray' Antigone to the king if he is just doing his job as a guard. Guards are supposed to capture criminals."

Lori listened to the group and her rewrite of the paragraph was much improved thanks to their suggestions.

The friction between the synthesized laws of a state and the natural dictates of conscience created conflict even 2,500 years ago, as *Antigone* by Sophocles demonstrates. The polarized concepts are embodied by a guard and Creon, on the one hand, and by Antigone on the other, with the tragic nature of the play stemming from the collision of the two perspectives. Responsible man-made laws are derived from consideration of the potential benefit for all members of a society, while the values which people develop emanate from their uniqueness as individuals. Poorly synthesized laws, however, can produce repression and injustice.

The rest of the paper went on to develop the ideas in the first paragraph, including a long discussion of the role of the guard in the play. But more important than the details of this paper is the fact that an idea was planted which grew as the process of writing within the class continued. Having discovered the significance of a minor character in *Antigone*, Lori began to look more closely at minor characters in other works of literature. Her first draft of her introduction to an essay on *Hippolytos* picked up a similar theme:

Although the character of the nurse in *Hippolytos* by Euripides may at first seem insignificant in regard to the tragic heights of the play, it nevertheless serves a vital function in intensifying conflicts and actually bringing about a tragedy. The nurse acts as a facilitator in the confrontation between Hippolytos, the son of Theseus, the king of Athens, and Phaidra, Theseus' wife.

The essay developed this point through an analysis of the nurse's character and her function in relationship to others. The first draft left a great deal to be desired in terms of proof of the basic thesis. The student seminar leader has the responsibility to comment in writing on the papers of all of the students within the seminar. Part of the response to this paper said, "Your structure and style are good as usual, but you didn't defend your point well. When I read an essay, I should be convinced of your point. Don't present your reasoning implicitly; do so explicitly." The criticism was apt, but the process is even more important. Each student receives carefully considered written comments to each piece of formal writing from a seminar leader who is usually another student. While the student who receives the comments often benefits from the help, the student making the comments receives an even greater benefit. To read and critique carefully six to ten papers a week is a powerful learning experience. An audience other than a teacher can motivate students to write more carefully and with greater thought. Both the read-around and the seminar leader expand the audience for a student's writing.

A next step in this process of helping Lori to see new relationships in the reading she was doing came during one of our conferences concerning her writing. Using students as seminar leaders allows me to spend class time talking to individual students about their writing because the work of the class is continuing, with the student leaders acting as teachers. As we reviewed the paper on *Hippolytos*, I commented that she was doing a good job of pursuing her concept, but that it was time she developed a name for it, so that it could be identified quickly and easily. We couldn't think of an appropriate name in the brief time we had, but she said that she would work on it.

It was a few weeks before she came back to the concept she had begun. Her writing in the interim had not been on topics that allowed her to deal with a similar topic. Most of the formal writing in the course comes out of the reading which the students choose to do from a number of options presented to them during each unit. When Lori joined a seminar on Shakespeare, she returned to her theme:

> The idea that even minor characters and factors contribute irrefutably to the whole has been widely applied in many disciplines, including literature. The concept, known informally as the Twig in the River Theory, finds applications in most of Shakespeare's works, with his *Twelfth Night* serving as a prime example. Two seemingly minor elements in the play, the character Sir Andrew Aguecheek and the clown's song, 'Come Away, Come Away, Death,' represent twigs in the elucidation process.

Lori has made an important leap forward in considering relationships in literature.

The name she selected was relatively unimportant except that it opened up the idea that not only minor *characters* could contribute to the significance of a work of literature, but also minor *factors*, such as a song. The use of the term "twigs" to represent the idea expands its meaning and allows the exploration of relationships within a work that would not have been possible if the name for the idea had been something like "The Role of Minor Characters." The metaphor selected opens the category rather than closes it and leads to a greater understanding of the topic.

By the time Lori had finished a paper on the role of Horatio in *Hamlet*, she had written four short essays that were all really a part of a longer essay on "Twigs in the River." The developmental process as she moved from section to section indicates the ways in which a writer can interact with other students, with the teacher and with the ideas being considered. A concluding activity could have been to take the four parts and write the necessary framework which would combine them into a longer paper. However, Lori chose to continue the development of the concept, but this time with a satiric rather than an analytic voice. Although the process of combining the papers into one unified essay would have been a worthwhile experience, taking the same material and using it for a completely different purpose was even more valuable in Lori's development as a writer. Further evidence of her ability to look at the ideas in a new way was demonstrated by the form she used for her writing. The final paper was a one act play rather than a formal essay. The best part of the play was Lori's inclusion of the mysterious Mrs. Brown, a representation of my role in the writing process as seen through satiric eyes. Mrs. Brown embodies the pedantic challenges I raised concerning points in the essays. Because it is humorous, it serves as a strong humanizing factor in a classroom which must often be serious and sober as we deal with improving skills and discussing ideas. The play makes fun of ideas I have introduced, such as the bihemispheric nature of the brain, as well as ideas of Lori's, the *Grand Hotel/ Airport* style reference which refers to another series of papers she wrote examining literary style.

"Twigs"

CHARACTERS:
Mrs. Brown
Guard
Antigone
Sir Andrew Aguecheek
Horatio
Hamlet

SCENE I: A dining room with four large chairs and a massive wooden table. Streamers of crepe paper are draped on the table and from the chandelier. A large sign hangs above the table which says "Welcome Western Wyoming College Alumni Literary Societé." A large tree is bolted to the stage to the right of the room set. The Guard, Sir Andrew Aguecheek, Horatio, and Mrs. Brown are standing or seated near the table. They are each wearing a party hat and are holding noisemakers. Mrs. Brown is wearing a Miss America-type banner which says, "Excellent — well-written, well-organized, and well-supported" and on her posterior the banner continues with "But . . ." The curtain rises to the fade-in of their voices talking in a cocktail party conversational style.

SIR ANDREW: Oh yes, he's very good, but his story line construction leaves something to be desired. Guard, have you read his latest?

GUARD: About right hemispheric external brain stimulation techniques?

SIR ANDREW: (listening to himself) Brilliant account of the coming trend of neoisolationism on a global scale. Fictional, of course, but the substance is still there. But again, his *Grand Hotel/Airport* style of plot construction is so poor and the overall effect is tres disappointing. (He throws his head back to keep his hair in place.) Mrs. Brown — are you still working on your book, *On Becoming Omniscient*?

MRS. BROWN: (Mrs. Brown looks up from her work at the mention of her name. She has been making comments in pencil at the top of Time Magazine and New Yorker articles.) I gave it up, Sir Andrew Aguecheek, because I discovered omniscience is innate and hence not a good subject for the self-help paperback market. But I disagree with you about his *Grand Hotel/Airport* idea. He's *marvelous*. He has excellent themes, good ideas, concrete examples and lots of specific support — just because he says nothing doesn't mean he's disappointing.

GUARD: At least it's selling among the intellectuals, and strangely enough, so is McFarland's new book, *Twig in the River Part II*.

MRS. BROWN: (shrieks) A-a-ah! That trivialized piece of refuse makes me ill! All that nonsense about minor characters and factors contributing to the resolution of conflict in a work is trash. I've been quashing the fad among my English students in no uncertain terms. (Emphatically) You and me both know who is responsible for a story's outcome: it's the protagonist, the protagonist, the protagonist. (She continues to roll it over her tongue quietly through the Guard's next few sentences.)

GUARD: (gets up and walks off dining room set toward the tree) Now, Ms. Brown, look at that durable classic *Antigone*. Where would that play have led without the guard, who was only a minor character in Sophocles' musings? (As he reaches the tree, the lights dim on the party and brighten on the tree. Antigone sits beneath it. The Guard breaks off a twig, and looking at it, recites:)

> I think that I shall never see
> A poem lovely as a tree
> Against the earth's sweet flowing breast
> A tree that looks at God all day
> And lifts her leafy arms to pray
> A nest of robins in her hair
> Upon whose bosom snow has lain
> Who intimately lives with rain
> Poems are made by fools like me
> But only God can make a tree.

(yelling over to Mrs. Brown) Ms. Brown, let's remove the Guard from the play and imagine what happens. (Guard dons a crown and sits in a chair; he impersonates Creon the King's voice.) The ground was hard and dry, unbroken, without track of wheel; the doer was one who had left no trace. The dead man was lightly strewn with dust, as by the hand of one who shunned the curse. (ghoulishly, and after a pause) If ye find not the very author of this burial, and produce him before mine eyes, *death alone* shall not be enough for you, till first, hung up alive, ye shall have revealed this outrage. (pause to remove crown) Now my fellow literary societé members, without a guard to hunt down Antigone (he looks at her) she will not be found, which leads us logically to a fundamental alteration in the play. The thrust of the play will shift from Antigone the Martyr to Creon the King (he dons the crown again and develops an obsessed expression on his face) who becomes a Hugo-style Javert, obsessed with hunting the unfortunate Antigone. You must admit, Ms. Brown, that although the drama without the guard may have possibilities, it surely ain't the same play. (He again removes the crown, breaks off a twig, and joins Antigone under the tree. Mrs. Brown continues to look dubious.)

SIR ANDREW AGUECHEEK: (Always a buffoon, and by this time a little tipsy. He jumps up on the table.) I rather agree with Guard. Although Miss McFarland's twig theory might be a little tenuous, I think it has some basis in truth. Take for example my character, Sir Andrew Aguecheek, in Shakespeare's *Twelfth Night*. (He heads for the tree with the lighting the same as before.) Imagine what Antonio might have been fated to had I not been in the scenes. Suppose Sir Toby Belch had described me to my prospective duel-mate Viola as a "knight," dubb'd with unhatched rapier and on carpet consideration; but that I was a devil in private brawl (with emphasis). Souls and bodies . . . Had I divorc'd thee . . . Strip your sword and then imagine I had not been present in the ensuing scene to attempt the duel. (Excitedly) Then — (he looks at the Societé) my dear friends, Viola's brother Antonio would never have been drawn into revealing himself to the authorities . . . and again, Mrs. Brown, the play would have taken a different twist. (He breaks off a twig and joins the players under the tree.)
(Mrs. Brown still looks undecided, so the previously silent Horatio puts down his noisemaker, removes his party hat, and makes a military Napoleon hat out of a party napkin, and elegantly cocks it on his head.)

HORATIO: (with a Danish accent) Ah, Fraulein Brown, you still do not believe us; (calls offstage) Hamlet! Hamlet! You will see the truth in Shakespeare's *Hamlet*, at least. Suppose I, as Hamlet's friend, I, Horatio, had been absent from the play. (He mimics the screechy, worried voices of Marcellus and Barnardo as he heads for the tree.) "Peace break thee off. Look where the ghost comes again . . . in the same figure like the king that's dead." Had I not been there to speculate as to the reasons behind the appearance of Hamlet's father, my old comrade Barnardo probably would have just ended speculation with "See, it stalks away." (He bounds to the other side of tree and removes his paper hat.) And even better, Mrs. Brown — what would Hamlet have done without me there as a catalyst for his feelings? What if I had never advised, "If your mind dislike anything, obey it not a whit." (Conceitedly and with an even heavier Danish accent) Hamlet needed me. (Hamlet finally appears and Horatio good-naturedly leans his elbow on Hamlet's shoulder.) . . . Of course, maybe he didn't need me when I drove him to the brink of desperate action when I said (looks at Hamlet) "You will lose this wager with Laertes," but at least I influenced him. Okay, Frau Brown, do you believe us now? (He breaks off a twig, but lets it fall to the ground. He sings.) I believe that every little twig that falls . . . (He smiles, joins the players under the tree, and the curtain falls.)

Chapter 11

I Wish the Punk Had Written Back

SHELLY WEINTRAUB and MARILEE STARK

In her six years as a social studies teacher in an urban school system, Shelly Weintraub has moved from junior high to senior high, working with progressively older students. Yet her goals have remained the same — to have her students actively involved, through various uses of oral and written language, in discovering the social and political aspects of their communities to the end of their becoming thoughtful, informed citizens.

Similar goals inform the work of Marilee Stark, a high school social studies teacher for nine years. Presently teaching in an alternative School-Within-A-School in a large suburban high school, Marilee offers a variety of integrated courses such as Oral History, Women's Literature, Afro-American Literature, and others in the school's interdisciplinary program.

✑

Making Plans

We had shared a political background which helped to shape the curriculum of the government course and the assumptions that lay beneath the surface. Both of us had been active in the anti- war and women's movements and felt the need to incorporate many of the lessons learned from that period into our classrooms.

In the government class this meant very specific things. We were faced with teaching a class that was required by the state — students took the class in order to graduate. Most students were disinterested in a political world as they understood politics. Our underlying curriculum was meant to make students feel that they, with others, had the possibility of power over their own lives. In order to have this, students had to understand power as it exists in America and also develop a sense of personal conviction combined with the ability to express those thoughts. These letters were one method for students to express their ideas and hear the opinions of others.

We had decided to work together planning the curriculum for our government classes. As we progressed and struggled with the best way to get across concepts such as Democracy, Equality, Justice, we realized that our students would be studying the same curriculum from divergent backgrounds. Their opinions and understandings of these concepts would reflect their varied experiences. We decided to take advantage of these differences in our communities and schools by initating a letter exchange between our students. Through writing we hoped they could reflect on themselves and their communities and their different and similar experiences with American law and government. Further, we hoped they would clarify their own values and opinions about various social, political, and economic problems by explaining them in letters to someone else in a very different area. Our students would then be educating themselves and each other. With so much to be learned, we were willing to take the risks of such a project.

Getting Started

We introduced the letter project to our classes as an opportunity for them to learn about another community and to have penpals from another high school. Independently we decided not to require the letters, not wanting the students to treat this as "just another assignment." Furthermore, we felt we could not require a project that we had never tried, and we didn't want to insist that students write letters that might (and did) become personal. Equally, we didn't want to risk students blaming us for exchanges that didn't work!

Those students who were at first reluctant to write were encouraged, but not required, to write. As it turned out, the personal ties formed between the students broke through the barriers raised by the segregated and isolated communities and made the question of requirements a moot issue. In fact, one of Marilee's students who refused to participate in the first exchange begged to be given a penpal after the first set of letters was received and discussed in class. In this way, we were able to minimize any potential backlash from this project, which cut across economic and racial lines.

The first letter was to serve as an introduction in which students described themselves, their schools, and their communities. As a class they brainstormed about the different ways to describe their environment, and we tried to get them to focus on what they liked and didn't like. We had to keep reminding the students that their penpals had probably never seen their street or town. Shelly told her students that they had to write more than simply "I live on East 14th Street." Marilee told her students to explain that their home was in a beach town and that they rode a bus 45 minutes over a mountain to get to school.

After a general class discussion of their community, writing key words and phrases on the board, students formed into groups of two or three to write one introductory letter. We wanted them to work in small groups so that they would be able to analyze their communities with each other. Another strategic reason for the small groups was that we wanted to assure the flow of letters. We were worried that some students might lose interest and discontinue writing after a couple of letters, wouldn't come to class after September, drop the class, or transfer to another school. With small groups, no single student would be responsible for an exchange. Also those reluctant or self-conscious about writing alone could, then, participate more easily in the small group. After the first exchange of letters, many students wanted to write individually and we felt it was important to be flexible on this question. Some students enjoyed the intensity of the more personal exchange between two individuals; others preferred the anonymity or the sharing of the small groups. This system made our record keeping difficult. It was often not clear to us who was writing to whom, though the students always seemed to know. They'd give the letters to us; we'd make copies and mail them.

The introductory letters reflected the great differences between our schools and communities. Our intial instructions were simply, "Describe yourself, your school, and your community." When students asked, "What do you want me to say about our school?" or "I don't know what to say about my community," we encouraged them to talk with others in the class and to write what *they* wanted — it was to be their letter. We had to keep telling them that there was no "right" nor "correct" way to describe their schools or communities. While we believed that it was important to give some direction to these first letters, we did not want to determine the content. We were as surprised as our students with the varied and often divergent descriptions.

Discovering Points of Contact

The following selections are from the inner city students' introductory letters.

I am writing to you with John, Jack and my name is Henry. We attend _____ high school in _____. I play football, baseball for (school). John and Jack don't. We are writing to you because we need a grade! Ms. Weintraub is a good teacher I think Ha Ha. Some problems at _____ is that we just got a new school and the outside is disgusting, Mexican writing is on wall, the Black smoke up the John. And the teachers don't understand you, But I like it here.

We don't fight here because we all like each other.

Hi, I'm Barry at _____ high school this is my last year and I hope its a good one. First week in a half enjoying it all ready, so it should be a good one. On my free time I enjoying lying in the park keeping cool. On the weekend I go Disco. Boy do I like to dance, I drive the girl crazy. I know everybody like to dance.

Some of the letters reflected student pride in themselves.

Dear pretty girl

My name is Jeff Sugar Daddy Johnson. But you can call me Brown Eyed Sugar Daddy of the West Coast. I am writing to you this letter to let you no about my community. Well I dont no where to start. Well why not with me and what I do in my community. I am a student at _____ where there is crime, drug, and a lote of other pretty girl. were I play Baskball. And that Enough of me and my school.

Other letters revealed pride in their newly built school and their surrounding community.

As you have probably heard, _____ has just be rebuilt. It looks very nice. We have a big courtyard, where we eat lunch, talk, listen to bands play some of the best music you would want to hear. We haven't had our 1st dance outside yet, but I do think that the senior class is planning to have one very soon.

We have open campus and we are free to go in a nutrition and lunch time. We have all sorts of places to go for lunch. There's a Church's Chicken, Burger King, Lucky's and many stores to go to for the students who don't want to each time in the cafeteroa.

There are some good and bad things to say about this city. The disco's are live and the after hours are even nicer. One of our newst disco's is the New Age, it is located on Grant Ave. It is open Friday, Saturday, and Sunday nights until 12 p.m. That is where more of our students hang out at on the weekend.

Others focused on the problems in their community:

The discription of are community is, like this we have many teen-agers in this district that are having problems with pregnantcy We are not talking about us so don't worry, we dont have any kids. We have many programs for teen agers who are in school that wish to work, we have many collages.

If you weren't raise in _____ I feel it's the worst place to live. Their is a lot of people out here that just don't care about no-body. They will try to still your head if it wasn't connected to your body. Oh these police is really something else other than crime preventer, their killers with a license. The only thing you hear out here is I got to get some money from somewhere. They're usually talking about stilling, robbing, gambling or pimping.

The introductory letters immediately highlighted the great diversity between and within our schools. The following are examples from the suburban school.

> Hi,
>
> The purpose of this letter is to serve as sort of an introduction, so . .. we would like to tell you a little about ourselves and the place we live in . . . Now because _____ is in _____ County, you might associate it with EST, TM, hot tubs, divorces, cocaine, and money. But being residents of this town, these things are not as evident to us. Granted, these things do go on, but they don't apply to everyone.
>
> Mary has lived in _____ for 9 years. Her interests run from photography to skiing. She plays the violin and is interested in music. She loves the outdoors particularly the beach. Her mother is the Northern California representative of the conservationist organization "Friends of the Earth."
>
> Meg has lived in _____ for 3½ years. She is also interested in photography. Her other interests are cartooning, running, and playing the piano. We are both seniors, and the issues that concern us most are nuclear power, the promotion of solar energy, preservation of natural resources, and others. We would like to know what kind of issues you have opinions on, how you feel about the issues that are important to us.
>
> Please write back and tell us . . . we're interested.

The suburban school draws from many different areas — a low income ghetto with a largely Black population, low middle and high income white areas and beach and artist communities. Class discussion helped students define their areas; a Black student from the low income area asked if her segregated community would be called a ghetto. This question led to much class discussion defining ghetto, segregation, etc. In her letter she wrote:

> Hello. Whats happ'n
>
> I'm a senior of _____ High school. I recide in _____ a small segregated community outside_____. I come from a large family of 14 and I'm the baby. I'm 17 years old Black and going somewhere in my life. My views of whats happ'n in this world are growing day by day, which I'm very proud of . . . I enjoy reading, writing, hiking, singing, and talking. In my spare time I

dig parting, traveling, drinking, tooking (smile) getting high'! But that doesn't make me a bad person. I consider myself as a person learning the will in life. Enough about me. What about you? What is your life like up to this point? What are your views of political aspects? I would like to here from you and be your friend. Thank you for taking the time out to read this letter.

Hi, I am a senior at _____ High School. I live in a town called _____. _____ is about 17 miles from my school and it takes me about an hour to get over the mountain to school in the morning. My community is a small town with about 300 people. It is a very small protected town and the majority of the people are high income. I am not one of the majority. My father works at the local service station and I work in a hamburger stand. Most of my friends and I like to party when we are not working . . . We often get in trouble because of our parties. Some of the things we are concerned about are off shore oil drilling and the draft . . .

Hello_____

It was a rough nite at work and have to work tomorrow. I've worked 4 nites this week but I'm maken some money doing it.

Do you have a job? If so doing what, do you like what you are doing?

It's hard to work and go to school. I get up at 7:30 go to school all day till 2:00 then have to be at work at 5:00 till 11:30, what a drag day after day after day . . . I've never been to a disco but may try it, who knows it may be fun burning up the dance floor.

An inner city student to a suburban one:

. . . Well I got your name to write to, and you got mine, _____. You asked some questions like where I live, I live in _____ on 40th. For fun man I go cruzing the Mission in _____ and check out the vatos (guys) on 24th Street, and after we go eat at ¼ lb thats were all the barrios go eat after they party. I am into Ranflas (cars) not engine wise. For example, my Ranfla is getting ready for new years it goin to be looking firme (good) it's a 68 Impala. Its ready to go into the shop its going to get painted candy Apple Green with a pearl green top, trued out (spoke's Rims) and dropped to the ground. I am into Low Riders (cars that have springs cut, and fixed up looking firme). All my family is into them. I have cousins in car clubs. Are there any fine dudes car clubs. Whats a Disco Sucks party? Give a more firme explanation . . .

Many of the students assumed that sterotypes of their community were widely known:

Dear friends at _____, Rolf and I are writing to you to start a friendly relationship. We are seniors at (the suburban high school). You probably watched the television program on NBC last fall and think our town is made of peacock feathers and hot tubs. It's not really like that. The people are very friendly and not snobby aristocrats like the television program portrayed. Arin and I are really into sports. If you are not or don't enjoy talking about sports please pass this letter to someone who does. I play golf on our championship golf team which plans to have a good year. Please write back soon.

Developing Relationships

After the introductory letters were written, we tried to match students by skill level and interests. With only a few exceptions, random selection would have been as effective as our efforts at matching. We had not anticipated that students would become attached to their own penpals; the penpal turned out to be a far more powerful link than shared interests and skills. In fact, the great differences that often existed between penpals forced them to be more detailed in their letters. They had to define words and describe lifestyles in response to questions from each other. In the exchange between Dan from the suburban school and Maria and Juan from the inner city, much detail is required to explain their differences.

Dan:

This is a weird pairing. I know absolutely nothing about the "lower rider scene" and I would guess you know just about as much about the Drama or punk scene. Oh yeah, what's the low rider scene like. What sort of things happen "on de Boulevard"?

Maria and Juan wrote back:

You asked about what is a low-rider? Well let us tell you all about low riders. The low riders have hydraulics and 5'20's. Those and tires they have a small chain steering wheel, and a crushed velvet interior, and tru-spokes. They also have a nice paint job and only Chicanos drive them. Over here when you see a low rider you know the person driving is a Chicano. My Ol' man has a '72 Monte Carlo and is dropped front and back. Well he's a low rider too. You know the D.M.V. made a new rule that low riders are getting busted for having 5-20's and chain steering wheels, don't you think that's all the way fucked-up? Most of the Chicanos here have a ride, and know we cant even party at our turben at East 14th St in this hamburger place its called ¼ pound. If a lowrider drives up a pig pulls him over and just starts hassling him for no damn reason.

Well I already told you about our rides now you tell me well really tell us about what's punk rock.

Dan responded:

Now I know what low riding is. Thank you.

Basically Punk is a state of mind. It started in England (London) with the kids rebelling against the establishment. The first true punks were Johnny Rotten and the Sex Pistols. But not all punks stay punk. Johnny Rotten is now living very happily and quite well in Jamacia.

I recently saw this statement written on a wall, "Hard Rock may rule but Punk is a culture." That's really pretty accurate. Punk is more than the spiked hair (mine isn't spiked) or the safety pins, it's a way of thinking. It's the poor people in the city saying, "We're as good as you shit we're better."

In S.F. in the mayor's race third place (behind Dianne Finestein and Quentin Kopp) was taken by Jello Biafra. Jello is the lead singer for the Dead Kennedys a local punk group. Punk is really gaining precedence.

Reading over the letter I've just written it seems to me that I'm defending punk and that's weird because punk needs no defense.

All that I can say is that you really have to experience it to totally understand it. I wish that I could have written as eloquently as you did in your description of low riders.

Finally Maria and Juan wrote:

Dan we understand this is the last letter we're going to write to you, and we wanted to tell you that it was fun doing it and it was nice knowing you this way. Dan do you ever go to San Fran and cruse at Mission? Well Juan sometimes goes up their he might see you some day up their, well that if you go . . . Well we don't know what else to say but thank you for taking the time to write back to us, and it was nice knowing what's punk-rock because you explain it to us and now we understand.

The exchange between Isabella and Carla shows how they began to get interested in each others lives. To student at the suburban school:

My name is Isabel, I work at The Parent Child Center and taking care of children is one of my favorite hobbies. I also like going swimming and do alot of sewing. I take up an electronics course at _____ H.S. and hope to continue in college to become an electronics technician.

We'd like to bring this subject up to you, to see what your opinion is it. First of all our city has the largest infant mortality rating in American other than New York. There's a debate on the cause of so many deaths of infants. For one — the blame is on the patients for not getting the proper medical care, not taking care of themselves properly while pregnant. 2. Under-staffed in hospitals and not enough caring for the infants is the other reason.

We hope we may one day get to meet you.

Carla's response:

What's happen,
How's life treating you, or should I say How are you treating life, either way I hope it's great.

Listen, I got your letter, and I found we shared the same intrest in child care and development. You mentioned something about infant mortality; I really know very little about it. If you could give me a little insight on it, I would really appreciate it. I also plan to check into myself as much as I can.

Anyway, in my first letter I really didn't talk to much about myself, so I'll try and give you some insight on the type of person you are writing to. I love children, and hope to share, learn and grow with them as much as I can. I am presently working at a private Montesorri school with children.

Rap to you later.

Isabella:

Dear Carla:

. . . I also see that you like working with children too, and that to me is one of my main things other than electronics . . . I took child care for two reasons, one is that I really like working with children and enjoy doing it. The other is that I'm a young high school mother with a son at the age of two and just wanted to learn more about children so it would help me be a good mother to and for my child. I also hope that later on I can open a childcare center of my own. You also said that you were interested in knowning more about infant mortality. Did you know that _____ has one of the largest number of infant deaths next to New York City? And there's a big debate going on about it now . . . I would have to keep gathering information before I give my decision or opinion of what I think! This to me is something very serious to think about. We'll talk more about it later. Be talking to you later!

Carla:

What's up,

How are you and your son? Working with kids is great. It helps me to create a positive attitude for myself as well as the children's and my co-workers . . . I got into it for several reasons (child care that is) one; I come from a large family and there are alot of cousins younger than I am, as a matter of fact the youngest right now is 1 yrs. old. So I grew up holding a baby in my arms; (so to speak) and I loved every minute of it. The second reason is because I think children are unique creatures, and theres so much you can learn from them. Observing their difference in personalities is a mind blower . . . I cannot give an opinion on Infant Mortality, because I still do not know much about it. I will also have to gather more information. I would like to know more about you. Your experience with pregnancy. The disadvantages and advantages of all. Please don't be affended. I have a couple of friends who are still in high school and have children, and do not knock anyone. Whatever makes them happy and you makes me happy. I hope to meet you soon.

Take care and give your son a hug for me. Talk to Ya

It seems to us that this exchange between Isabella and Carla is an excellent example of how students developed a personal relationship with each other. While Isabella started writing on a relatively academic level — the topic of infant mortality — the warmth of Carla's response allowed her to reveal that she had a young son. We were pleased that the correspondence allowed these young women gradually to share more and more of themselves.

Reflecting on Issues Together

In addition to exchange of information about their own lives, students asked each other questions about the problems that were facing them and these exchanges were also successful. Here are three brief examples from the suburban students:

It was very nice to receive your letter. I'm glad you told me what things are like over in your town. They sound pretty tough. Even though I believe that every society has its flaws.

My town isn't really all peaches and cream but I don't believe that its as violent as yours. The kids around here are bored I don't really think that there are alot of activities going on, so they get really rowdy. We have vandalism, robing and rape and their are some groups that go around and get roudy. _____ is a pretty mellow town but there are other towns around here that get pretty bad.

We (our class) heard in a lot of letters that you have a lot of gangs and that the police cause a lot of hastles. Is that tru? We don't have anything like that. I even had a friend who is a police officer and he and some of his friends got together and they put on Friday Night Teen Dances at the Rec Center.

The police dept here doesn't do much of anything except give citations for jaywalking and being out after curfew. They also give traffic tickets.

Martha from the inner city school wrote to Jim:

What do you think about the Iranians and the draft would you like to get drafted and go fight for your country. They say that they are going to draft ladies I know if they try and draft me I am not going to go Ill do something to get out of it, like cut off my thumb get pregnant, speaking of pregnancy how would you feel if your old lady had an abortion would you try to stop her an would you rather have your own flesh and blood killed I know I would spit in his face if my old man told me anything like have an abortion. He should be happy.

Jim writes back:

You asked if I would go and fight for my country — the answer is yes and no — yes for a good cause and no for Iran to me its not worth getting shot at for oil. My problem if they do start the draft is I can't get pregnant — if they tried to draft me I would go to Canada and hide out.

Thoughts on abortion are difficult for everyone. I think it is up to the couple. They started it together they should make the decision together . . . Oh if they do reinstate the draft get pregnant its much more fun than cutting off your thumb.

Sometimes questions from one school provoked discussion at the other which resulted in more detailed returned letters. Janine from the inner city school wrote Steve and Jim:

I Have a question for you guys and I want both of you opinions. If you have a girl friend and she ends up pregnant would you have her get an abortion or would you tell her to keep it and you will marry her. If you disagree with my answer tell me why. I feel that if you take a chance and you get the girl pregnant both you and your girl friend should suffer the consequences. I'm strongly against abortion because it's not fair to kill a human being for the mistake you made. The reason I'm asking you guys is because the guys out here are a trip (funny). When their girl friend tells them that she's pregnant they will leave her and never see her again. I've asked a lot of guys that question and they say that they don't want to be tied down with one girl. They say if she gets pregnant thats her problem not mine. Please answer my question I want to hear your side of it. P.S. I hope I'm not being too hard on you guys but thats a woman for you. bye.

Jim read his inner city letter to the class. Heated class discussion followed on the pros and cons of abortion. Jim then selected four points from the wide-ranging discussion to include in his letter. Since he had given little thought to this issue prior to the discussion, his advice clearly reflected his *need* to know in order to write a reply:

Whether to have the baby or to get it aborted is a difficult question to answer. I guess you have to take in many considerations. 1) Is the girl old enough to deliver the baby safely 2) Will they both get married and bring up the baby 3) Who will suffer the most the child, the parents 4) Will the baby screw up the parents, since the parents are so young. Those are only a few questions you have to think about before you make that important decision.

Before you get yourself in that situation has anyone over there ever heard of birth control devices? It seems if the guys and gals are playing Russian Roulett, it would be a lot safer if they would use something for protection. What are your views about birth control? Teenage Sex?

In addition to sharing advice on personal problems, students exchanged opinions regarding the subjects under discussion in class. The following excerpts reflect the classroom debates on democracy:

An inner city student defining democracy from her experience: "My opinion of democracy is that we are given the freedom to express our thoughts but we have to make an effort to make things better for all human being, not just whites, but all minorities."

Another view from the inner city: "I say we are a democratic nation. The reason I say this is in order to have democracy the people of that nation should have equal rights to do any thing they want, live anywhere they want, and vote for any person running for condidate in an election. I would like to know from you whether or not you believe this is a democratic nation, if so, why? and if not why?

A suburban student replying to an inner city student: "So you say you believe that we live in a democratic country. I hope after the Federalist, anti-federalist debate you had, that you've seen the light. Our country is set up to be democratic but in fact it's more of a capitalist nation. If you have alot of money, you can easily get yourself into or out of something you desire. This happens a lot in todays society."

Students even questioned each other's definitions: An inner city student wrote: "I think democracy will and can destroy a nation. I would like your opinion."

A suburban student replied: "We don't really understand what you mean by 'Democracy will and can destroy a nation.' We believe in democracy but we're not sure if we really have one here. Sometimes we think it's more of a bureaucracky.

Often students would include information about subjects interspersed with friendly chatter: An inner-city letter to suburban:

What's been happening babe? I'm doing alright. You were wondering what type of sports and activities I am into well, I play football, track and some wrestling. I'm a jazz musicians and have been for quite sometime; the instrument I play is the saxophone. In my spare time I play chess and backgammon . . . Do you have a man? If so is he supporting you in any way: Do you have a job? What's your sign? I'm a Pisces. Patty as you may already know we had a debate in my Amer. Gov't class. I was on the side of the Federalist *arguing* against the Anti Feds. We practically had everyone on the side of the Anti. Feds. confused, and worried that most of their group would change sides and go with the views of the Federalist. But our closing was to weak and the debate ended in a stalemate.

In your last letter you were asking me my views on the draft, well it's like this, I don't believe that the policy of a draft will be voted in. Anyway I don't believe in men and women being to put to war against their own will.

A suburban student to an inner city student:

Boy, your job sounds really interesting! All I do is make sandwiches. Do you ski? I was wondering because everyone around here is getting really excited because ski season is going to be so early this year . . . Anyway I suppose I should be telling you a little about what we're doing in class. It's actually pretty interesting. We're about in the middle of our mock Senate. I'm a Senator from Missouri and a radical democrat. The radical democrats are in the majority so we hope to get all our bills passed so that we sort of have control. It's really pretty fun. The bill I worked on had to do with socializing all the oil companies — turning them ino one, government regulated utility . . . Propositions A, B, f and G were hot issues around here on the past ballot. Speakers came to our class and gave a slide show about solar village . . . Do you ever hear anything about that? But, back to me. I've never been to a real disco! On weekends I usually just go out partying with my friends, or to the movies . . . We don't have too many low riders around here. I havent been able to get a hold of a picture of our school yet — but I'll work on it.

An inner city student to a suburban student:

I got picked for a senator from the state of Vermont. Of all thing I
turn out to be a republican and I know for sure that I'm democrat
but that's the way things turn out and also got pick from a boring
state like Vermont. Our class got the subject of South Africa and
there will be a speaker coming to our class and talking about South
Africa.

A suburban student to an inner city student:

I am a liberal democrat from the state of New Mexico. I am writing
a bill about U.S. trade in South Africa. I don't know how much you
know about it, and I didn't know anything until last week, but its a
white racist govern country meaning that 4 million white people
govern the over 17 million black people. The black people have no
say in their gov't at all. I feel that the United States would have
nothing to do with a government like that. See the government
system is called aparthied (prounced apart-hate) Its laws say white
people are supreme and that *they* should be kept separate from
blacks . . . Well I gotta go, good luck at your singing and someday
I'll come hear you. Why don't you tell me the time and place of
where you'll be singing on the 26th. Oh yeah where do you live I
mean what town? P.S. Sorry if this is boring but its kinda hard
writing to someone you don't know.

The shared curriculum turned out to be an important area the students shared in common, and they easily exchanged information about
it. Because they were not required to write about their course work in
the letters, we were always surprised to discover which students included it. We were also interested in learning which parts of the curriculum they included in their letters. Often their descriptions of class
projects and discussions were quite detailed and indicated a level of understanding previously not evident to us nor to them.

Exploring The Key Issue: Prejudice

"Nice people but highly eliterit . . ."
As students tried to explain differences in language and culture
they also spoke directly and indirectly to the issue of prejudice. Their
letters continually revealed how prejudice is so often a result of ignorance.
As more letters were exchanged students began to rely on their
own writing as a way to discuss the problems. As a white teacher in a
predominately Black school, Shelly was unsure how to deal with the
hostility expressed by her students towards the white students in the
suburbs, especially as her students saw her as part of the inner city and
not part of suburbia.

As a white teacher in a largely white school Marilee had also to deal with the prejudice and stereotypes expressed by many of her students. Both relied on the letters themselves and the class discussions to break through the differences. As long as there was open, honest communication the problems with hostility and prejudice could be worked on.

From a suburban student to an inner city student:

Our teacher has informed us that some of you took offense by some of our letters. We just want you to know that we meant no offense at all. We get alot of racism from your letter. It sounds pretty competitive over there. Michael says his skin is dark but he's no minority . . . I've never been exposed to real racism before. I've been to your city many times but I guess I never really looked below the surface. It doesn't seem at all fair. . .

The following is an interchange between an inner city girl and a suburban boy:

Inner city: You said you make 5 dollars a week why don't sent me some because our minimum wage is only $2.90 hour . . . In my last letter I told you that I wanted to meet you personally because I hate writing to someone I never seen. You didn't respond to it. I don't have any prejudices either. As you may or may not know but I'm black . . .

And about your truck if you make so much why don't you buy you another truck. I know you don't drive your girlfriend around in a truck . . .

Suburban response to inner city student:

. . . In your last letter you asked me if I liked all that "white boy music". Well I don't know what your definition of white boy music is? The kind of music I like is music by Al Green, Crosby, Stills, Nash and Young and the Rolling Stones. What kind of music do you like?

What's wrong with driving my girl friend around in my truck. I think its a pretty nice truck but I must admit that it is a little confining.

The following are typical of the racial comments which occurrred in letters from both schools:

I hope it doesn't matter, but I am white. Seeing as this might be my last letter to you, at least in this class, I want to say that if your ever in my town go to Ed's superette and ask for me.

Have a good day.

What's happening Claire and Scott?

What would we do if the draft would start? Well it's simple! We ain't going. Truley spoken. What we mean by niggers in our letter, well its like this, because we said niggers, that don't - mean just Blacks. It means all color. All that acts crazy. That could be Black, White, Red, Blue, or Purple. Anybody. . . . .

My name is Joseph. I think I am almost a one-of-a-kind at this school. This school is sixty % Black, 30% Chicano, and ten % all others. There is about 10 true white rock'N' Rollers here. I feel so outnumbered.

We took a lot of risks by initiating this exchange between students from such different backgrounds, but we had hoped from the start that the letters would not simply be an exchange in stereotypes and prejudice. We wanted the exchange to help the students see themselves and their communities more clearly, but we were concerned that some inner city students might become self-conscious about their skills or feel bad or hostile about the inequalities between the two communities. In a similar way, some suburban students might act superior to those "less fortunate" or perhaps feel guilty about the disparities in schools and other areas.

Our fears were balanced by our faith in the students being able to teach and learn from each other. As the problems were raised, we discussed them in class and the students continued to write their letters. Problems were not ignored. Our discussions had to be as honest as the students' exchanges.

Shelly had to deal with the hostility and resentment many of her students expressed over the inequality between the communities. Her students wrote on their evaluations:

It gives me the feeling that they are middle and high class people only. It also gives me a feeling that they have cleaner air over there.

They are rich white kids who know they are rich and don't mind telling you about it.

One student was so curious about the suburban school he even took a trip out there and reported:

There places are world's apart. About two weeks ago my friend and I took a drive down there to see how it is it's lke the oppisite of this city, nice big house green grass and fresher air then here. I thought it was sort of like this city (before) but now "oh boy" I had the wrong idea.

I enjoyed writing the letters to people who are more fortunate then ourselves can have a first hand view of how city life is truely like for the underprivilege. My impressions of (the suburbs) from the beginning did not change. They live in a world where they are blinded from the fact that in this country many people suffer worser than they realize.

However, the power of personal contact helped to offset the hostility Shelly encountered. For the students, receiving a letter with their name on it became the most important part of the exchange; it hardly mattered what the content of the letter was. Students became possessive and defensive of their penpals.

Inner city students explained the ways their impressions of suburban students had changed through the letter exchange:

I felt that (the suburban town) was a mainly white town. I felt that some of the students would be real snobbish. My impression changed a little. The students that I wrote to didn't seem that way at all.

Well (suburban town) seams like were people with mony live and I thought I would be writting to some high class person by my impression was wrong there just as the same as us.

That white people would write Black people and tell them about thereself.

One student shared our pleasure and astonishment in her evaluation:

At first I thought it was not going to work nobody would want to do it. I was amazed to see pratically everyone in the room writing letters to their penpals, or someone they never met and really did care.

The first set of letters from the inner city confirmed the stereotypes some suburban students held of the cities as dangerous, violent places where they wouldn't want to live and made them feel fortunate that they didn't live there. However, through the continuing exchange of letters and intense class discussion, students began to describe and define, rather than judge the differences between the communities. Their prejudices, largely based upon ignorance and isolation, were continually challenged by the information coming from their penpals in the inner city:

I learned that high schools though very close are very different. (The inner city) is a more dangerous place, and many of the kids are concerned with just surviving. Their high school, their goals and expectations of life are incredibly different from ours.

I will start with the differences. (The inner city) High is totally different from our school. The kids have to deal with a whole different life style getting in fights, taking loads of drugs, stealing so you can get food or just something you really want.

I have found that they have basically the same three track minds most student's have (sex, drugs, rock and roll) However their interpretations of these tracks are somewhat different. Disco, lowriders, etc.

The letter exchange allowed some suburban students to learn more about their own community:

We learned that people around here are more prejudiced then we thought and more judgemental of different value systems. Their culture is totally different although we're geographically close.

The suburban kids are spoiled and we/they can never really know what it's like in the inner city.

Inner city student aren't sheltered and protected as they are in the suburbs.

During class discussions regarding the similarities and differences between the city and the suburbs special insight was provided by those inner city students who themselves bridged the race, class and cultural gaps. A Black student from a low income ghetto in the suburbs commented:

The environment and living conditions often reflects how we are our opinions, achievements and failures. This county is one of the richest counties in America, so it's rich, predominantly white, upper middle class, better education systems, high employment, greater opportunities, safe environment. The inner city in contrast has a high percentage of minorities, great percentage of poverty-stricken neighborhoods, high rate of infant mortality, crime rate is high, segregated low income housing.

This student went on to further point out a unique aspect of the letter exchange that we had not realized:

Another thing we have in common is that both schools were brought together to try to understand and communicate with one another in an intellectual level, and not on another basis.

After reading her evaluation we recognized that most inter-school contact, especially across social and economic lines is focused on sports, music, and academic competition. Not often is this contact a non-competitive exchange of ideas and information.

Often Marilee was asked fundmental questions about the inequality of the educational system which she found difficult to answer: "How come they can't read and write?" In an evaluation a suburban student wrote:

The students could not write very well. Thier use of the English language was poor. They sounded as if they liked school and what they were doing, but they still couldn't write.

or:

I learned that the way they talked is in pretty poor grammar.
Another student commented, "Nice people but highly eliterit."

Marilee began to answer some of these questions through her government curriculum. For example, her students debated privilege and opportunity as it was raised in the area of affirmative action. Some students, who couldn't see the need for affirmative action in general, became the first to defend the need for affirmative action when it affected their penpals in the inner city. For example, one of the student "lawyers" opposed to preferential admissions programs wrote on his evaluation:

There's more money in this county than in the inner city. And since there's more money it seems we have a definite educational advantage which is sad.

Another example, "Politics hurts education in less rich neighborhoods. Prop. 13 didn't affect all schools equally."

Some students were unable to accept and comprehend the inequality between the two communities:

I noticed that they think about very much the same things that we do, and are, disregarding monetary and financial status and educational opportunities, exactly the same as us.

Planning the Next Time Around

We had no idea that the letter exchange between our schools would be so exciting. As teachers we were delighted to notice that students were exchanging views of themselves, their schools, communities, national political problems as well as incorporating the class curriculum into their letters. However, the success of the project was largely due to students receiving letters addressed to them personally. They wanted to write for an audience. While we are pleased with our first letter exchange, we view this project as an experiment-in-progress. Based on our evaluation and those from the students, we would propose several changes in structure and organization:

(1) Provide a regular time in class for writing letters. Students unanimously agreed that the exchange needed more and better organization. Since we had developed the idea late in the planning stages for the class, we had not allowed class time for writing and discussing the letters. Also we weren't willing to risk setting aside time for an experiment that might not work. Shelly was teaching new classes in a new school and didn't need additional unknowns. Neither of us had tried

letter projects within our own classes and certainly never between schools.

We did set aside time in class to introduce the idea and write the first letters. This was followed with more class time to read and discuss the first letters received. After this initial exchange our lack of organization severely limited the success of the project. We had not anticipated that the letters would mean so much to our students. Many expressed great disappointment when they didn't get a letter back. One of the two white students from the inner city said he enjoyed writing the letter because "I could explain my position here at this school to an almost white school but the punk never wrote me back . . . I wish that punk would have written back."

Without class time for letter writing we couldn't guarantee a regular exchange. But even this limitation didn't prevent students from writing letters on their own time; many were surprisingly responsible for making sure their letters made "the mail." On several occasions students rushed in after school with their letters.

Next time we would set aside a "letter day" every two weeks. We lost the momentum and excitement created by the first letters because we didn't allow follow-up time. A "letter day" would allow the exchanges to develop more fully for individual students and the classes as a whole.

(2) Set aside classroom space for a bulletin board focused on the material from the letters. All letters, sent and received, are sources for information about the respective communities. In addition we would include maps, photographs of students and their schools, relevant news clippings, and any letters students would share. We would arrange the boards to include material from and about both communities.

(3) Give students some responsiblity for the organization. We found that there was too much paper work for us in this project. We would recommend that students be placed in charge of filing and xeroxing the letters. Letters must be copied before they are distributed because they become the personal property of the students and they take their letters home. We found that students were eager and willing to take responsiblity for organizing the letters. They are personally involved through their own letters and giving them this responsiblity simply enhances their interest, concern and commitment. Spending less time on the paper work would give us more time to work with students on the content of the letters and their writing skills. On the evaluations from the inner city over half of the students commented that they preferred writing the letters instead of talking to their penpal. Shelly found this a significant statement because many of these students do not have a favorable image of writing. If they were to be asked directly "Do you like to write?" they would probably say "No." However, given a concrete situation where they were getting a response,

their attitudes about writing changed drastically.

(4) Begin the exchange with only one class writing and then the other class can respond. We began the project with all the classes writing simultaneously. In this way we hoped to match students with similar interests. As pointed out before, our match-ups had little effect on the success of the exchanges. Instead, we created unnecessary confusion for ourselves and the students by the letters crossing at the same time. Record keeping became an almost impossible task.

(5) Students must use first and last names when addressing their penpals. A letter addressed to Susan at one school from Jim at another was not enough to assure delivery. Using last names became especially difficult to enforce as the letters became more personal.

(6) Plan for meetings between the schools. We would recommend at least one meeting at the end of the semester. Our students requested to meet each other many times. If possible we would arrange two meetings — the first one could be small (20 students representing each school); the purpose would be to exchange information about the schools and communities. This could be done with slide shows, tapes and other media to supplement the letters. This group could then make plans for the second meeting which could be a more social event (potluck or picnic) involving all students who participated in the exchange.

(7) We found that it was important to keep the focus on the students and their correspondence with each other. For example when students misunderstood each other they would ask us, "Why did _____ say this?" or "What does she mean by this?" We told the students to ask these questions of each other and clarify their own differences directly. As teachers we had to keep ourselves separate from their exchanges. Our role was to help direct and focus the exchanges and not to become personally involved in the communication.

(8) Common curriculum is not necessary for a successful letter exchange. The personal contact between the students is the basis for a successful project. However, our students found it helpful to rely on their shared curriculum for topics to write about in their letters. This occurred more frequently in the first letters when the students were still overwhelmed by the dramatic differences in their schools, backgrounds and communities.

As teachers we agreed on our goals and strategies. We also were able to trust each other especially when our students, schools and communities are very different. Even though we hold similar ideas about teaching and learning and are good friends, we still had a tendency to become protective of our students. However, we managed to laugh when we caught ourselves defending a student's behavior. We even pressured each other for the next set of letters in the same way our students pressured us!

Chapter 12

"This Guy Can Really Write"

DIANE COOKSTON

Sixteen years of teaching high school English — on and off with time out for child-rearing — have convinced Diane Cookston that what she likes best about her students are first, the adolescent sense of humor — "They're always ready to laugh and so am I." — and, second, that her students are not cemented into one pattern of living or reacting. As this chapter illustrates, Diane encourages individual reaction to what is read, short-cutting the possibility for distanced, stereotyped responses. A writer herself, she knows the value of daily, informal writing to get the flow of thought going, and she uses the reading logs to help her students make personal connections with literature previously unfamiliar to them.

✑

Each class takes on a character of its own, and my afternoon junior English class of sixteen and seventeen year olds had grown into a combination of warmth, brilliance, and absurdity. The final spring quarter stretched in front of us, seeming both too long for us to maintain any imitation of decorous and scholarly behavior, and too short to read and write about our last two novels, *East of Eden* by John Steinbeck and *The Great Gatsby* by F. Scott Fitzgerald. On the first day of the nine week quarter they had *East of Eden* in their hands.

"My god, Mrs. Cookston, this book is 691 pages long!" complained Helmuth, a conscientious student who preferred writing five-paragraph essays to what he called my "strange writing assignments." His other claim to fame was that I had lost my temper and called him a "stupid baby" when I caught him trying to pierce an orange with a table leg near his seat in the back of the room. "You think we're going to read this in four weeks?" he wailed. Then came the classic. "We've got other classes, you know. You must think this is the only class we've got!"

I stifled the impulse to call him a "stupid baby" again, which would have brought forth a shout of laughter, for the students had loved the moment when, overcome with anger and speechless from a desire to swear, I had babbled that childish epithet. What they needed now was a sense of purpose, not humor. I loved teaching Steinbeck's great flawed novel, and previous students had liked it. I would have preferred to have taught it in five weeks, but the demands of our book schedule were inflexible. I was determined they would read *East of Eden* and love *East of Eden*.

"All right," I began. "This is going to be hard, but it's going to be worth it. We've read Steinbeck before — *Grapes of Wrath* and *The Long Valley* — but his philosophy and style have evolved into something different in *East of Eden*. You won't have much sense of reading the same author.

"We won't have any extra writing assignments while we're reading. We'll continue our vocabulary study for the college entrance tests, write great Reading Logs, and write an in-class final essay as an exam when we finish the book. It will be intensive, but you can do it. My classes last year got a lot out of this book, and I'm sure you will, too."

My students were familiar with Reading Logs, for they had written them on and off all year. The four works we had written Logs for were Mark Twain's *The Adventures of Huckleberry Finn*, John Steinbeck's *Grapes of Wrath* and *The Long Valley*, and Ken Kesey's *One Flew over the Cuckoo's Nest*.

"Reading Logs!" Helmuth groaned, grinning, brown eyes snapping with suppressed laughter, knowing his comments were obnoxious to me, but popular with the class.

Several pairs of serious eyes, belonging to students at tables nearer the front of the room, looked up from the dittoed reading schedule I had given them to see my reaction to Helmuth's new tack. I ignored him and continued, "Notice the directions for Reading Logs on the bottom of the calendar of reading assignments I've given you. It says:

Reading Log — These will take the place of quizzes.

1. One-half page minimum response for each night's assignment. Please date your Logs.
2. Due at the completion of each "Part" of the novel. Lateness will be penalized.
3. For an "A," responses must go beyond plot summary. Be thoughtful.

I read from the ditto like a primary teacher reading to seven year olds, wanting everything to be clear, adding, "A set of Reading Logs is due at the completion of each part of the book — one thoughtful Log for each night's reading assignment. Logs should be a minimum of a half a page. There is no maximum. I'll gladly read and respond to everything you write. Four dated Logs will be due Friday. We'll write one together in class tomorrow. Questions?"

"Can we read now?" asked Kate, who gets the point quickly and doesn't care for elaborate class discussion.

"I'm going to read Chapter One aloud to you now," I answered, bracing myself for the look of friendly disgust she predictably shot my way.

"I know how you like to read to us, Mrs. Cookston," she smiled tolerantly.

"At the beginning of each part is a chapter of historical or philosophical background," I introduced bravely, wishing it was September and they didn't all know me so well. "These chapters will remind you of the intercalary chapters in *Grapes of Wrath*.

The Salinas Valley is in Northern California. It is a long narrow swale between two ranges of mountains, and the Salinas River winds and twists up the center until it falls at last into Monterey Bay. I remember my childhood names for grasses and secret flowers. I remember where a toad may live and what time the birds awaken in the summer — and what trees and seasons smelled like — how people looked and walked and . . ."

I read happily, "just to get them started," until the bell rang.

*   *   *

Last summer I was a part of the Mt. Diablo Writing Project, an offshoot of the Bay Area Writing Project, sharing experiences with other teachers of writing — kindergarten through secondary school — and with BAWP consultants. I encountered the idea of using Reading Logs there through such teacher-consultants as Mary K. Healy and Dave Holden. I saw the method of having students respond in writing to each night's reading, at first, merely as good practice in writing, or as a practical way for students to keep track of the plot of a novel or short story. For example, the Logs for *Huck Finn* and *The Long Valley* emerged almost exclusively as plot summaries and were very useful to the students during examinations. Then the Logs' value as a reading check, taking the place of shallow, though easy to grade, objective reading quizzes, or even short answer essay quizzes, occurred to me.

At Northgate High School in Walnut Creek, California, where I teach, English teachers compete with the rigor demanded by other highly academic courses offered to our mainly college-bound student body. We compete, in a sense, for students' study time, and if they must choose between reading a selection from *East of Eden* for class discussion, or tackling six calculus problems, students often choose calculus over English. Our students are fanatically grade-oriented and are from a culture where study of the arts is thought frivolous. So, our situation necessitates regular grading following reading assignments.

I have always hated the questions I have used for reading checks preceding discussion of literature. Valuable time and energy are wasted in providing the motivation of a grade. Also, reading for names and places and events interferes with reading for understanding.

Earlier in the school year, I had accepted any level of response — summarizing the plot, reflecting on an idea, or relating a fictional incident to personal experience. I was satisfied with their entries, which seemed to mirror each student's capability and maturity, since I assumed many were not yet dealing with abstractions. We were free from the debilitating superficiality of content quizzes. The summaries helped the class to write better supported essays, and in the time I spent grading Reading Logs, I was dealing with higher quality student writing.

As we began *East of Eden*, I wanted more than writing practice and reading checks and study notes. I wanted to encourage each student to experience the human meaning in the novel — the love and hate, the hope and despair — hoping he or she would grow emotionally and intellectually. I had not forgotten that we write well when we are deeply involved and have something that we really want to say. So with good writing still an inseparable part of my goal, genuine exploration of the literature became my crusade.

*   *   *

The second day of Spring Quarter, my juniors wandered in after noon, taking their usual five minutes to stop munching the remnants of lunch and settle down into their bright-colored plastic chairs.

"We're supposed to be on page 43 of *East of Eden* today, Mrs. Cookston?" asked Betsy with genuine amazement, even though I had distributed a schedule and written the week's reading assignments on the board. "It's impossible to read that much in one night." Near her sat students who I knew had done the reading, but they listened silently.

I responded patiently, "I read 13 pages to you in class yesterday, Betsy, and we're using some class time for reading today. I'm going to give you all the help I can. And you have weekends if you get behind. You can do it." Betsy sighed, her round, freckled face set in an expression of stubborn disbelief.

"Today," I addressed the class, "we're going to read for fifteen minutes, write Logs for fifteen minutes, and share what we've written for fifteen minutes by reading our entries aloud. I'll read and write and share with you. Then you should have an idea of what the possibilities are. Remember — no "A's" unless you reflect or relate, and no above-average grades if your Logs are turned in late. Unless you were absent, this should be Log No. 2."

We settled down behind our rectangular, simulated-wood tables, bending, focusing on our orange paperbacked copies of *East of Eden*. The cover picture of James Dean and Julie Harris on a grassy knoll, portraying Cal and Abra in the Hollywood film version of the novel, faced me from all parts of the room. I had re-read the current assignment the night before, so I took only a few minutes to find the paragraph I wanted to write about, and started my Log. Actually, the task I had set for myself was to write four Logs, each a different type, to use for examples in case one or another approach was missing from those the students were about to share.

After fifteen minutes I checked my watch — our open plan school does not provide a clock in each classroom — and, squirming a bit, the class switched from reading to writing. Some well-organized students pulled out the notebooks they had been using for Reading Logs through the year, others reached for lined paper they would later staple into crude booklets when it came time to hand in the Logs.

"I can't get started unless I write about the plot," said Betsy, taking her pen out of her mouth to speak.

"A combination is fine," I said, walking over to her, hoping not to disturb everyone, "but don't use plot summary exclusively."

"Oh, I won't," she said reassuringly. I angled back to my table to finish my writing, looking curiously over a few shoulders as I went.

"I'll read first, Mrs. Cookston," called Helmuth from the notorious back row, noticing that the second fifteen minutes was up.

These chapters further depict the plight of the Trasks and Hamiltons. There is a great Biblical connotation after the episode involving the attempted murder of Adam by Charles. This parallels the myth about Cain and Abel. The scar which Charles receives, occurs while he attempts to move a rock. The earth is now unyielding to him and he loses control of himself. I think that Steinbeck is trying to show how great the Hamiltons are in Salinas while the hobo Adam, who wanders the country, and his hermit brother who gallavants only to the neighborhood whorehouse appear to me as natural losers in life. Even though the Hamiltons have a hard time in life, by losing patents and being cheated, no one ever dies in their family, and they seem to be always happy.

"Thank you, Helmuth. That's good. What phrase or sentence do you remember from his Log, Karen?"

Karen pushed her light brown hair out of her eyes as she thought. "The hobo Adam and his hermit brother," she answered steadily.

"How would you describe his Log, Karen? Is it a reflection, a summary, a related personal anecdote, what?"

"He talks about some ideas in the book."

"So what would you call it?"

"A reflection."

"Good. You said 'ideas.' How many?"

"Two, I guess," she frowned, "the Cain and Abel story and the contrast between the Hamiltons and the Trasks."

"Does everyone agree with Helmuth's analysis so far?" I asked.

There was movement and muttering, and I was certain that not everyone did agree with Helmuth, especially about no one's ever dying in the Hamilton family. We weren't very far into the book, leaving room for misinterpretation. It seemed unfair to argue with anyone's guesses about the author's intentions at this point. We continued sharing, basing our comments on the language of the Logs, analyzing, looking for memorable bits of writing and different approaches to responding. The dialogue, however, was usually between me, the teacher, and one reluctantly responding student.

Even though I enjoyed the sharing time, and their entries were varied enough so that my models were superfluous, my class begged me not to have them share Logs again. They said they wanted to write personally and were embarrassed to share. Also, they would rather use class time working on their reading and Log writing individually. In thinking their request over, I decided that writing honestly, responding deeply, admitting confusion, feeling free to question — these were my goals for them. If sharing would inhibit these processes, then sharing would be sacrificed.

The day was valuable, especially since everyone got a feeling for what was acceptable, or even excellent, but we never read our Logs aloud again. These Logs were also shared that day:

This short Log, written by tall, aloof, not-into-the-Northgate-scene Ken, is not really much more than plot summary. I gave him full credit, however, because I love his ironic, irreverent tone.

> This reading assignment goes into detail into the Hamilton family and the separation of Adam and Charles. We read how exciting a good firm-grounded family like the Hamiltons can be. Adam joins the army and when he gets out he becomes a tramp. Adam manages a few amusing plights. Charles stays home to work the farm, visit the local whorehouse every two weeks, and grows into a hermit. They later reunite to collect off their father's inheritance.

Linda wrote, responding with her own anger.

> When I read the part about Lizzie Hamilton, I began to think of myself. I have a capacity for hatred and bitterness. I've been saving up and dreaming about the time that I will no longer be at home. I've been trying to get good grades ever since ninth grade to be able to be accepted to a University far away. I absolutely can't stand being home. Just as I'm writing this paper, my mom comes into my room and makes a bitchy remark. I guess I don't want to be seen at only funerals, but I don't want to come back to this house for a long, long time.

Julie rambled from one idea to another, letting her mind play over what she had just read.

I know the feeling of knowing someone better from letters. My best friend lives in Alabama and she probably knows me better than any one in California or anywhere else for that matter. I've got a few friends that I write to and I know that the majority of the time, I tell them more than the friends I see everyday. Also I have two pen-pals, and sometimes I feel closer to them than my every-day friends. From this experience I believe that letters are a way of keeping friends and relatives closer in the heart, though they are far away in distance.

I love the way he talks about Samuel. It does take time to be accepted by a new town, city, etc., as it does to be a new student in a new school.

I can't really understand the significance of Adam's conversation about birthmarks with the bartender. Except I once had one similar to it with a friend who noticed that my birthmark looked somewhat like a heart. I think that Steinbeck wanted to give the impression that birthmarks showed some personality traits. (I really don't know. I just some how get that feeling.)

I thought that was a very nice thing of Charles to reply in a letter, "I didn't hardly expect you any ways." For Adam was embarrassed as it was.

I can't believe Steinbeck; this guy can really write. I have to admit I wasn't too thrilled over *Grapes of Wrath*. I like the way he writes about all the characters, and the way he describes how he feels towards certain things.

*   *   *

Before the second set of Reading Logs was due (based on Part II of *East of Eden*), I responded to some students' pleas for inspiration by reading them a Log I had written earlier:

On the night when Cyrus Trask tells Adam that he loves him better than he loves Charles, Adam shows his father the little nestlike hollow near a stump where he goes to hide when he is hurt and troubled. Adam is surprised when his father tells him that he knew about the hiding place.

When I was a little girl, we moved a lot, and since I was an only child, I spent a great deal of time alone. Near each house we had, I would find a secret place, a private place, where I felt no one could find me. At one house, it was beneath the thick, dark branches of an orange tree that drooped to the ground. At another house, my place was high in a smooth-barked walnut tree. In Texas, I found a hiding place beside a muddy crayfish pond in a grove of mesquite. If I had time to plan my secret hour, I took an old green cotton blanket with me for comfort, and, of course, I took a book. Sometimes I went to my secret place so no one would see me cry. I always planned to spend a long time there when I cried, so that all the traces of tears, puffy eyes, red, runny nose, would be gone when I came back into the house. Once I had a great hiding place in a closet inside the house, behind my mother's orangey squirrel coat with the fox collar, but our collie would always find me there and give me away.

After Adam's and Cyrus's talk about the hiding place, Cyrus tells his son why he never came looking for him by the stump. "No, I wouldn't do that. You can drive a human too far. I wouldn't do that. Always you must leave a man one escape before death. Remember that! I knew, I guess, how hard I was pressing you. I didn't want to push you over the edge."

I know how vital my hiding places were to me, and how exposed and defenseless I would have felt without them. Cyrus's words ring terribly true to me, and no doubt, to Adam, too. I think he did remember them always.

The class, gratifyingly, responded with wonder. "We can't write anything that good," lamented Cathy.

"Yes, you can," I answered. "You already have. And look at my years of practice. Think how beautifully you'll all write when you're forty-four. You're pretty awesome already."

"You use so many details," Cathy, at the table right in front of me, observed, almost accusingly.

"What effect did that have?" I questioned, pleased to be talking about writing style.

"It made it more interesting," said Kate.

I smiled appreciatively at the rare compliment. "Remember that technique when you're writing. And notice that they're sensory details; they make you see and feel."

Although I have had other, more intense, experiences in writing with and sharing with students, the "hiding place" Log had its effect on the class's attitude toward writing. They saw my self-consciousness, my blushing, my fidgeting with the edge of my paper before I began to read. As usual, I started apologetically, "I didn't have much time to work on this." Then I caught myself, and said, "But I'm not supposed to apologize, am I. So, here is what I've written. I hope it says what I intended to say."

As I shared my writing with them, I demonstrated my willingness to risk, my struggle with thought and form. We became, as we had on other occasions, a community of writers working to better our products, each one, even the teacher, benefitting from the successes and mistakes of the others.

Interestingly, as we worked on reading and writing in Part II of
East of Eden, even some of the best students asked for ideas to write
about. At first their requests offended me. I felt something basic would
be missing from the process if they didn't respond to an idea that sparkled up at them from one of the novel's pages. Thinking it through,
however, I reasoned that I was training these students to think their
way through a book, to read for reality in the fiction that was truly
theirs, not just the author's, or, worse yet, the teacher's. I wasn't testing
this skill, I was building it, and, for a while at least, I would provide any
help they needed. I read them this list of Reading Log ideas, and many
used them. Next year I may ditto similar lists for Parts I and II, then
leave them on their own for Parts III and IV.

Reading Log Suggestions (Part II)

You might respond to —
—nostalgia for the past.
—hope for the future.
—"And I guess a man's importance in the world can be measured
    by the quality and number of his glories."
—"Our species is the only creative species, and it has only one cre-
    ative instrument, the individual mind and spirit of a man.
    Nothing was ever created by two men."
—Adam's blindness to Cathy's flaws.
—Cathy's attempt at aborting her baby.
—Adam's desire to create an "Eden" in the Salinas Valley.
—the decency of the Hamilton family.
—Cathy's distrust of Lee.
—Lee's reasons for pretending to be illiterate when he is college
    educated.
—Liza's domination of the Hamilton household.
—Cathy's abandonment of Adam and the twins.
—Samuel's advice to Adam: "Act out being alive, like a play. And
    after a while, a long while, it will be true."
—Kate's plot against Faye.
—the naming of the twins.
—the significance of the story of Cain and Abel from the Book of
    Genesis.

*   *   *

As we worked on in our focused way, Steinbeck's novel came to
dominate the classroom. Before-class conversation, although not notice-
ably quieter than before, and still accompanied by perching on table
edges and waving at friends in the hall, centered on *East of Eden*.

"Cathy's perverted, for sure," said Eric.

"He makes it sound like she was born that way," answered Jeff.

"Nobody's *born* perverted."

"Olaf was," Jeff's eyes rolled towards one of the class's off-beat characters sitting slouched in his too-small chair. The speakers laughed, as lanky Olaf ignored them with preoccupied dignity.

Kate sat quietly at a nearby table, her hands folded over a large green leather photo album of 1940's vintage.

"Kate brought her pictures of the Hamiltons," announced Carrie.

I immediately started toward her table, joined by a few other students who had heard Carrie. "Oh, let's see them," three of us said in a chorus, as Kate moved to open the large, unwieldy book. Kate is John Steinbeck's grandniece, so her family's album has wonderful, somber old photographs of his mother's family, the Hamiltons. *East of Eden* began as a family chronicle for John Steinbeck's sons, and although it evolved into a complex novel, a large section of it concerns the family.

Kate wanted me to do the showing and telling, so, with her help, we went through the huge pages, deciding whether or not various Hamiltons looked the way we had pictured them. Our favorites were Samuel and Liza — Sam, twinkly-eyed and bearded; Liza, thin-lipped and stern. As the album circulated around the room, I kept a nervous eye on it, but the big book and its historic photos met only fascination and respect.

Not every day brought us family portraits, but every day, because of the different level of involvement required by Reading Logs, did bring us more of John Steinbeck, and more of ourselves.

*   *   *

Jeff — warm, friendly, honest, and known for his love of girls and roller-skating disco dancing — was just recovering from hand surgery when *East of Eden* was issued to the class. He had been unable to do any writing for weeks, so he was eager to get back to work on a new effort. The timing, for Jeff, was perfect. He had always been open to new ideas, but during our month of *East of Eden* he blossomed as a reader, as a writer, willing to make the book his own. He beamed a loud, "All *right!*" at me when he read my rave comment, written at the end of his forthright, insightful Logs.

Pages 3-42
Chapters 1-4
April 15, 1980

During Adam's life as a soldier, he revolted against violence. He knew at the time that this was an act of treason against his men and the government. But he did not seem to care. He just could not bring himself to inflict pain or death on another human being. Perhaps this is why he never tried to protect himself from his brother, Charles.

I'm going to relate his feelings toward mine. Adam could not bring himself to even protect himself if it meant harming his opponent. Now if I was in a war with the Russians 10 years from now, I would probably develop an increasing feeling to kill, simply because I hated them for starting it (relying on the fact that they would). Plus seeing my buddies fall right and left to the ground. I'd go crazy.

But Adam has no prejudicial feelings toward anybody or any race. He is a true human being who believes one should not destroy his own kind.

This feeling of love toward all he comes in contact with is displayed in his bravery and efforts. Especially behind the lines, and in the hospital. This quality is very unique in a man. Well, at least that's my opinion.

Pages 43-81
Chapters 5-7
April 16, 1980

The only thing I can relate to in these chapters is the pages about the whores and the inn. Not that I go to a whorehouse every 3 weeks but the skittish feeling about settling down.

Up till this day, I haven't gone with a girl. Except once. That was in the 8th grade. I just can't handle being tied down. I need my freedom. So many times I've wanted to ask a girl to "go steady." But every time I change my mind. I picture myself not being able to put my arm around a female friend, let alone talk to her without my girlfriend exploding. Plus, I always say to myself, "You're gonna break up sooner or later, why go through hell." I enjoy my freedom, because I can get much closer to a girl, but not get involved with her. Sure we go to the movies and "make-out" (I had to put that in.) but that's all. We don't get serious. I guess you're using each other.

Well, anyway, that's how I think Charles feels. He's lonely, bored, overworked and has few friends. So, he makes use the best he can. He's just not ready to settle down with a wife and kids. He needs his freedom, but he also has his sexual desires.

Pages 82-114
Chapters 8-10
April, 17, 1980

When the fire broke out at the Ames's house, questions and suspicions rose. Why is it that every time something bad happens people look at the "low," "poor," or lonely people. That's discrimination, and against the law. But everybody does it, and our police departments contribute a lot to it also. Why must we discriminate?

People are always speaking of the Bible. How great it is, how important. Well, I'm part atheist. Now if people believed, truly believed in God, they'd follow his thoughts, rules and commandments. The Bible says God created man equally. Well, as far as history goes, we've been discriminating against one another for thousands of years. In every book I've read for this English class there's been discrimination. I'm sick of it.

Sure, I go down the Main at night and see a scummed-out low rider and say something under my breath. But that's for what he is in reality. Not his color, sex, or religion.

That's the only thing I thought of to write about.

Pages 114-143
Chapter 11
April 18, 1980

Charles and Adam have a problem. They fight, like all brothers do, but they fight with feelings. It's not over who gets the front seat when Mom goes to the store or who's got the right to a certain rock album. They fight about their parents. Yes, their mom and dad and how they treated the boys.

Charles has a bigger problem. He's shy and unable to express his feelings in words. His father and him never had a close relationship. This always bothered Charles. He was jealous of Adam. He wondered why their relationship was better. But it wasn't, not according to Adam.

My brother and I used to fight all the time over insignificant things. But never over the love of our father. Boy, am I confused.

Earlier I stated something about Charles and his shyness. I find myself at nighttime writing down what's on my mind. Mainly because I can't put it into words.

That's funny, because I have no problem in communicating with people that I know of. But some people are like that. Charles is like that.

Pages 179-211
Chapters 15-16
April 22, 1980

We're introduced to Lee in these chapters. What kind of man is he? I don't understand how a man's customs, traditions and cultural background can retain him from being free. Why does he feel he must serve somebody?

This is kinda my idea of craziness, like the kamikazes I'm writing a term paper on. They're willing to die for their country. Well, once you enlist in the army, you've taken on that part already. But these guys get in specially rigged planes carrying a form of nitroglycerine that's very explosive. Then they fly their planes head on into enemy ships in order to perform a strike, defense, for their homeland. It's ridiculous. I guess we never will understand everybody's culture totally.

Pages 317-356
Chapters 23-24
April 25, 1980

I've noticed through this whole novel that the family was most important to everybody. If somebody did something good on purpose, it was usually towards the good of the family. As on Thanksgiving. Everybody was there in 1911. The feeling of security and togetherness was very abundant.

Well, nowadays it's not like that. Kids are off goofing around, watching a movie, parents are working. I mean, the only time you see your whole family at once is at dinner. Sometimes not even there. This doesn't really bother me, it just attracted my attention. I guess all families are like that now. Everybody has something to do instead of sitting around and vegetating.

I wonder why Steinbeck called this book *East of Eden*. I wonder if any of this was part of his decision to entitle this book that way exactly. It seems like he wanted to tell a story that's totally different from a man's dreams or homeland. I'm confused.

Pages 448-471
Chapters 32-33
April 30, 1980

Tom speaks of suicide in these pages. He remembers his mother's strong distaste for suicide. She thought it was a combination of bad manners, cowardliness and sin. I think it's none of the above. Suicide is something that everybody has thought about doing at one time or the other. But few of us can truly try and kill ourselves. If a person really wanted to kill himself he would do it in a drastic manner. Like shooting himself or jumping off a building. For instance, when people think of slicing their wrists they usually cut crossways. That's because they really don't wish to end their lives. No, if they did it long ways, they're either crazy or they truly want to die.

My comment to Jeff was not as specific as most of my comments written on students' Logs. He handed in all his responses, these and nine more, at the same time because of his hand surgery absences. Also, we had talked, day-to-day, often walking down the hall together, about his ideas.

Jeff – Who but you could write so cheerfully and matter-of-factly about suicide?

Your whole Log is so fantastic that I hardly know what to write to you. You've done everything I've asked – read, related reading to your experience, expanded on the author's ideas, been honest, asked questions, admitted confusion, discovered your own ideas as you wrote them. I'm impressed.

The personal dialogues bouncing back and forth between me and the students during those four weeks were important to us. I was eager for the papers to be handed in; the students were eager to get them back. Eric and Beyat, however, hastily snatched theirs back off of my table one day when they saw I was going to read their Logs during class. "What's the problem?" I frowned at them.

"We don't want you to read them *now*," answered Eric, stuffing his little green notebook into his binder.

"Good grief; why not?" I answered in surprise.

They grinned sheepishly, faces red with self-consciousness. I concluded that their thoughtful, personal writing left them feeling exposed, and they couldn't bear to see me as I read and responded. They trusted my written response, but feared a smirk, a stifled grimace or a questioning look that would demean the great risk they had taken.

Understanding their sensitivity, that night at home I read these Logs and commented on them.

First, Beyat struggled with theological questions:

4/29/80

One Bible says, "Do thou," while another says, "Thou shalt," which indicates the inaccuracy of the *book*. I don't believe too much in the Old Testament, even though I am a Roman Catholic. It has not enough truth in it for me to believe in it.

I absolutely don't believe in the Adam and Eve, Cain and Abel story. For instance, where did Cain find a wife to give children after Abel died? This, of course, is not mentioned in the Bible because it is trivial.

Another is the famous Creation in seven days. It talks about the days and what happens on those specific days. Well, how long was a day in those years since there was no sun or planets? It could have been 36 hours or longer and not 24 hours.

Noah's Ark is a farce. How can you possibly collect two of each animal and put them into a small boat? How did the tiny animals get caught and what about the different kinds of species of animals in the entire world? As I said, many things that people live for are, I believe, just stories made up for the benefit of mankind.

4/29/80

I'm getting so involved in the last entry that I have to continue on it some more. I said that many of the stories from the Old Testament are false, because of the benefit to mankind. I believe that there is a supreme being (God) somewhere, but there is a limit to my beliefs. For instance, I look at the creation of the universe and solar system as a scientific stand rather than religious.

I believe also that since the Earth is such a small planet drifting around a star which is just a speck in the universe, that people must believe in something or there is nothing to live for. Now I have no idea if there is a heaven, but people believe so much that there is, even though there is no proof, that they are willing to kill themselves in order to go or to fight for their beliefs. Perhaps, many of these so-called miracles were from a race of beings that came from space, I don't know. All I can say is that ever since the death of Christ almost 2,000 years ago, there has been no miracle performed. Two-hundred or so years ago people would have killed me for my beliefs, but this is how I view it.

Beyat— It is such a miracle that mankind exists at all, that if I weren't convinced of my own existence, I wouldn't believe it. I, too, am offended by the myths man has invented to explain himself, when they are taken too seriously. The "genius from outer space" theory offends me as much as the beautiful Old Testament myth. Until I can know why I'm here, I'm going to stick with it — enjoy, produce, help, love—whatever seems good to me in my ignorance.

It's great that you can think through your ideas, groping for the clarity we all seek in vain.

Now, Eric's well-focused observations:

4-28-80

I think it was you, Mrs. Cookston, who said you read something that discussed Lee's character. The article said Lee was too extraordinary and unreal. I didn't think anything of it until now. Early in the novel, Lee's character is sketchy, but now it is much more clear. What is a guy like Lee doing in a place like that?

Lee is intelligent, clever, sophisticated, and dedicated. I guess it is dedication that keeps him at Adam's. Dedication toward Cal and Aron, and dedication to his boss. Finally his intelligence outweighed his dedication, so he told Adam he wanted to leave. Lee became lonely — he wanted to move to Salinas and open his own bookstore. It took Lee a long time to come to that decision, a decision that I believe to be a good one since you only go through life once. Lee must have felt obligated to stay after Cathy left, and he probably felt sorry for the twins. He knew that Adam would do a lousy job taking care of them, so he took it as his responsibility to bring them up correctly and teach them correct manners, etc. My hat is off to Lee for his dedication during those years with Adam and Cal and Aron.

Eric — As a stepmother who has raised four children not her own, my hat is off to him also. Real people do sacrifice themselves to take care of others' needs.

4/28/80

The sibling rivalry between Aron and Caleb is very strange but believable. The good-looking, great personality, out-going Aron versus the clever, intelligent, sneaky Cal. I'm sure after I have received more clues and witnessed other events between the two boys I may have different views of them. After the first chapter of their rivalry, though, that's the way I view them and I put Cal ahead after the first round.

Cal could out-trick Aron, but Aron could out-look Cal. So far, the tricks are beating the looks. Sometimes I wonder how it would be to have a twin brother. Sometimes I think how fun it would be to have someone my own age to play catch with and talk to, but other times I think about the bad parts. The competition, at least with the kind of personality I have now, would be unbearable. Not so much that I would want to do better in everything than my brother, but the thought of other people, including my parents, constantly comparing us.

I have a brother now, but he's two years older and our interests are different so we can't really be compared to each other, but I can't really say that with a straight face. We are compared — in school.

Eric — What honesty. I understand your feeling. Ideally, there should be no comparison; realistically, it's there.

I marveled at how far these boys had come in their ability to think through abstract thoughts on paper. I wanted to read their Logs to the class, but how could I? It would have been a violation of trust. I hope that some day I will be able to create a classroom atmosphere where students will share their deepest thoughts with one another.

During the month, our weekly class routine consisted of one and a half days of teacher presentation/discussion, one and a half days of college entrance test vocabulary study, and two days of quiet reading and writing Logs in class, usually preceded by informal talk. I introduced each Part to them, reading sections from the introductory chapters under Kate's tolerant gaze. Other times I read sections from *The Journal of a Novel* (Steinbeck's letters to Pascal Covici, his editor, which he wrote daily before beginning his *East of Eden* work) that I thought would interest them. I spent one day on the Book of Genesis and the significance of Steinbeck's translation of "Timshel" as "Thou mayest." Another day I distributed and read aloud the poem "With Cain" by James Kavanaugh, asking merely for their response to it in a class discussion.

My final presentation was to read and distribute the "Original Draft for the Dedication of East of Eden," a humorous, ironic dialogue with Covici outlining Steinbeck's defenses for all the editors' criticisms of his book. Two short paragraphs near the end of the Dedication spoke to us all.

Well, by God, Pat, he's (the reader) just like me. No stranger at all. He'll take from my book what he can bring to it. The dull witted will get dullness and the brilliant may find things in my book I didn't know were there.

And just as he is like me, I hope my book is enough like him so that he may find in it interest and recognition and some beauty as one finds in a friend.

One student who made *East of Eden* his friend was Ron, tall, dark-haired, brilliant and sensitive. Ron, interestingly, had studied Hebrew, could write the word "Timshel" in Hebrew characters, and had his own interpretation of the grammatical niceties that could distinguish among "Thou shalt," "Thou wilt," and "Thou mayest." He disagreed with Steinbeck's choice of "Thou mayest," but was willing to suspend his disbelief because he believes in Steinbeck's concept of Free Will.

Pages 317-356
April 30, 1980

This is one of those sections that requires very little summary, but a lot of interpreting. First, however, the summary is in order. The Trask children decide to take Samuel and Liza to live with them one at a time. Samuel and Liza decide to go and leave Tom behind to run the ranch. Before they leave, Samuel goes around and says good-bye to all his friends.

Now for the hard part: interpreting. This section had a strange effect on me. I can't really describe it or tell why it happened. All I know is that I felt terribly sad while reading this section. Not just because someone was growing old. It's more than that. First, though, I'll start at the beginning. When Una died, it was really the beginning of the end. To see a daughter that had died out of "pain and despair." Words could never describe such a feeling, especially for a man such as Samuel. To see the very life flow out of him. God, I never want to see that happen to anyone. Seeing things where they never were and letting them get to you. No matter how resistant you are it hits, and when it does it hurts, and ever so hard. I remember the will to go out and do things slowly drain from my grandfather, and when he died, how they drained out of my grandmother. The knowing that you must keep on going but not being able to do it. And the talk of the children when their parents get old. That dreadful talk, realizing what will and must happen. And the people who say you deserve a rest so why work so hard. With that rest comes age and with age comes death. No other way around it. And still people keep on saying it, convincing the people they are talking to. Why not let people work as long as possible? That length of "possible" time will get longer and happier. This is shown by Adam asking Samuel to finally build his "Garden of Eden." Maybe we should all keep on building our own "gardens."

The Chinese that Lee was talking about were still building. Whether it be by hand or, as they were, with the mind. At ninety, they learned a whole new language and after four years of patience came upon what they were after. And now they are learning Greek. Now that is a way to build a "garden."

The other main point to be discussed is in the interpretation of the Old Testament. The people that say "Do thou rule" and feel they must and the others say "Thou shalt" and believe they have no control over anything. And finally "Thou mayest rule it." We have a choice. We can do one thing or another. This at times can be the greatest gift to man and at other times the greatest curse. But it is what is and we should all be thankful for that.

Ron – Your reading logs are excellent. Are you aware of how much more you have to say than earlier; how much more fluent you are? You're working that careful stiffness out of your sentences: Also, you're doing what great writers do when *you end your Logs by universalizing your idea, when you talk about "everyone" and "the world."*

Another who found recognition of self in Steinbeck's novel was blond, broad-shouldered Dave, a fine swimmer whose health food snack, an orange, got Helmuth in trouble.

4-15-80

"As with many people, Charles, who could not talk, wrote with fullness. He set down his loneliness and his perplexities, and he put on paper many things he did not know about himself."

When I read this quote, I realized how much I am like this. When I have to talk to someone about something personal, such as my brother, sister, girlfriend, friend, etc., I find it easier to relate my feelings on paper. I find it easier because I can find the words when I have the time. I'm not too quick-witted, but sometimes I can be intelligent. I've often surprised myself in English by writing something I didn't think was possible from me. It is possible to learn something about yourself from your writing. You keep on digging to find out what to write, and things about yourself that you never thought about start appearing.

Dave—That's one of the things writing Logs is all about. I'm happy you agree.

The rewards of the Reading Log method lay in the dynamics created by the Logs themselves. The final essays written under pressure during a fifty-minute class period were good, but anti-climactic after the intensity of the reading experience. I was pleased, though, with the students' ability to return successfully to a more conventional literary essay stance.

Kelly, always a carefully correct writer, wrote:

East of Eden

In John Steinbeck's novel *East of Eden* the Cain type and Abel type characters are presented very strongly. The ideas of sin and whether man is predestined to evil or not are presented through the characters of Aron and Caleb. Another point of question is one which asks, "Does man have the ability to choose between good and evil for himself?"

Aron, along with his father Adam both represent the Abel type characters. They both had the experience of being accepted by their fathers, just as Abel was accepted by God. None of them ever really had to worry, as they were the victims of the jealousy which each of their brothers possessed. They all had positive-type qualities and never had trouble being accepted.

Caleb represents the Cain type character, as does Charles, Adam's brother. In the same sense, Cathy or Kate falls along the lines of Cain also. Cathy was an evil person, and when Caleb, her son, found out about her ways he automatically thought that he was an evil person. His jealousies of Aron contributed to this effect.

Lee, the Chinese who helped raise Aron and Caleb, noticed the feelings that Caleb had one day when talking. Lee was careful to set Caleb straight with one word, "Timshel," which means "thou mayest." He told Caleb that he had the ability to conquer the jealousy inside of him, and that he shouldn't feel that he should be jealous just because of Cathy.

John Steinbeck believes that man does have the ability to make of himself and his life what he wants. He proves this through Cal in the end when Adam is dying. Lee and Cal go to visit him, and Lee asks, "Is Cal forgiven?" Adam replies affirmatively.

Good and evil are both present in man. What a person chooses is of his own volition and there is no one to tell him which way to go. It can be summed up in one phrase, the words of Samuel Hamilton, "Sin is our own designing."

Kelly — Magnificent quote chosen for your ending. It is not one that I remembered, but I will now. Wasn't Samuel an amazingly wise man? The strong points of this essay are organization, balance, idea and correctness. There are flaws in style and (This is a recorded message.) there could be more supportive detail. You did a good job.

Jim, who does not consider himself a "good" writer, but who was deeply engaged by the book, wrote:

Essay: East of Eden

His whispered word seemed to hang in the air — "Timshel." This was the last word that Adam muttered in the book, *East of Eden*. John Steinbeck uses this ending to show us that everyone can choose his/her own destiny, either good or evil.

"Timshel" is described in the book by Samuel and Lee as meaning "Thou mayest." They said that ". . . it carried a man's greatness if he wanted to take advantage of it" and Samuel Hamilton said that he felt good about the word. He said that it set him free, it gave him a right to be a man separate from every man.

As he dies and speaks this word, Adam actually does conquer evil. He does not condemn Cal for what he did, but gives him a chance to condemn himself or make himself better. He holds no outright grudge against Cal for what he did, but, he does not forgive him either. Cal must help himself and realize that no one is pure and perfect.

I feel that this word, at the end of the book, sets Cal free to make his own life, what he wants or can make of it. He must have some help from some people like Abra and Lee, but on the whole, he must do most of it alone. Abra helps him realize that everyone is not perfect and Lee helps make him a man and makes him face himself.

He always thought that he was evil like his mother and that's the way it was. But towards the end of the book we start to see the tide turning. An example is when he has the urge to bring flowers to his mother's grave. He has good in him and bad. But in the end Adam sets him free.

"Timshel — thou mayest."

Jim — Excellent literary quality and original thinking in your essay — your most mature and polished writing of the year. I'm very proud of you. This paper was a joy to read.

Using responsive Reading Logs, my students could react to *East of Eden* as individuals, each student "making" his own book, writing in his own voice, sensing his own worth. Too often we tell students what their response should be, imply that only one response is right, analyzing and explaining and defining a work until it dies in the student's hands before it can live in his imagination. My long term goal for students is a love of good literature, a celebration of humanity — theirs and others! All other benefits aside — reading, writing and study skill development, elimination of insulting quizzes, even exciting class atmosphere — the opportunities for personal growth through good reading combined with good writing emerge as the outstanding benefit of using Reading Logs. Looking back, the preservation of the writers' privacy was one of the factors that made the experience work, this time. Certainly not for every writing experience, but appropriate for this one, was this quote from *East of Eden*: "The preciousness lies in the lonely mind of a man."

On the Monday after the *East of Eden* exam, I stood behind my table, elbows on my flimsy speakers' stand, trying to whip up enough energy to thrill the class with a vivacious introduction to Fitzgerald's *The Great Gatsby*. Its best recommendation, at that moment, was its compactness — just a hundred pages or so.

Two giggling sophomore girls wandered by, calling to Kyle, a quarterback on our football team, the Broncos. "Hey, Kyle, who should we take for English next year? Is this class easy?"

As the rest of us stared at the girls with annoyance, Kyle nailed them with a stern, upperclassman look. Without elaboration and without a glance in my direction, he said firmly, "This is a *good* class."

Imitating his tone, including the whole class, wanting to preserve our feeling of exhausted satisfaction an instant longer, I added, "That was a *good* response."

Chatper 13

Connecting Ideas and Expression

SAM TURNER

Sam Turner's a teacher of writing. A former high school teacher, he moved several years ago to a newly opened suburban community college where he and one other teacher form the English department. With the focus on the development of writing skills, one might expect an emphasis on usage and form. True, Sam's course *does* include reference to rhetorical devices like the inductive and deductive paragraph, but they are connected to, arise out of, the vitality of the student's ideas. His students reflect a wide diversity in experience and intention, so he capitalizes on it in a classroom organized as a workshop in which the teacher collaborates with students as they write to learn to write.

Recently I sat in a circle of chairs and talked with new students in my freshman composition class in a community college. They were a richly divergent group: some retired, many (women) returning to college as "displaced homemakers," a few veterans in their mid to late 20's, a couple of foreign students, and the rest kids right out of high school.

I remember beginning my writing class as follows: "I believe that the effective classroom for teaching writing should be organized around the perception of you, the students, as writers who learn by writing. This belief has forced me to reorganize my classroom from lecture hall to workshop, and I want the class to become a community of writers assisting one another in their work."

Over the past five years, my writing workshop classes stress student choice, self- and peer-evaluation, and writing for specific audiences. The students write what they want, in the genres they want, and they determine which works are to be evaluated. These are duplicated and read aloud in small groups for response and evaluation before being turned in for a grade. Often, these writings are for larger, more significant audiences than teachers: they write to each other, to the school, and to the public at large. As a result, in the past few years, many of the students have had works published in state and national magazines.

The writing class as workshop often appears chaotic and unstructured, but it is not. I believe what students must do in my classroom is what writers do: they have choice of subject and form, some control over deadlines, total control over whether or not a piece is finished and whether or not to submit it. The process of composing is circular: writers move from insight or idea, to writing, to evaluation, back to insight (now revision), and often they will go through this cycle many times before the writing satisfies them.

After this introduction to the course, Midge replied to my question, "What do you expect of this course as a writer exploring your own meaning rather than the cautious student seeking teacher approval?"

This Course: My Goals

I expect this course to help me communicate. I know I have something to say, yet my conversations are daunted by fear to speak, or inarticulateness. Many times I am a silent part of someone else's story, merely acknowledging their messages, while my own thoughts ripen and rot inside me.

I have a history of confusion and searching, wishing things were otherwise, false starts toward something better, and failure. The one thing life has taught me thus far is to lose, though seldom gracefully. I am defensive, frightened, and given to attacks of emotion which are very embarrassing. I guess I just don't have a good conception of what I want from life, and self-expression is the best release I have found.

I'm not really concerned with grades. I rate myself much more harshly than anyone else could and all I can hope for is to be enriched by this experience. I hate schools, classrooms, structure, and grades. I love to learn, grow, blossom, unfold. Maybe school strikes me as a denatured version of the real thing, like junk-food cereal merely resembles the grain from which it came. I expect to winnow the chaff from the usable, valid and pertinent and carry on.

In other words, to be a writer would be a dream I've only glimpsed could come true; it's too much to hope for and my dreams have come to dust before. Hopes have been dashed too many times for me to expect so much from one class. Nevertheless, I'm here and out of politeness or fear I probably won't say that I want this class to reveal me as a genius with a great gift of touching chords in the psyche which is universal and human and real.

That would require a risk on my part. Am I ready for it? Are you ready for me? By taking this step I am vulnerable to criticism, but the alternative is being destroyed by my inner conflict, so at least I've shared some of myself. Perhaps in retrospect, I'll be able to understand what I'm going through and laugh at my foolish fears, filing another vain attempt in the circular file and forgetting this, too. On the other hand, I could find a means of connecting ideas with expression. In that case, it's worth the risk.

"Writing is thinking" and Midge's page is alive with thoughts. The process slowed the rapidity of ideas and allowed Midge, writer, and me, reader, a connection not possible to the lecturer and notetaker.

With Midge's permission, I duplicated her paper, handed it out, and then the class engaged in a stimulating discussion on education in general and on writing and grading in particular. That, I can remember, was a fun class period.

What my students write fascinates me and I am often eager to read and respond. Perhaps this comes because my students most often write from stances of authority, of knowing, of experience, which is what all of us do when we are writing our best. All too often in the past I had asked students to write about something in which I was seen as the acknowledged specialist. For example, I would explain how Keats structured sonnets differently from Shakespeare and then assign a process paper on Keats's sonnets. I stopped making those assignments because of the consequences. Papers were dead and spoke with artificial voices. I observed that few students worked with pride or enthusiasm when they wrote to me about what I already knew. Now I prefer to ask them to write a paper explaining any process which they know well. I stress *any* process. The benefits are not only to the students!

Through their writing I learn much about them. One day I had just reminded them about the upcoming "read-arounds": "Each student will bring a piece of writing; we'll duplicate it and hand it out to other students sitting in a circle, listen to the writer read, and then we'll all respond." Consider what Sue wrote one week before we had our first read-around:

> I've got to admit that I'm a little scared of the read-arounds. I guess I have this fear that no one will understand my work, my style, or my techniques. I am most deathly afraid of letting anyone even read my work let alone criticize it. At home, I have a desk full of pieces mostly unfinished. I always found something else to do other than finish; when I came close to completion, I would get cold feet. I'm afraid of rejection. I think the read-arounds will help me in this and give me courage.

When their comments are so courageous, I become encouraging by explaining how I've felt before reading aloud my own work and how countless other students have felt the same way. I'm not eager to allow that enthusiasm in students to wane. But, sometimes, I get negative comments, too. I'll find through writings that they see no merit, no value to a particular activity or study. On those days no matter how well prepared the lesson, I must move away from subject matter to attend to attitudinal matters. Often, I think, most of us teachers know the worth, the value of an activity, and we assume that students are aware of our viewpoints when that's not the case.

For instance, one student didn't see any value in writing daily in order to meet my requirement of four rough pages per week, especially since these pages were not to be typed and submitted to me for a grade. He responded positively when I compared writing frequently to a jogger's running daily; he could understand, by analogy, that the frequent practice allows him to do well on the days that count.

Just as certain practices benefit the jogger, certain types of daily writing seem to aid student writers in their growth. The most demanding decision, as James Moffett discovered, is to properly sequence "the trials so that learning is transferred from one to the next." The sequence I currently follow arranges assignments so that they extend scope (starting with brevity and stretching toward length) and expand perspective (moving from personal narrative to specialized pieces such as literary analysis or the research paper).

A half page writing is the logical starting point; it's simple, yet demanding. I begin by distinguishing between details and assertions: details refer to sentences which describe, show, or report on facts and observations; assertions refer to analyzing, telling, or making interpretations and giving opinions. Students understand quickly through examples. "The 1979 Chevy came equipped with mag wheels" is a detailing sentence, but "Custom autos are outrageous" is assertive; or, "John Keats wrote for a brief ten years before his death at the age of 26" as opposed to "JK's sonnets reveal a growth unparalleled in English literary history."

Once students can distinguish between the two, I discuss three organizational patterns: beginning with details and concluding with assertions, vice versa, and using all details so that the assertion is not stated but implied. In class, I have them quickly write brief pieces using any one of the patterns. Afterward, I coax volunteers to read aloud their writings and ask the other members to listen carefully to hear what is said and how it is said.

Karen wrote during class:

Four years ago was the last time I visited New York. I arrived on Christmas Day full of expectations and in a great mood. On my way to my grandparent's house, a car tried to run me over while I was in a crosswalk. After catching my breath, I laughed and went on my way. A few days later I stood on a crowded subway while a lady yelled at me for accidentally touching her. Shocked, I said I was sorry, but she didn't listen. Later, on a rush hour bus, a person leaned on me and I told him to knock it off. Boy, did I forget how mean and nasty people can be. By the end of my stay, I was no longer Miss Polite from California, but I looked forward to my next visit when I would be able to utilize all my new-found aggressive tendencies.

Everyone laughed and felt good about her conclusions since we were all living in Southern California. When asked, though, they saw the benefit of holding her assertion until last because her examples had readied her readers for her conclusion. At this point, Michael volunteered his writing:

Imagination represents the most powerful force on earth. Yet it lurks in the black abyss of the human mind. Shift your thoughts into high gear and let imagination run free, like the unharnessed wind waving across the open sea. Catch a fleeting inspiration, hold it up, admire it, poke and toy with it, then let it loose to run its course.

Students concurred that his, too, was all right, but different. Without the assertion first, his abstract, metaphorical advice would not make sense to the listeners. Invariably, they turned back to me and asked which is the best method. My answer: "Whatever serves your purpose best." This was the first time of many that I attempted to teach the relationship between idea and structure. The class continued these brief writings until everyone had experienced the three patterns and questioned the advantages of explicitness and implicitness. With each piece I asked them to extend the length until they were ready to write pieces of two or more pages to be submitted for grades.

Within the scope of three to five graded papers, I like to move the students from self toward subject. The first writings allow them to narrate a recent personal experience. As such, no research other than recollection is necessary, and my students often appear eager, rather than reticent to do the papers. I structure assignments only in suggestions; the responsibility in my class is to write, rather than to follow a particular assignment.

Smokey Wilson's *Struggles with Bears* (1973) and Ken Macrorie's *Writing to Be Read* (1976) are full of excellent suggestions for meaningful writings. Wilson suggests, for instance, that students describe "one of those horrible instances when they stood before the world as the laughing stock, egg dripping from the face — a moment when they could label themselves Dope for a Day." I draw upon the previous experiences of ending a brief writing with an assertion by suggesting that they conclude this new paper, their narration, with an epiphany, James Joyce's term for that moment in which the main character comes to recognize something about himself or his universe.

Ted brought to the read-around this account of his human error while in the Navy:

First Reveille

As I opened the car door, I felt my stomach tighten and a chill run up my spine. With a slight hint of a tear, my father hugged me and wished me luck. I closed the door as the first light of day broke through the buildings and the bare-limbed trees. Standing alone on the street, I watched the exhaust cloud of Dad's car vanish around the corner, then stared at the building across the street. The large block letters above the entrance were still shaded, but loomed out at me in the early morning cold: DENVER FEDERAL BUILDING.

My head was filled with my friends' stories of being terrorized by fire breathing ogres as I pushed through the revolving door and slowly climbed the stairs to the third floor. There I spotted the conveniently located office. Taking a deep breath, I grabbed the ice cold knob and opened the door marked U.S. NAVY RECEIVING STATION.

By early evening, after much processing and many forms, I hadn't seen or heard any ogres. The people who processed the recruits smiled and treated me nicely; I realized my friends were kidding me. Soon after dinner, I was on a plane headed for San Diego, looking forward to fun and adventure. When I arrived at the base, I was given linen and assigned a bunk. There was still no sign of the ogres. At lights out, I crawled into my bunk feeling at ease; sleep came quickly after the long day.

My eyes suddenly opened, as I was tossed upward, but closed again after being stabbed by the harsh light. My ears were ringing with the sounds of a blacksmith at work. Off in the distance I heard a voice calling, but I couldn't understand what it was saying. With a clouded mind, I squinted at my watch: 4 A.M.

My blanket no longer offered its warm protection, it had been ripped from the bed. The calling voice was no longer distant. It erupted from all directions, repeating the same message over and over:

Hit the deck ya squirrel! Rise and Shine!

With a shiver, I sat up and looked out the dark fog-shrouded window. This certainly could not be the warm and friendly place I came to six hours ago. Gazing around the room, I found the source of the noise. The blacksmith was a squat looking specter dressed in black. His shoulders were as wide as he was tall. His smithing tools included a broom handle and a 30 gallon steel trash can. In his booming voice, which was a cross between a volcano and a typhoon, he issued directions:

Get yer butts dressed and downstairs, on the yellow circle. Ya got five minutes!

The floor was ice cold when I made my run for the bathroom. All the other people in the barracks, about 60, had the same urge. Jamming into the doorway, like cattle going through the chute, we were dismayed to find it would service only six at a time. Circling our compact group were four of the specter's helpers. They proceeded to divide us into small groups and regulated the use of the bathroom. Time was running out when my turn came, so I forgot about washing up and ran downstairs to find a yellow circle.

Standing with my feet together and chest out, I watched the adjutant make the late arrivals do 30 pushups. This couldn't be the place where I was supposed to be; it was the middle of the night, an ice cold night, with a madman screaming at me. Looking around, I did not see a friendly face anywhere, just the intimidated and the intimidators. My eyes rested on a dimly lit sign above the adjutant. The sign which was welcoming people to the RECRUIT TRAINING COMMAND didn't provide any comfort.

My mind raced with confusing thoughts, but finally settled in on one idea; this man must be an ogre! My friends had been right. I had become a willing victim of the fire breathers. All fantasies of fun and adventure vanished and were replaced with anxiety. What seemed to be the beginning of a good time had turned into a night of fear.

When Ted finished reading, the group broke instantly into animated discussion praising his piece. Students felt unanimous about the success of the writing, and one by one they responded to Ted.

Karen said, "You really captured what I imagined an inductee's experiences to be like. It was a unique telling of a not so unique experience. That's about it — I really like it."

There was a dead-like silence while the responsibility to talk inevitably shifted from one responder to the next.

Michael was next. "Ted, your details were really moving. I wish I could write that way." (I interrupted here: "In what way were the details good?") "'Oh, I don't know why they appealed to me. They just started the story in a good way."

Midge offered her opinion, "It's good, but I didn't like that it started in Denver, but finished in San Diego. It's too long or too much passage of time, I guess."

Many disagreed audibly, in no order: "No! . . . Heck, no." . . . "It's fine." . . . "Didn't bother me."

Ted responded. "I felt that I had to describe Denver. Otherwise, I'd have to start in San Diego and tell what had happened and I remember strong feelings in Denver so I just began there."

Michael jumped back in. "I want to say something more, Okay?"

I nod, "Sure."

"The details of your opening in Denver sort of anticipate the later action. All that (he stops and looks back at the draft in his hand) . . . All that cold and bare limbs and your dad's goodbye and that government building looming up in the early cold, oh, that's great. I knew something bad would happen. Those descriptions set the stage for your story."

Others concurred, until Sharon interrupted: "I felt that the way you indented the shouted commands really made them stand out and almost startle me. It's very good to set up dialogue, or rather what they shout at you, like that. Also I liked all the building's names in capitals. May I ask, where did you get the idea to do those things?"

"I don't know, not from any of our readings." Ted was smiling now, pleased. "At first, I didn't write it that way. When typing it out, I just indented the shouting and really liked the way it looked."

Pat asked, "Why didn't you tell more about what happened during that 'night of fear'? Wouldn't that be a better story?"

"I thought about that, but really it seemed that it would be too long and I felt that my point was made." He turned to me, "What about it, Mr. Turner? Should I have written more?"

I held off commenting for just a second, long enough to ask if anyone else in the circle had any further responses about Ted's story. I feel that somehow students always see my statements as final and authoritative, and generally I want their comments candid and truthful to come out first. All seemed finished.

"I really can't answer the question except to hedge. Your ending, Ted, is sufficient for me, and I suspect that further examples of your being harassed would not necessarily enhance the story. That's the reader in me speaking. If, however, I were the writer, I might play with it some more and try feeling out one or two different endings to see which satisfies me the most. I suppose that not knowing exactly which option to choose is a common dilemma of the writer." I looked around and they seemed satisfied. Then I summarized, smiling that there was little or nothing new I could add. Their comments had made me proud of them and secure in the effectiveness of the read-around process. Ted wanted to keep the piece over the weekend to see what other endings would do to his story.

From personal narrative, I pull students toward topics that move gradually from self toward subject. Usually, these kinds of papers are easily generated: I recommend that students write about their thoughts or feelings regarding another person's idea or belief. This assignment is a step away from narrating a personal experience, but it is still couched in the comfort of expressing a personal view.

Laura's exposition blends details and assertions perfectly:

Redressing Mr. Molloy

Certain forms of dress are always appropriate for certain job settings. If one worked in a law firm, bank, or corporate headquarters, that individual would want a more understated form of dress than if the job were in the creative department of an advertising agency or a magazine. Neatness and good taste are always important when choosing business attire. But such obvious good sense is not what John T. Molloy is selling in his *The Woman's Dress for Success Book*.

Instead, this self-proclaimed fashion "engineer" asserts that only when a woman discards everything in her wardrobe in favor of the ultimate uniform, a "skirted suit," can she make any progress toward professional equality with men. This skirted suit must be made of either wool or linen material in a subtle plaid, "bushy" English tweed, or solid (preferably grey) color. This suit should be worn with a white blouse (Although a black blouse may be more impressive, it may offend one's male co-workers) and plain dark pumps. Molloy stipulates that "this suit should be worn without a vest. Vests make women more sexually attractive and, therefore, less authoritative. When a woman wears a vest, she draws attention to her bust. With most women this is sexy, and with a busty woman this can be very sexy."

Not only are vests out as far as Molloy is concerned, but boots, pocketbooks, dresses that are either too short or too long, pant suits, sweaters, pastel or bright colors are all unacceptable attire for the working woman.

What Molloy implies is that the outline of a woman's body and characteristically feminine accessories are too distracting to male co-workers for her performance to be evaluated objectively. "Wearing feminine prints with flowers, birds, sailboats and the like will make men think that a woman is frilly and ineffective. Many abstract prints should also be avoided." According to Molloy the pattern with the worst effect in the office was floral: "I would even advise against wearing it socially."

It seems as if Molloy is proving that one reason men were so anxious in the past to keep women at home is the fear of some mysterious female power — sexual as well as intellectual. Molloy is teaching women how to disguise the fact that they are women, so that men can adjust to their presence without feeling threatened.

I believe that it is about time for women to attain success, and I believe that many books and articles offer intelligent advice on how to get ahead in the business world. Unfortunately, in my opinion, John T. Molloy is not the author of one. Not only does this book contain bad advice, it paints an unflattering picture of the successful business man. If the average male executive were to be as easily distracted by a woman's presence as Molloy seems to think, he would certainly not be qualified for his position., If persons, male or female, have the ability to do their jobs effectively, they should be able to dress the way they please.

From this position, the personal point of view, I move students toward the specialized papers required in college. We write explications of poems, analyses of short stories, plays or novels, and research papers.

The final step necessary to develop successful writers, ironically, does not involve students, but me, the teacher. When I see my students as writers, my expectation of their ability seems to shape their performance and self-confidence, but how have I modified my behavior?

First, I've found it effective to write with my students. By continual writing, I discover the sheer pleasure of creating and I delight in my accomplishments. More practically, I experience what my students are experiencing and my participation serves as my license to teach well. Perhaps, I am a teacher best when I am closest to being a student. Regardless, they have commented favorably about my writing in class, and, certainly, it affords me a connection with my students.

Second, I share with other teachers the exploration of similar successes and similar shortcomings. I "open" my classroom door because for too long my profession has been "close doored." The last time a fellow teacher visited my classroom, I saw my students and my teaching in a different light. The last time I worked out a teaching strategy with a colleague I could hardly wait to return to class to try it out. If I discover that we all have the same dilemmas, then I begin to share in the achievement of excellence in teaching.

Not long ago, I asked my students to write about someone whom they had hurt or betrayed, and they asked me to do the same. I did and I discovered an unexpected story as I wrote. Often I take it out of my file folder and reread it:

From the first day Emma Lloyd sat in the back desk of the back row; from my podium at the front of the classroom she was physically further from me than any student in the room. Daily she took her seat, sat quietly among the noisy students, and remained anonymous throughout the semester. She had no grades, since she handed in no work. Because she was unobtrusive, I divided my time between the good students and the trouble makers. I sensed that we shared an unstated, but fully understood agreement:

"Leave well enough alone." On Wednesday of the last week I went home only to find her manuscript propped against my front door. On the cover, the simple statement, "Thank you so much," forced me to read every word. What talent she had. Every piece sparkled with life, pushed forth its existence, and read professionally crisp. She missed Thursday and Friday and I never saw her again except at graduation when she stood with her class. I lost her after the recessional as I had lost her in the classroom. I'll never lose Emma Lloyd again though. The first weeks of every class I look for her in every student. I'll never have another Emma Lloyd.

Writing is difficult; let's not be misled. But it can be useful and exhilarating for the student and for the teacher. I must not lose perspective, though; it can't be done in one semester — it never is. The real test of my worth as a teacher of writing will be measured by how much writing students do after my class, after the final grade is entered on the transcript.